PUBLICATIONS
of the
American Ethnological Society
Edited by FRANZ BOAS

VOLUME V

KORYAK TEXTS

BY

WALDEMAR BOGORAS

E. J. BRILL, Limited
PUBLISHERS AND PRINTERS
LEYDEN, 1917

G. E. STECHERT & Co., New York, Agents.

NOTE.

The present volume was intended to include a collection of Kamchadal texts. Owing to the war, it has been impossible to communicate with Mr. Bogoras; and since the volume has been in type for over two years, it seems best to publish the collection of Koryak texts alone.

There is some inconsistency in spelling the verbal endings -*lin* and -*len*. These ought to be read consistently as given here. The forms -*lin* and -*len* are incorrect. There is no *g* in Koryak. Wherever this occurs, it should be read ǥ.

EDITOR.

November, 1916.

PRINTED BY E. J. BRILL, LEYDEN (HOLLAND).

CONTENTS.

ERRATA.

p. 15, lines 4, 5, for "geiʹɫıɫin" read "gaiʹɫıɫin."

p. 50, line 1, interlinear translation, for "that, what was" read "with that which was."

p. 66, last line of footnote, for "bring" read "being."

p. 74, line 26, for "yaʹtti" read "yaʹti."

p. 76, line 6, for "mıntaiʹkir" read "mıntaiʹkin."

p. 76, line 17, for "tıyeiʹɫıñın" read "tıyaiʹɫıñın."

p. 78, line 18, for "ñênvêʹthıčñın" read "ñenveʹthıčñın."

p. 82, title, for footnote reference "1" read "2."

p. 82, footnote, for "1" read "2."

p. 86, last line of footnote, for "part ii" read "part i."

p. 91, title, omit reference 1.

p. 93, 6th line from bottom of text, for "came" read "come."

p. 97, footnote, for "2" read "1."

p. 102, line 11, for "nekaʹlkıḷat" read "nekaʹɫkıḷat."

p. 102, line 13, for "MuⅬiʹtıḷkıḷat" read "MuⅬiʹtıḷkıḷat."

p. 105, 3d line from bottom of text, for "carier" read "carrier."

p. 105, last line of text, for "kantc" read "kantcx."

INTRODUCTION.

THE collection of Koryak texts here published was made as part of the field-work of the Jesup North Pacific Expedition of the American Museum of Natural History. Since the Museum does not allow sufficient space for the publication of all the linguistic material, which naturally forms one of the most important aspects of the work of the Expedition, the American Ethnological Society has undertaken the publication of part of it.

The texts contained in this volume were collected by me between December, 1900, and April, 1901. While Mr. Waldemar Jochelson, my colleague in the ethnological work of the Expedition in northeastern Siberia, investigated the ethnology of the Koryak, I undertook the study of their language, because my practical knowledge and previous studies of the Chukchee language put me in a position to acquire with ease a knowledge of the Koryak, which is closely related to the Chukchee.

I left the Anadyr country in December, 1900, and travelled to the village of Kamenskoye, on Penshina Bay, where I met Mr. Jochelson. I staid with him one month, after which time I proceeded to the southeast, to the eastern branch of the Koryak, and also visited the Kamchadal. I travelled among these tribes for two months, until my return to the mouth of the Anadyr, on April 8, 1901. A considerable part of this time was spent in covering the long distances between the villages, the journey bring made by reindeer or dog sledge and on

snowhsoes. Some parts of this territory had never been
visited by any white man, not even by a single Russian
trader, and I met camps and villages the inhabitants of
which did not even know the taste of brandy, — in these
countries, the foremost product of civilization, and the first
to arrive. The last fifteen days of the journey between
the Ke'rek region and Anadyr Bay[1] were spent in going
without a guide through a country wholly uninhabited;
for the Ke'rek, who have but few dogs, do not go very
far from their villages on the coast, and are unfamiliar
with the hills of the interior.

We travelled up-stream along several small rivers that
flow into Bering Sea on the Ke'rek coast, and then, passing over the divide, followed the rivers that belong to
the Anadyr system, and finally reached the first camps
of the Telqäp Chukchee. This is the method of travelling
adopted by the ancient cossacks, the conquerors of Siberia.

All the time that was not taken up by travel, and that
was available for study, was devoted to an investigation
of the languages of the Eastern Koryak and Kamchadal
tribes. The study of the Koryak was the more extensive,
owing to its closer affinity to the Chukchee in grammar
as well as in vocabulary.

The Koryak dialects may be divided into two large
groups, — the western branch, which includes the Maritime
Koryak of Penshina Bay and also the Reindeer Koryak;
and the eastern branch, which includes the Maritime
Koryak of Kamchatka, and also the inhabitants of the
villages Rekr'nnok, Pustoretzk, and Podkaguirnoye, to the
south of Parapolski Dol. These last belong ethnographi-
cally to the Kamchatka Koryak, although they are counted
by the Russian Administration as belonging to the Gishiga
district. The eastern branch includes also the Maritime

---

[1] See map, Publications of the Jesup North Pacific Expedition, vol. vii.

Koryak of the villages on the Pacific coast around Alutor Bay, and those of the Pacific villages still farther east. The Ke'rek stand apart, and form perhaps a third dialect, although, on the whole, similar to the western branch.

The most obvious point of difference between the two branches is that the sound *r*, which occurs frequently in the eastern branch of the Koryak and in the Chukchee, is wholly missing in the western branch, and is there replaced either by *y* or (less frequently) by *t*, *č*, *s*. The natives are well aware of this difference; and in the tales of the Penshina Koryak, as may be seen from the texts, the use of *r* in the pronunciation of certain words is ascribed to evil spirits.

The inhabitants of villages on the rivers Vi'rnĭk, Poqa'č, and Opu'ka (i. e., between the Alutor Koryak and the Ke'rek), explained to me that, though leading the settled life of sea-hunters, they belong by origin to the Reindeer Koryak. In proof of this they pointed to their pronunciation. They said, "We say *yaya'ña* (HOUSE), and the Alutor people say *rara'ña*."

Instead of the classification "western and eastern groups," we might just as well have said "northern and southern groups;" but I prefer the former designation, because the pronunciation of the eastern branch is nearer to that of the Chukchee, who live to the east.

The Koryak language, in contrast to the Chukchee, which has almost no dialects, is furthermore divided into several local dialects. Each bay and river, with its few villages, has a dialect of its own, differing from the others in pronunciation and vocabulary; and a dialect of Kamchatka may in some respects be nearer to a dialect of Penshina Bay than to that of its immediate neighbor.

The following series of texts was collected chiefly in the village of Kamenskoye (Koryak, Vai'kenan), on Penshina Bay, with the help of Nicholas Vilkhin, Mr. Jochelson's interpreter. The correct transcription of Koryak phonetics offered considerable difficulty, since Nicholas Vilkhin, a half-Russianized Koryak raised in Gishiginsk, belongs by birth to the village of Paren (Koryak, Poi′tɪn). Now, the dialects of Paren and Kamenskoye, though very much alike, present several points of difference. Some of these are, that *e* of Paren is replaced by *a* in Kamenskoye; *tk*, by *tč* (*čč*); *y*, by *s*. The people of Kamenskoye are well acquainted with the Paren pronunciation, because the intercourse between the villages is considerable. Therefore many of them, when talking with the interpreter, would assume his style of pronunciation. I have tried to avoid confounding the two systems of pronunciation, but I am not sure that I have succeeded in doing so in all cases. Besides this, the rules of pronunciation, which are strict and consistent in the Chukchee language, are quite lax in all the Koryak dialects.

The harmony of vowels, which exists in Chukchee, is unstable in Koryak, and often inconsistent. Chukchee has two groups of long vowels, —

$$i \qquad e\ (\ddot{a}) \qquad u$$
$$\hat{e} \qquad a \qquad o\ (\theta)$$

The vowels of the one group cannot be combined with those of the other, either in single words or in compounds such as are in use in this group of languages. The other vowels of the Chukchee are short, obscure, and neutral. Therefore they may form combinations with either group of long vowels. In compounds, the vowels of the first group are replaced by the corresponding vowels of the second group whenever the word contains a single vowel of the second group in any position whatsoever. There are also some stems containing only neutral vowels, which nevertheless require the exclusive use of vowels of the second group in the other parts of the word.

In Koryak, with its constant dialectical changes from *a* to *e*, this pair of vowels is excluded from the action of the vocalic harmony just described, and both *a* and *e* are considered as neutral. Thus, in the dialect of Kamenskoye, *nu′tanut* (EARTH) changes in the dative to *notai″tĩn*. The two remaining pairs (*i-ê*,[1] *u-o*) also admit many exceptions, in contrast to the strictness of the rule of harmony prevailing in Chukchee. Owing to the intermarriage between the people of different villages, *a, e, ä, ɪ,* may also be used in the same place by different persons, especially when not under accent; for instance, *na′nako* and *na′nɪko*. In the same way, *uu* and *oo*, *aa* and *ā*, the verbal suffixes -*lin* and -*len*, interchange; for instance, some people of Kamenskoye say *nuu′wge* (COOKED MEAT), others *noo′wge*.

There are also dialectic differences in the use of consonants; for instance, intervocalic *y*, which is omitted in Chukchee and preserved in the Paren dialect of the Koryak, may be omitted in the Kamenskoye dialects, although it is sometimes pronounced, but less distinctly than in the Paren dialect. The sound *č* may to a considerable extent be replaced by *s, s·, t.* Chukchee has for this sound two different pronunciations, — *č* by men, and *š* by women. A slight difference in the pronunciation by the sexes exists among the Koryak, but much less strict and regular than in Chukchee. Men use the pronunciation *č*, while women employ *s·* or *t.*[2] The sound-group *nͅnɪ* is replaced individually by *nni*; *q*, by *k*; *wg*, by *ww* or *wx*; *y*, by *g̣*; etc.

---

[1] I use in Koryak, instead of this *ê*, simply *e*.

[2] It is interesting to note that the possessive adjective Quyqɪnn·a′qučhin, BIG-RAVEN'S (literally, RAVEN-BIG-HIS), has *č*; and Miti′s·hin, MITI'S (literally, MITI′-HER), has the corresponding *s·*.

Except when otherwise stated, the texts were taken down in the village of Kamenskoye, from the lips of Maritime Koryak women or girls, as follows: 1, 2, 12—14, 18, from Pa′qa; 3, 17, from Ai′wan-ñaw; 4, 5, 8—10, 16, from Anne; 6, from Yu′ḷta-ña′ut; 7, 19, 20, from A′qan-ñaw; 11, from Ai′u-ña′ut; 15, from ɪpɪña′.

Text No. 21 is in the dialect of Pa′llan, a large village of northern Kamchatka on the Okhotsk Sea, and was related to me by Basile, a Maritime Koryak man.

Text No. 22 is in the Paren dialect, taken down in the village of Kamenskoye from the words of Nicholas Vilkhin, a native of Paren, Mr. Jochelson's interpreter.

Text No. 23 is in six languages, — in Chukchee; in Koryak of Kamenskoye, Qare′ñɪn,[1] and Lesna;[2] and in Kamchadal of the Okhotsk shore and of the village Sedanka (Kamchadal, E′sxlin) in the mountains, the dialect of which has undergone a great change through Koryak influences. The original text is from Kamenskoye, and was dictated by Anne, a Koryak woman of that village. The Chukchee translation was made by Aqan·kau′, a Maritime Chukchee man at the mouth of the Anadyr; the Qare′ñɪn version, by Maria, a Koryak woman of the village Qare′ñɪn; the Lesna version, by Andrew, a Maritime Koryak man from Lesna; the first Kamchadal version, by Ivan Kulagin, a Kamchadal man from the village Napana (Kamchadal, Na′pno); and the second Kamchadal version, by Tatiana, a Kamchadal woman from Sedanka.

Text No. 24 is in three dialects, — Kamenskoye, Paren, and Qare′ñɪn. The original text was recorded from dictation by Pa′qa, a Koryak girl of the village of Kamenskoye. The Paren translation was made by Nicholas

---

[1] Russian, Kapara, a large village in northern Kamchatka on the Pacific coast.
[2] A village of northern Kamchatka, on the Sea of Okhotsk, called in Koryak Vei′emḷin (THAT OF THE RIVER).

Vilkhin; and the Qare'ñın translation, by Maria of Qare'ñın, mentioned before.

These texts may serve very well for a comparative study of all three languages. I took care to have the translation made as literally as possible, although a few changes were unavoidable. Thus, for instance, the Koryak *Quyqınn·aqu'nu*, which is simply the plural of *Quiqınn·a'qu*, is translated in Kamchadal as *K!u'txen k!č!a'mjanl·a^εn* (KUTX'S MEN). The Chukchee *erre'č* (Kamenskoye Koryak *ačco'č*), which signifies THAT IS ALL, in the Qare'ñın Koryak is replaced by *tenma'wılen*, which signifies THE FINISHED ONE. *Ge'tkurlı*, added in two Kamchatka Koryak texts, signifies DID ALL AT ONCE, and indicates the suddenness of action, etc.

The affinity between the Chukchee and the various dialects of the Koryak is evident; but in reality it is still greater than it appears after a hasty comparison. For instance, HE BROUGHT HER HOME, in Qare'ñın Koryak, is *ganrai'talen*; and in Chukchee, *rırai'tannen*. The Chukchee, however, has also the form *ganrai'taʟen*, only it is used syntactically in a different manner.

Free translations of a part of these tales were published in Mr. Jochelson's work on the Koryak ("Publications of the Jesup North Pacific Expedition," Vol. VI), together with other Koryak and Kamchadal tales which I collected without original texts. References to Mr. Jochelson's versions are here given in footnotes to the tales.

A number of tales are given with interlinear translation and free translation; others, only with free translation. The attempt has been made to render the texts as accurately as possible; but it has been found necessary to omit in the translations many of the particles, which are as numerous in Koryak as in Chukchee, and hardly admit of adequate translation.

Words added in translations for the sake of clearness are placed in parentheses. Literal translations of Koryak words or phrases are enclosed in brackets.

The Koryak here given may be compared with the Chukchee texts published by me in Vol. VIII of the "Publications of the Jesup North Pacific Expedition" and in the "Publications of the Russian Imperial Academy of Sciences." [1]

Few Koryak or Chukchee tales are known under definite names. Titles indicating the contents have been added by me. I have transcribed the name of BIG-RAVEN in the form most frequently met with, *Quyqınn·a′qu*, although Mr. Jochelson prefers *Quikınn·a′qu*. In Chukchee are found the forms *Ku′rkıl* or *Ku′urkıl*; and in Kamchadal, *K!utx*. In Koryak I write the third letter as *y*, because it replaces Chukchee *r*; the fourth letter as *q*, because of the corresponding Kamchadal *x*. For *Emé′mqut*, in the English translation, I have retained the Paren pronunciation adopted by Mr. Jochelson, although in these texts the Kamenskoye pronunciation Ama′mqut was used more frequently.

The following alphabet has been used for transcribing Koryak and Kamchadal sounds: —

VOWELS.

	ë	ä	ö	ü
ʽi	ê	ạ̈	ɵ	
i	e	a	o	u
ɪ	E	ʌ		ŭ

---

a, e, i, u . have their continental sounds (mostly long).

o. . . . . . like *o* in *nor*.

ë. . . . . . like *a* in *make*.

ö. . . . . . like German *ŏ* in *Möwe*.

ü. . . . . . like French *u* in *lune*.

ä. . . . . . obscure vowel (mostly long).

ê. . . . . . like *e* in *bell*, but prolonged.

ᵉi . . . . . a diphthong with an accent on *i*. It always has a laryingeal intonation *ᵉi*ᵉ.

å. . . . . . between *a* and *o*, long.

ө . . . . . between *o* and *u*, long.

ŭ . . . . . posterior part of mouth in *i* position, lips in *u* position (short).

A, E, I . . obscure short vowels.

Very long and very short vowels are indicated by the macron and breve respectively.

The diphthongs are formed by combining any of the vowels with *i* and *u*. Thus, —

ai . . . . . like *i* in *hide*.

ei . . . . . " *ei* in *vein*.

oi . . . . . " *oi* in *choice*.

au . . . . . " *ow* in *how*.

CONSONANTS.

	Stops		Continuant		Affricative		Nasal	Trill	Spirans
	Surd	Sonant	Surd	Sonant	Surd	Sonant			
Glottal	ɛ								
Velar	q	g̈	x	—	—	—	—	ɾ	h
Palatal	k	—	x·	—	—	—	ñ	—	
Anterior palatal .	t·	d·	s·	—	č·	ǰ·	n·	—	—
Alveolar	t	d	s, c	z, j	š, č	ǰ	n	r, ř	—
Labial	p	b	f	v	—	—	m	—	—
Lateral	L	Ḷ	—	l, ḷ	—	—	—	—	—
w, y									

b‘, p‘, d‘, t‘, k‘, g‘, w‘, l‘, m‘, n‘ have a spirant added (*Gehauchter Absatz* of Sievers).

! . . . . designates the increased stress of articulation. K!, p!, č!, t!, are pronounced with a sudden explosion, which gives them a clicking sound.

’ . . . . a full pause between two sounds: yiñe’a, att’ɪ’yuḷ.

- . . . . used to connect the parts of a compound word.

l . . . . as in German.

ḷ . . . . the tip of the tongue touching the alveoli of the upper jaw, back of the tongue free.

ʟ . . . . posterior palatal *l*, surd and exploded, the tip of the tongue touching the alveoli of the upper jaw, back of the tongue pressed against the hard palate.

ʟ̣ . . . . posterior palatal *l*, like ʟ, but sonant. The Chukchee has both the surd ʟ and the sonant ʟ̣. The Koryak has only the sonant ʟ̣, which, however, is pronounced differently from the Chukchee sonant ʟ̣, in that the back of the tongue touches the hard palate with less pressure. And the Koryak sound ʟ̣ is almost similar to double *ll*. I use, however, the same transcription for both sounds, the Chukchee and the Koryak, because they fully correspond to each other.

r . . . . as in French.

ř . . . . dental, with slight trill.

ṛ . . . . velar.

m . . . . as in English.

n . . . . as in English.

ñ . . . . nasal of the *k* series, like *n* in *sing*.

n· . . . . palatized *n* sound (similar to *ny*).

b, p . . . as in English.

v . . . . bilabial.

w . . . . always consonantic, and in Koryak nearer to *v* than in Chukchee.

y . . . . always consonantic.

f . . . . pronounced somewhat as a compound of *hv*, bilabial.

h . . . . as in English.

g . . . . velar *g*.

x . . . . like *ch* in German *Bach*.

x· . . . . like *ch* in German *ich*.

d, t . . . as in English.

d·, t· . . palatized (similar to *dy* and *ty*).

s . . . . as in English.

s· . . . . palatized (similar to *sy*).

š . . . . like German *z*.

z . . . .   "   English *s* in *rose*.

c . . . .   "   English *sh*.

č . . . .   "   English *ch*.

j . . . .   "   French *jour*.

ǰ . . . .   "   English *joy*.

č· . . . . strongly palatized *č*.

ǰ· . . . . strongly palatized *ǰ*.

Sounds ë, ü, ö, å, x·, j, z, belong only to the Kamchadal.

Since in the western branch of the Koryak the Chuk-chee *r* is replaced by consonantic *y*, there appear the combinations *ay*, *oy*, which are distinct from the diphthongs *ai̯*, *oi*. They are pronounced like the respective diphthongs, but their *y* replaces the corresponding Chukchee *r*.

In Koryak the compound sound *ẉg*, *gẉ*, replaces the Chukchee sound *wkw*.

x in Koryak occurs but rarely, and replaces the velar *q*.

In Koryak as well as in Chukchee, *ı* terminal and un-accented is frequently pronounced with a slight nasal sound; but in Koryak the nasal sound is often pronounced quite distinctly. I do not use any additional sign to indicate the nasal character of this sound. On the other hand, I preferred to add *ñ* when the nasal sound was pronounced quite distinctly. Therefore, for instance, the dative of the noun has been transcribed in some cases as *yayai̯'tı* TO THE HOUSE, and in others as *notai̯'tı̃ñ* TO THE OPEN COUNTRY.

In Kamchadal, the Chukchee *r* is replaced by *j*. This *j* sound is often pronounced with a light *r* trill, somewhat like the Polish sound *rz*.

In the second Kamchadal dialect,[1] *ļ* sometimes has a slight nasal sound. This nasal *ļ* replaces the usual *n* of the first Kamchadal dialect.[2] No special symbol was adopted for this nasal *ļ* sound.

The Koryak as well as the Chukchee, in order to express a strong exclamation, transfer the accent to the last syllable. Under this transferred accent, *i* is changed to *e*; and *a*, *ı*, *u*, are changed to *o*. For instance, *ᴇ'nki* becomes *ᴇnke'*; *ñawa'kak* becomes *ñawako'k*. At the end of tales, *a'ččıč* becomes *aččo'č*.

---

[1] That of the village Sedanka.   [2] That of the Okhotsk shore.

1. Little-Bird-Man and Raven-Man.[1]

Raven-Man and Little-Bird-Man wooed (the daughter) of Big-Raven. Big-Raven preferred Little-Bird-Man. He said, "I will give my daughter to Little-Bird-Man." Miti′ said, "I will give my daughter to Raven-Man." After that Raven-Man would go out secretly. He would eat excrement and dog-carrion. (In the morning) they would wake up, and several wolverene-skins and wolf-skins would be there. They would ask both of the suitors, "Who killed those?" and Raven-Man would answer, "I killed them."

Vaḷvɪmtɪḷaᵋ′ninti ɛ′ččɪ Pĭči′qaḷaᵋn ñawɪnyoñvo′yke Quy-
Raven-Man (dual)   they   Little-Bird-Man   want a wife   with

qɪnn·aqu′yɪk. Quyqɪnn·a′qu Pĭčê′qaḷaᵋnañ gaimanñɪvo′ykɪn,
Raven-Big.   Raven-Big   for Little-Bird-Man   has a desire,

e′wañ, "Gŭmna′n ñawa′kak Pĭčê′qaḷaᵋnañ tĭyai′ḷɪñɪn."
he says,   "I   female child   to Little-Bird-Man   will give her."

Miti′ e′wañ, "Gŭmna′n ñawa′kak Vaḷvɪ′mtɪḷaᵋnañ tĭyai′ḷɪñɪn."
Miti′   says,   "I   female child   to Raven-Man   will give her."

5 Vaᵋ′yuk Vaḷvɪ′mtɪḷaᵋn vɪ′n·va ñɪto′ykɪn, aᵋḷa′ta awyeñvo′y-
Afterwards   Raven-Man   secretly   goes out,   excrement   he eats,

kɪn, attaᵋ′wawa awyeñvo′ykɪn. Kɪyaw′ḷaike, ɛ′nkɪ vañvo-
dog's carrion   he eats.   They wake up,   there   are

ḷai′ke qapa′au qu′tti iᵋu′wi. Newñɪvo′ykɪnenat, "Mi′kinak
(lying)   wolverene-skins   and wolf-skins   some   They began to say to both of them,   "By whom

ga′nmɪḷenau?" Vaḷvɪ′mtɪḷaᵋn, "Gŭmna′n."
are they killed?"   Raven-Man (says),   "I (killed them)."

---

[1] Compare W. Jochelson, The Koryak (Publications of the Jesup North Pacific Expedition, vol. vi), No. 82, p. 250.

Then a snow-storm broke out, and continued for a long time with unabated violence. Big-Raven said to the suitors, "Go and try to calm this storm! To the one who calms it, to that one will I give my daughter to wife." Raven-Man said, "I will calm the storm." He said, "Prepare some provisions for me." They prepared several pairs of boots. He went out, and staid near by under a cliff, eating. Little-Bird-Man went out, and there he stood eating of the provisions. Raven-Man gave to Little-Bird-Man a wicked look. Little-Bird-Man entered again, and did not say anything.

Raven-Man staid at the same place. The snow-storm

Va⁸'yuk gawya'ḷyoḷen. Qo'npŭ ᴇñña⁸'an ama'ḷatča.
Afterwards snow-storm came. Altogether thus not growing better.

Quyqɪnn·aqu'nak gêwñɪvo'ḷenat,[1] "Toq, qamaḷɪtva'thɪtɪk!
By Raven-Big they were told (dual), "There, make it better (dual)!

Ma'ki yamaḷɪtva'tɪñ, ña'nyen tǐyanñawtɪña'nñɪn." Vaḷ-
Who will make it better, to that one I will give the wife." Raven-

vɪ'mtiḷa⁸n, "Ġŭ'mma mɪmaḷɪtva'tɪk." E'wañ, "Qinatinuñ-
Man said, "I will make it better." He said, "Provision prepare

5 ḷa'tɪk." Ñɪnvo'q pḷa'kɪḷñu gatai'kɪḷinau. Ġa'ḷqaᴛin. ᴇ'ñkɪ
for me." A number of boots they prepared them. He went. There

vañvo'ykɪn e'n·mɪgenka, yenotčoñvo'ykɪn. Pɪči'qaḷa⁸n
he stays under a cliff, he is eating. Little-Bird-Man

ñɪtoñvo'ykɪn, ᴇnke' vañvo'ykɪn, awyeñvo'ykɪn. Čemya'q
goes out and there he stays, he eats. Of course

Pǐčeqaḷanai'tɪñ Vaḷvɪ'mtiḷa⁸n aqaᴛapñɪvo'ykɪn. Pǐči'qaḷa⁸n
on Little-Bird-Man Raven-Man badly looks. Little-Bird-Man

yaḷqɪ'wikɪn, ui'ña i'wka enñɪvo'ykɪn.
enters, not saying he is.

10 Vaḷvɪ'mtiḷa⁸n ᴇ'nki va'ykɪn. ᴇñña⁸'an qo'npŭ vŭyaḷan-
Raven-Man there stays. Thus altogether it

---

[1] This form is inchoative. It presents a compound of the stem *ñɪvo* TO BEGIN. It is used quite frequently to express a prolonged action: THEY WERE TOLD ALL THE TIME. Almost the same as the corresponding Chukchee plural form *gêuñño'lěnat.*

continued with the same vigor, without abating. Oh, at last Raven-Man entered. His boots were all covered with ice, for he would make water in his boots. That is the reason why the boots had ice. He said, "It is impossible! there is a crack in the heavens." After a while they said to Little-Bird-Man, "Now, then, calm this storm!" He said, "It is impossible. Shall I also go out and make water in my boots, like Raven-Man?" Then Big-Raven said to both suitors, "Go away! None of you shall marry here." Then Little-Bird-Man said, "All right! I will try." He took a round stopper, a shovel, and some fat, and went up to heaven. He flew up, and came to the crack in the heavens. He stopped it with a stopper, and threw the fat on the heavens all around it. For a while it grew calmer.

ñıvo′ykın, ui′ña ama′ļatča. Ģo, va⁸′yuk ģaya′ļqıwlin, ı′mı
storms,   not   not growing   Oh, afterwards   he entered,   all
           better.

pļa′ku   ģaqi′tilinau,   qačı′n   pļakgeñe′tıñ   na⁸′čañvoqen,
boots   were frozen,   and   into the boots   he made water,
           meantime

iñi′nñinık pļa′ku ģaqi′tilinau. "Q̈ıyı̆me′wun, i′ya⁸n ģači′-
therefore   boots   were frozen.   "Impossible,   heaven   is

malin." Va⁸′yuk Pı̆či′kaļa⁸n gewñıvo′ļen, "Toq, ģın-ya′q
broken."   Afterwards   Little-Bird-Man   they said to him,   "Oh,   thou now

5 qmaļatva′t." — "Qıyıme⁸′en, ģı′niw ģŭ′mma tıyanto′ykın,
make it better."   —   "Impossible,   like thee   I   shall I go out,

pļakgeñe′tıñ tıyaa⁸čañvo′ykın?" Ģewñıvo′ļenau Quyqın-
into the boots   shall I make water?"   They were told   by

n·aqu′nak, "Qaļqaļa′tık, kıtta′ñ aña′wtıñka." Va⁸′yuk
Raven-Big,   "Go away!   there   unmarried."   Afterwards

gewñıvo′ļen, "Atau′-qun." Qo′ļa ača′pil ģa′kmiʟin, qaļ-
he said,   "Well, now."   Some   fat small   he took it,

te′nñın, wŭlpa′pel, ga′ļqaʟin e⁸e′tı, ģayı′ñalin, ģaļa′lin,
stopper,   shovel small,   he went   to the sky,   he flew up,   he came,

10 iya⁸′kin čema′thıtñın qaļte′nña ģai′pıļen, ača′pil e⁸e′tıñ
of the sky   the cleft   with the stopper he stopped up,   fat small   to the sky

gani′ñļalin, pıče′ gama′ļalin.
he threw it, for a while it grew better.

He came home, and the snow-storm broke out again.
Even the stopper was thrust back into the house. It
was too small. He said, "It is impossible. The heavens
have a crack." Big-Raven made another stopper, a larger
one, and gave it to Little-Bird-Man. He also gave him
a larger piece of fat. Little-Bird-Man flew up to the
same place and put this stopper into the crack. It fitted
well. He drove it in with a mallet. He spread the fat
around over the heavens, shovelled the snow around the
hole, and covered it. Then it grew quite calm.

He came back, and then Raven-Man grew hateful to
all of them. He took a place close to Miti'; and she
said to him, "How is it that you smell of excrement?" —

 G̣ŭ′mḷañ gayai′tiḷen, g̣ŭ′mḷañ g̣awyalyo′ḷen. Ña′nyen
Again   he came home,   again   it stormed.   That

qaḷte′nñɪn g̣anqu′ḷin yayačɪkoi′tiñ, nɛpplu′qin mi′qun.
stopper   was thrust out   into the house,   small one   namely.

E′wañ, "Q̣ɪyɪme′wun. I′yaᵋn g̣ači′malin." Quyqɪnn·aqu′nak
He said,   "Impossible.   Sky   is broken."   By Raven-Big

qaḷte′nñɪn va′sqɪn g̣atai′kɪlin nɪma′yɪñqin, gei′ḷɪɪ̣in, a′čɪn
stopper   another one   he made it   big one,   he gave it,   fat

5 o′pta nɪma′yɪnqin gei′ḷɪɪ̣in, g̣a′ḷqaɪ̣in g̣ŭ′mḷañ, panenai′tiñ
also   big one   he gave it,   he went   again,   to the same place

g̣ayi′ñalin. G̣aḷa′lin, pa′nena ña′nyen qaḷte′nñɪn mal-kit
he flew up.   He came,   another time   that   stopper   all right

g̣a′npɪlen, taḷa′wg̣a g̣ata′ḷaḷen, ña′nyen a′čɪn eᵋe′tiñ g̣ani′ñ-
he stuffed in,   with the   he struck it,   that   fat   to the sky   he threw
    mallet

ḷalin, g̣ŭ′mḷañ äᵋ′ḷäḷa g̣aᵋ′ḷmelin, qoqḷo′wɪčñɪn; qo′npŭ
it,   again   with snow   he shovelled up,   the hole;   altogether

g̣ama′ḷalin.
it grew better.

10 G̣aḷa′lin; ña′nyen Vaḷvɪ′mtɪḷaᵋn aqa′nn·u g̣a′ččɪḷin.
He came;   that   Raven-Man   to hate   they had.

Miti′nak eñyei′ña vag̣a′ḷekɪn, newñɪvo′ykɪn Vaḷvɪ′mtɪḷaᵋn,
To Miti'   close   he sits,   she says to him   Raven-Man,

"Why! it is because I have had no bread for a long time." She said to him, "Enough, go away! You have done nothing to quiet this storm." He went away. Little-Bird-Man married Yini′a-ña′wgut.

Summer came. It was raining hard. Then Raven-Man put the sun into his mouth; so it grew quite dark. After that they said to Čan·ai′, "Čan·ai′, go and fetch water!" — "How shall I fetch water? (It is too dark)." After a while they said to her, "Why, we are quite thirsty. We are going to die." She went groping in the dark, then she stopped and began to sing. She sang, "Both small

---

"Meñqañqa′če enñɪvo′ykɪn, nɪme′ aᵉḷatčɪñvo′ykɪn?" —
"Wherefore   it happens to   quite   thou smellest with
             thee,   excrement?"   —

"Mi′qun, ui′ña yu′ḷaq akle′woka tɪnaᵉ′ḷɪk." Ģewñɪvo′len,
"Why,   not   for long   without bread¹ I remained."   She said to him,
             time

"I′n·ač, ga′ḷqata! Ui′ña mi′qun amaḷatva′tča i′tɪ!" Ģä′ḷ-
"Enough,   go away!   Not   even   not made better   thou   He
                                                    wert!"

qaᴛin. Pĭči′qaḷaᵉnak ña′nyen Yini′a-ña′wgut gama′taḷen.
went.   Little-Bird-Man   that   Yini′a-ña′wgut   married.

5   Toq, gaḷai′ulin, inya′wut gamuqai′ulin. Vaḷvɪ′mtɪḷaᵉn
Oh,   it came summer,   then   it rained.   Raven-Man

ti′ykɪtiy gaya′ḷuplin. Qačɪ′n qo′npŭ nɪki′ta ganaᵉ′ᴛen.
the sun   used for a quid.   So   altogether   night   grew.

Vaᵉ′yuk gewñɪvo′ḷen, "Čan·ai′, qaimŭ′ge!" — "Me′ñqač
Afterwards   they said to her,   "Čan·ai′,   fetch water!"   —   "In what
                                                                    manner

mi′qun mai′mɪk?" Vaᵉ′yuk gewñɪvo′ḷen, "Me′ñqañ nɪme′
namely   shall I fetch   Afterwards   they said to her,   "Why   very
water?"

mɪtɪpaᵉḷai′kɪnen. Vaᵉ′yuk mɪssavɪᵉ′yaḷa." Ģa′ḷqaᴛin qai-
we are thirsty.   Afterwards   we shall die."   She went

10   čayiči′ña, ᴇñaᵉ′an wŭs·qŭ′mčɪku, vaᵉ′yuk ga′ñvɪlin, gañ-
groping,   thus   in the dark,   afterwards   she stopped,   she

---

¹ This is meant sarcastically. Bread is considered a delicacy among the Koryak. The Raven, who eats excrement, pretends to feed on bread.

rivers are stingy (with their water)." Then a small river came to that place, bubbling. She filled her pail bought from the Russians (i. e., an iron pail), and carried it on her back. (Suddenly) a man came to her. She could not carry the pail. He said, "I will carry the pail (for you)." She came home in the dark. The man followed. It was River-Man. They said to her, "Who is this man?" He said, "I am River-Man. I took pity on that singer." They scolded their daughter. Nevertheless River-Man married her.

After that they remained still in complete darkness. They said to River-Man, "Why are we living in darkness?" He said, "Why, indeed?" He put on a head-

---

voḷen gɪya'pčak. E'wañ, "ı'mɪn qai-vai'amti aḷña'we°ye."
began   to sing.   She said,   "All   small rivers (dual) are stingy."

Va°'yuk gani'kalin ᴇnkai'tɪ vai'ampiḷñ, gañvo'ḷen čilala'tik.
Afterwards it made so to that place river small,   began   to bubble.

Ģayɪ'ččalin miḷh-u'kkam, yaite'tɪ ga'ḷqaɹin, miḷh-u'kkam
She filled   Russian vessel, to the house she went,   Russian vessel

gemtei'pɪlin, qḷa'wuḷ gaḷa'lin. Ģapkau'ḷen, e'wañ, "Ģŭm-
she carried on   a man   came.   She could not   he said,   "I,
her back,   (carry),

5 na'n, gŭmna'n mɪ'mtɪn." Ģayai'tɪḷen wŭs·qŭ'mčɪku ña'nyen
         I   shall carry it." She came home in the dark.   That one

gaḷɪmñena'ḷen. Vai'am. Ģewñɪvo'ḷen, "ᴇni'n ma'ki?"
followed.   River.   They said to her, "That one who?"

E'wañ, "Ģu'mma Vaiamenai'-gŭm. Ģŭmna'n yai'vaču
He said,   "I   River-am-I.   I   to compassion

tɪ'tčɪn ᴇna'n gɪya'pčaḷa°n." Ģañvo'ḷen ñawa'kak kitai'ñak.
had   that   singer."   They began female-child to scold.

Ña'nyen Vaia'mɪnak gama'taḷen.
That one   by the River   was married.

10 To, va°'yuk qo'npŭ wŭs·qŭ'mčɪku vañvoḷai'ke. Gew-
Oh, afterwards altogether in the dark   they remained.   They

ñɪvo'ḷen Vai'am, "Me'ñqañ nɪki'ta mɪtɪtvañvoḷai'kɪn?"
began to say   to River,   "Why   in the night   we remain?"

E'wañ, "Me'nqañ mi'qun?" Ḷawtɪkɪ'ḷčɪčñɪn vi'tvitin gai'-
He said,   "Why,   indeed?"   Head-band   of ringed- he
                                              seal thong

band of ringed-seal thong. He went out (and practised magic). Then at least a little light appeared. The day dawned. They spoke among themselves, "How shall we do it?" Then Yini′a-ña′wg̣ut prepared for a journey. She went to Raven-Man and asked, "Halloo! Is Raven-Man at home?" Raven-Woman said, "He is." She said to Raven-Man, "Since you went away, I have been feeling dull all the time." She found Raven-Man, and said to him, "Did not you feel dull (since that time)? Will you stay so?" He turned his back to her, but she wanted to turn him (so that he should look with) his face to her. But he turned his back to her. Then she tickled him under the arms. She put her hands under his armpits. His sister said to him, "What is the matter with you?

---

pıḷen, g̣anto′ḷen, ayi′kvan g̣aqayıchıḷanñivo′ḷen vantıge′ñın
put on, he went out. at least small light came, dawn

g̣ato′mwaḷen. Va⁣ᵋyuk gewñıvo′ḷen, "Me′ñqañ mı′ntın?"
was created. Afterwards they began to talk, "In what manner we shall do it?"

Yini′a-ña′wg̣ut g̣anvo′ḷen tenma′witčuk, Vaḷvımtıḷaᵋyıkıñ
Yini′a-ña′wg̣ut began to prepare, to Raven-Man

g̣aḷa′lin, "Mai, Vaḷvı′mtıḷaᵋn va′ykın?" Va′čvı-ña′ut e′wañ,
she came, "Halloo! Raven-Man is (at home)?" Raven-Woman said,

5 "Va′ykın." Gewñıvo′ḷen Vaḷvı′mtıḷaᵋn "As·s·o′ qati′,
"He is." She began to say to Raven-Man "Since you went away,

qo′npŭ a′ḷva tıtva′ñvok." G̣ayoᵋoḷen Vaḷvı′mtıḷaᵋn, gew-
altogether wrongly I was." She found the Raven-Man, she

ñıvo′ḷen, "Gı′ssa qa′čık ui′ña a′ḷva a′tvaka? Qe′nñıvo?"
began to say, "Thou really not wrongly not wert? Will you stay so?"

Qa′pten g̣ayı′ḷtıḷen, yai′na yıli′ykının. G̣ŭ′mḷañ qa′pten
The back he turned, to the front side she turns him. Again the back

li′ykın. Va⁣ᵋyuk g̣anvo′ḷen čıchi′ñık yıyıgıcha′wik, g̣ačečeñ-
he turns. Afterwards she began in the armpits to tickle him, she put her

10 qatvıñvo′ḷen; čake′ta gewñıvo′ḷen, "Quya′qı? I′n·ač.
hands under his armpits; by the sister he was told, "What is the matter with you? Enough.

Stop it! This is a good girl." After that he began to
make sounds in her direction, "Ġm, ġm, ġm!" She turned
him around, and at last he laughed out, "Ha, ha, ha!"
The sun jumped out and fastened itself to the sky. It
grew daylight.

After that they slept together. She said to him, "Have
you a tent?" — "No!" — "Have you a fork?" — "No!"
— "Have you a plate?" — "No!" She said, "Then let
us go home! I have all those things at home." They
moved on to Big-Raven's house. She said to Raven-Man,
"Oh, you are a good man!" and he felt flattered. Afterwards she killed him.

E′nnu maḷ-ña′wɪtkata." Vaᵋ′yuk ᴇnkai′tɪ gañvo′ḷen, "Ġm,
This one is a woman." Afterwards to that he began, "Ġm,
good direction

ġm, ġm." Qo′yɪñ yɪḷeñvo′ykɪnen. Vaᵋ′yuk ġaktača′čhaʟen,
ġm, ġm." To this side she turns him. Afterwards he laughed loudly,

"Ġa, ġa, ġa!" Ti′ykɪtiy ġače′pñɪtoḷen, i′yaᵋġ ga′plin,
"Ha, ha, ha!" The sun peeped out, to the fastened
sky itself,

qo′npŭ ġecha′ʟen.
altogether it grew light.

5 Vaᵋ′yuk gayɪ′ḷqalinat Yini′a-ña′wġutinti, gewñɪvo′ḷen,
Afterwards they slept (dual) Yini′a-ña′wġut (dual, i. e., she told him,
with the man),

"Ma′ččɪ yɪ′nna va′ykɪn, poḷa′tka¹ va′ykɪn?" — "Ui′ña." —
"Now what is, tent is?" — "No." —

"Ma′ččɪ vi′ḷka¹ va′ykɪn?" E′wañ, "Ui′ña." — "Toreḷ′ka¹
"And fork is?" He said, "No!" — "Plate

va′ykɪn?" Ġŭ′mḷañ e′wañ, "Ui′ña." E′wañ, "Mɪnyai′tɪmɪk.
is?" Again he said, "No!" She said, "Let us go home!

Ġŭmni′n ya′yak vaḷai′ke." Ye′lɪñ gata′wañḷenat Qoyqɪn-
My things at home are." There they moved on to

10 nˑaqoyɪkai′tɪ. Ewñɪvo′ykɪnen Vaḷvɪ′mtɪḷaᵋn, "Eᵋ′n, maḷ-
Raven-Big. She began to say to the Raven-Man, "Oh, well, a good

qḷa′wuḷ." Ačačhitčoñvo′ykɪn. Vaᵋ′yuk ñe′nako ga′nmɪḷen.
man!" He felt flattered. Afterwards there she killed him.

¹ Words borrowed from the Russian: палатка TENT, тарелка PLATE, вилка FORK.

Yini′a-ña′wgut put Raven-Man's (head) on above. She said, "That spotted palate of yours, let it grow to be a fine cloudless sky!" [1]

She came home. And they said to her, "What have you been doing?" She said, "I killed Raven-Man. He had the sun in his mouth." From that time on it was quite calm. Raven-Woman said, "Well, now, does my brother remember me? (Probably) he has plenty to eat." She said, "Let me visit him." She visited him, and he was dead. Then she cried (and said), "He caused annoyance to the other people. (Therefore he is dead.)" She left him there. There was nothing else to do.

Yini′a-ña′wgutınak Vaḷvı′mtıḷaᵋn gıčgoḷai′tı goi′pıḷen.
By Yini′a-ña′wgut   Raven-Man   to the upper part   was stuck in.

E′wañ, "Gıni′n ka′li-qa′nyan maḷ-iᵋ′yu nına ᵋ′ḷın, tañ-iᵋ′yu
She said,   "Thy   spotted-palate   to a sky   let it grow,   to a fine sky good

nına ᵋ′ḷın."
let it grow."

Gayai′tıḷen, gewñıvo′ḷen, "Me′ñqañ i′tı?" E′wañ,
She came home,   they told her,   "How thou wert?"   She said,

5 "Vaḷvı′mtıḷaᵋn tı′nmın, ɛna′n ti′ykıtiy gaya′ḷuplin." Ačiva′n
"Raven-Man   I killed,   he   the sun   used for a quid."   From that time

qo′npú maḷa′tı. Va′čvı-ña′ut e′wañ, "Iñei′! Yiča′myi-
altogether   it grew better.   Raven-Woman   said,   "Well now!   By the

tu′mga ḷı′gi ina′tčı? Tañ-a′wyeñvoi." E′wañ, "Mıyoᵋ′ogan!"
brother   to his mind   I am put to?   Good he began to eat."   She said,   "Let me visit him!"

Gayoᵋ′oḷen. Eᵋ′en gavıᵋ′yalin. Gañvo′ḷen qaḷhai′ak, "ɛna′n
She visited him.   And   he was dead.   She began to cry,   "He

tu′mkıñ ya′notı vetke′gıčıın tai′kınin." Gape′ḷaḷen.
to the other people   at first   annoyance   did."   She left him.

10 Me′ñqañ nı′ntınin?
How   was she to act?

---

[1] These words are used also as an incantation against bad weather.

Then those people said to Little-Bird-Man, "Go home, both of you!" They said to them, "Go away with a caravan of pack-sledges!" He replied, "We will go on foot." They went away on foot, and came to a river. Little-Bird-Man said to the woman, "Let me carry you (across)!" The woman said to him, "Do not do it!" He said, "It is all right." He carried her, and in doing so he died. Yini'a-ña'wgut slept a night among stone-pines and was almost frozen to death. On the following morning it dawned, and close to that place a reindeer-herd was walking. All the reindeer had iron antlers. A man was walking there too. He said, "Oh, come here!" She said, "I will not come. My husband has

---

Ña'nyeu   gewñıvo'ļenau   Pĭči'qala⁸n,   "Qıyai'tıtık."
Those   began to say   to Little-Bird-Man,   "Go home (dual)."

Ģi'wlinat,   "Mu'uta   qi'thıtık."   Ģi'wlin   ᴇnna⁸'an,   "A'ļımı,
They told them   "With a   be (dual)."   He said   thus,   "Well,
(dual),   caravan of
sledges

vai'čita."   Ģaļqa'ʟinat vai'čita.   Va⁸'yuk ģayo⁸'oļen vai'am-
on foot."   They went (dual) on foot.   Afterwards   they found   a river

n·aqu.   Pĭči'qala⁸n   e'wañ   ña'wıtkatıñ,   "Mıtı'mtıngi!"
big.   Little-Bird-Man   said   to the woman,   "I will carry thee!"

5 Ña'wıtqata   gewñıvo'ļen,   "Qıye'm-e⁸'en."   E'wañ,   "Mal-
By the woman   he was told,   "Not needed."   He said,   "All

kı'tıl."   Ģati'mtiñlin,   va⁸'yuk Pĭči'qala⁸n ģavı⁸'yalin.   Yini'a-
right!"   He carried her,   after that Little-Bird-Man   died.   Yini'a-

ña'wgut ģaļa'lin qas·wuge'ñkı kc'vıñvoñ, kĭma'k ququi'tıñ.
ña'wgut   came   to the stone-pine   to stay for a   almost   she was
bushes   night,   frozen.

Miti'w gečha'ʟen, ᴇnka'ta tīļai'vıkın ñe'ʟa, pı̣ļvı'ntı-yı'nnala⁸n.
To-   it dawned,   on that   is walking   a herd,   with iron antlers.
morrow   place
around

Qļa'wuļ   o'pta   ᴇnka'ta   tīļai'vıkın.   Gewñıvo'ļen,   "Toq,
Man   also   on that place   is walking.   He told her,   "Oh,

10 qıya'thi!"   Gewñıvo'ļen,   "Qıyo'm   mıla'k!   Ģűmni'n i'pa
come!"   She told him,   "I will not   come.   My   actual

died." He said to her, "I am he, I am your husband."
He took out his gloves. "These you made for me. I
am your husband. I am Little-Bird-Man."

A house was there, also reindeer (for driving). He
said to her, "Let us go to Big-Raven! Now let them
say again that you have a bad husband!" They went
with a caravan of pack-sledges, and they arrived. The
people said to Big-Raven, "Oh, your daughter has come
with a caravan." Big-Raven said, "Our daughter went
away on foot." She said, "Here I am, I have been
brought home by Little-Bird-Man." Little-Bird-Man made
numerous driving-sledges, all of silver. They lived there

---

qɪa′wuɭ viɛ′gi." Gewñɪvo′len, "Wutɪnnaɭai′-gŭm qɪa′wuɭ-e-
man   died."   He told her,   "This-am-I   man-am-

gŭm." Yɪ′ɭhɪɭɪu gaito′lenau. "Wutɪssau′ gɪna′n gatai′kɪ-
I."   Finger-gloves he took them out.   "These   thou   hast made.

linau. Wutɪssaɭai′-gŭm, Pĭčiqalaɛnai′-gŭm."
    This-am-I,   Little-Bird-Man-am-I."

ᴇnke′ yaya′ña va′ykɪn, gŭ′mɭañ qoya′we. Gewñɪvo′len,
There   a house   is,   also   reindeer.   He told her,

5 "Qoyqɪnn·aqoyɪkai′tɪ mɪnɪ′ɭqat. Če′čve yewñɪvoɭa′ñe,
"To Raven-Big   let us go!   Openly   they shall tell,

'Aɛ′ččiñ qɪa′wuɭ yawa′ykɪnen.'" Ga′ɭqaɭinat mu′uta,
'Bad   man   she has him.'"   They went (dual)   with the
caravan,

gaɭa′linat. Gewñɪvo′lenau, "Ñawako′k! naya′tɪn, mu′uta!"
they came.   They began to say,   "Female child!   came,   with the
caravan!"

Gewñɪvo′len, "Mu′čhin ñawa′kak vai′čita qatha′ai."
He said.   "Our   female child   on foot   they went
away" (dual).

Gewñɪvo′len, "Wuttɪnaɭai′-gŭm. Pĭči′qalaɛnak inaya′tɪ."
She said,   "This-am-I.   By Little-Bird-Man   I was
brought."

10 Pĭči′qalaɛn neɭhepɪto′nqen yaqa′n-uya′tikiu am čerepro′nau.[1]
Little-Bird-Man   many created   driving-sledges   all   of silver.

---

[1] Borrowed from the Russian серебро SILVER.

all together, and travelled about in all directions with a caravan of pack-sledges. They lived in joy. They staid there.

E'nki   oma'ka   gatvañvo'ļenau,   ga'lñıl   gaļaivıñvo'ļenau
There   together   they lived,   in all   they walked around
directions

mu'uta,   gaaimıyo'oļenau,   gatvañvo'ļenau.   Aččo'č.
with a   they lived in joy,   they lived.   That is all.
caravan,

---

2. Big-Raven and the Mice.[1]

Some Mouse-Girls walked along the seashore. The youngest Mouse also wanted to follow. Her mother said, "Tie her (and leave her) on the seashore." They bound her with two strings of her diaper. She began to squeal, "Pawawawa'!" and they said, "What is it?" — "I have found a genuine small nail." — "Go to her!" They went to her. "What is it that you have found?" But it was only a small shell. "Oh, strike her!" They struck her, and she whimpered, "Igigi'!"

Pipi'kča-ña'wgutinu gas·hıntıļı'linau. ıla'lu ļúmñena'ykın.
Mouse-Women   on the seashore walked. The   is following.
youngest

Ma'ma e'wañ, "As·hı'ñka qwuļa'gıtča." A'men gawgu'ļın
Mamma   said, "On the seashore   tie her."   And   they bound her

5 am-ma'kil-ñe'eta.   Tawtawanñıvo'ykın,   "Pawawawa'!"
with diaper- with two.   She began to squeal,   "Pawawawa'!"
only- strings-

A'men e'wañ, "Yı'nna wot?" — "Tıļa'go'n! Ta'qıñ-
And   they said, "What   this?" —   "I found!   Genuine

va'gıļñıpel." — "ıļa'ñı qıyoᵉoļa'gıtča." Gayoᵉ'olen. "Yı'nnaqi
nail small." — "The   you visit her." They visited her. "What then
youngest

ļuᵉ'waᵉn?" Qa'čın milya'qpil. "Qaykıpla'gıtča!" Gañvo'ļen
thou foundest?" And only a shell small.   "Strike her!"   They began

kı'pļık, gañvo'ļen qaļhai'ak, "Igigi'."
to strike,   she began   to cry,   "Igigi'."

---

[1] See Jochelson, The Koryak, l. c., No. 88, p. 260.

After a while she turned to them again, and began as before, "What is it that I have found? Oh, indeed, it has nails! Oh, indeed, it has eyes! Oh, indeed, it has whiskers!" — "Go to her and see what she has found!" They came to her, and really it was a small ringed seal.

Big-Raven said, "Eh, eh! Why are those Mouse-Girls shouting and dancing?" Miti′ said, "Oh, leave off! Why do you want to go to them?" But he went to them. "Well, there! Mouse-Girls, what is the matter with you?" — "Oh, nothing! only this Hairless-One grew angry with us." He said, "Louse me, (one of you!)" One Mouse-Girl said, "I have pricked myself with my father's awl."

Gŭ′mlañ ᴇnkai′ti gañvo′len, "Yı′nna wot tıḷaᵉgo′n?
Again in the same she began, "What this I found?
  direction

Ča′myeq gavaɣınña′ḷen, ča′myeq gaṛa′lin, ča′myeq gaḷa-
Indeed with nails, indeed with eyes, indeed with

ḷu′lin." — "Qıyoᵉola′ɣıtča ıḷa′ñi, yı′nna ḷuᵉ′nin." Ɡayoᵉ′oḷen,
whiskers." — "Go to the youngest, what she has They visited her,
  (and see) found."

qačı′n vi′tvitpıl.
and really a ringed
  seal small.

5 Quyqınn·a′qu e′wañ, "Eei! ya′qḷau Pipı′kča-ña′wɡutinu
Raven-Big said, "Eh, eh! what are Mouse-Women
  they doing,

ıs·hımḷavai′ñaḷai?" Miti′ e′wañ, "Qanqa′wɡi. Ya′qkınau
loudly dance shouting Miti′ said, "Cease. What for
  they are?"

nayoᵉ′onau?" Ɡayoᵉ′oḷenau. "Amei′! Pipı′kča-ña′wɡutinu,
will you visit them?" He visited them. "Well there! Mouse-Women,

yaqḷaikıne′tık?" — "Ui′ña aya′qka. Atau′ A′xɡıke
what are you doing?" — "Not not anything. Simply Hairless-One

kŭmaᵉ′ti." E′wañ, "Qinamḷıḷa′tik." Qo′ḷḷa e′wañ, "Appa′-
is angry." He said, "Louse me." One said, "With

10 nak [1] inassına′ñik toi′pŭk." Naniᵉ′wın tami′nñı-qḷa′wuḷen
father on an awl I pricked One could say handicraft-man's
  myself."

---

[1] *A′ppa, a′pa* in some Koryak dialects, FATHER; in others, GRANDFATHER. Here it is used with both meanings indiscriminately.

One might think she were the daughter of some artisan. He said to another small girl, "Louse me!" — "I have pricked myself with my mother's needle." One might think she were the daughter of some seamstress. "O Hairless-One! louse me." She said, "Eh, all right!" She loused him. (He said,) "Oh, say (these words): 'Grandfather's lice taste of fat!'"[1]

Then he shook his head, and the small mice were scattered in all directions. Some fell into the sea, some into the coast-slime, others into the river, and others again on the pebbles. Big-Raven took the little ringed seal and carried it home. The Mouse-Girls crawled to the shore

---

ñawa'kak. Va's·qɪn ña'nyen qai-ña'wɪs·qat, "Qinamḷu'wi!" —
female child. Another   that   small-woman,   "Louse me!"   —

" G̣ŭ'mma mama'nak[2] tetei'tɪñ toi'pŭk." Nani⁸wɪn, awa'nñɪ-
"I   with mamma   on a needle I pricked   One could say, sewing
                              myself."

ña'wɪn ñawa'kak. "Axg̣ɪke, qina'mḷu." E'wañ, "I, toq!"
woman's female child. "Hairless-One, louse me." She said, "Eh, well!"

G̣añvo'ḷen mĭḷu'k. "Qiwiykɪn-i'-g̣i, 'Appanau' mɪmḷu'wg̣i
She began to louse him. "Say you,   'Grandfather's   lice

5 nanyamča'čaqenau.'"
    are tasting of fat.'"

ᴇ'nki g̣aḷawtɪme'lin, ña'nyau qai-pipi'kaḷñu am-ma'na
Then   he shook his head,   those   small   mice   to different
                                                        directions

g̣anɪya'linau, — qu'tčau a'ñqak, qu'tčau wapɪ's·qalqak,
he scattered them, — some to the sea, some   to the slime,

qu'tčau va'yamɪlqak, qu'tčau wu'g̣wulqak. Quyqinn·aqu'nak
some   to the river,   some to the pebbles.   Raven-Big

ña'nyen vi'tvitpiḷɪñ g̣anyai'tɪlen. Ña'nyau g̣awḷɪñvo'ḷenau,
that   ringed seal small he took it home. Those   came to the shore,

---

[1] It seems that the Hairless Mouse-Girl, according to the custom of many native tribes of this country, was killing the lice with her teeth.

[2] *Ma'ma*, probably from the Russian мама. The proper Koryak term with endearing sense is *a'mma*.

and asked one another, "Where did you fall?" — "I fell into the sea." — "Then you were cold." — "And where did you fall?" — "I fell on the small pebbles." — "Then you were pricked." — "And where did you fall?" — "I fell into the coast-slime." — "Then you were cold." — "And you, Hairless-One, where did you fall?" — "I fell on the moss [1] spread by mother." — "Then you fell easy."

They said, "Let us go home!" They went home and told their mother, "See, mamma! we have found a small ringed seal, but grandfather took it away." — "Did he? Then we will fetch it back. O daughters! go and look

---

es·he′lvīñ uwi′kiu gapñiḷañvo′ḷenau. "Gɪ′ssa mi′ñki i′yi?" —
between themselves / their bodies / they told about. / "Thou / where / hittest?" —

"Gumma a′ñqak ti′yak." — "Vɪ′yañ iskuḷa′ti." — "Gɪ′ssa
"I / to the sea / hit." — "Then / thou wert cold." — "Thou

mi′ñki i′yi?" — "Gu′mma ti′yak čegai′lɪkɪk." — "Vɪ′yañ
where / hittest?" — "I / hit / on the small pebbles." — "Then

isvɪḷa′ti." — "Gɪ′ssa mi′ñki i′yi?" — "Gumma vapi′s·qalqak
thou wert pricked." — "Thou / where / hittest?" — "I / on the slime

5 ti′yak." — "Vɪ′yañ iskuḷa′ti." — "Gɪ′ssa, A′xhɪke, mi′ñki
hit." — "Then / thou wert cold." — "Thou, / Hairless-One, / where

i′yi?" — "Gu′mma mama′nak veta°niya′tɪk." — "To, gɪ′ssa
hittest?" — "I / to mamma / on the moss spread." — "Oh, / thou

yiykuḷa′ti."
wert on soft!"

Gewñivo′ḷenau, "Mɪnyaitɪḷa′mik!" Gayai′tɪḷenau, gañvo′-
They began to say, / "Let us go home!" / They came home, / they

ḷenau pñaḷte′lɪk, "Ki′wan, ma′ma, ya′nut vi′tvɪpil mɪtḷa°′wḷa°n,
began to narrate, / "Truly, / mamma, / at first / ringed seal / we found it, small

10 appa′nak i′tčanin." — "Ya′qkɪnki! Nayanva′nñɪnɪn, mɪs-
by the grandfather / he took it away." — "What for! / Let them skin it, / we

---

[1] Used as a child's diaper. See W. Jochelson, The Koryak, *l. c.*, p. 252.

into his house." They looked in. Then they came back and said, "Eme′mqut is skinning it." — "Now you there, [you Mouse-Girl,] go and look in!" She looked in. "Just now they are cooking it." — "Now, you there, this one, go and look in there!" She looked in. "Just now they are taking the meat out of the kettle." Mouse-Woman said, "Oh, I wish Big-Raven would say, 'We will eat it to-morrow!' We must find a shaman's small stick (used in magic). Oh, you there, small Mouse-Girl! take this bundle of grass (on which magic had been practised) and carry it to Big-Raven's house. There drop it through the vent-hole."

They (the Mice) took it and carried it there, and dropped it into the house. Big-Raven immediately said, "Miti′,

---

saitıḷa′ñın. Ñawa′kku, qawas·vıḷa′tık." Ġawa′s·vılinau,
will fetch it. Female children, look in." They looked in,

gaya′ʟinau, gi′wlinau, "Amamqu′tinak yıwa′ññıykınin." —
they came, they said, "Eme′mqut he is skinning it." —

"Am-ñu′nin qai-ña′wıs·qat, qawas·vu′gi." Ġawa′s·vilin.
"Now this one small-woman, look in." She looked in.

"Akiḷaᵘ′č kokaiviḷai′ke." — "Am-ñu′nin qai-ña′wıs·qat,
"Just now they are cooking it." — "Now this one small-woman,

5 qawas·vu′gi." Ġawa′s·vilin. "Akiḷaᵘ′t kokañpaḷai′ke."
look in." She looked in. "Just now they take (the meat) out of the kettle."

Gewñıvo′ḷen Pipi′kča-ña′wġut, "Iñe′! Quyqınna′qu ne′wñıvon,
She began to say Mouse-Woman, "Oh, Raven-Big would he say,

'Tañ-miti′w mına′wyeḷa,' Iḷuᵘ′pılñ ti′ta mĭneḷoᵘ′čoḷa! Qai-
'Well to-morrow we will eat it,' Shaman's when we shall find! Small
small stick

ña′wıs·qat em-ña′no qıyaᵘ′thın vai-kı′ltıpılñ. Qıḷaḷaġı′tča
woman there-that one bring grass-bundle small. Carry it away

Qoyqınn·aqoyıkai′tñ, qĭnayaḷa′ġıtča."
to Raven-Big's (house), drop it."

10 Ġaʟa′lin, gana′yalin. Quyqınn·a′qu e′wañ, "Mitei′,
They carried dropped it. Raven-Big said, "Miti′,
it away,

we had better eat this meat to-morrow." And she said,
"All right!" — "Oh, you, small Mouse-Girl! go and look
into the house!" — "Just now Miti′ is arranging the bed."
— "And now you, go and have a look!" — "Just now
they have gone to sleep, they are snoring." — "Now,
there, let us go!" They took bags and iron pails, went
there, and put all the cooked meat into them, also what
was left of the broth. They defecated (into the kettle),
also filled Miti′'s and Big-Raven's boots with small pebbles.

Next morning they awoke. "Miti′, get up! Let us eat!"
Miti′ began to put on her boots. "Ah, ah, ah! ah, ah,
ah!" — "What is the matter with you?" — "Oh, nothing!"

---

miti′u mɪnnu′nau noo′wge." A′men e′wañ "I, i′nmi-
to-morrow we will eat the cooked meat." And she said "Eh, all

qu′nŭm." — "A′men yɪ′nna, qai-ña′wɪs·qat qawa′s·vugɪn." —
right!" — "Oh, what, small-woman look in there." —

"Akiḷaᵉ′č taka′wñekɪn Miti′." — "Am-ɪnyi′n qai-ña′wɪs·qat,
"Just now prepares the bed Miti′." — "Now this small-woman

qawa′s·vɪ." — "Akiḷaᵉ′č gayi′ḷqalinau, ɪnkayalai′ke." —
look in." — "Just now they are gone to they are snoring." —
sleep,

5 "Toq, mɪnɪḷqaḷa′mɪk." Milh-u′kkamau a′gɪmu ga′kmiɪinau,
"There, let us go!" Russian vessels bags they took them,

ga′ḷqaɪinau, ɪ′mñ noo′wge gayo′oḷenau, a′kyeḷ ipa′ña
they went, all the cooked they put in, also broth
meat

paio′čɪpɪt. Gaᵉḷai′oḷen, ɪ′mñ Miti′s·hinau Quyqɪnn·aqu′čhi-
remainder. They defecated, also Miti′s Raven-Big's

nau pḷa′ku wu′gwa gaye′lin.
boots with pebbles they filled.

Miti′u gakya′wlinat. "Mitei′, qakya′wgi, mina′wyi."
Next day they awoke. "Miti′, get up! Let us eat!"

10 Miti′ gapḷaitiñvo′ḷen. "Mɪkɪkɪkɪ′k, mɪkɪkɪkɪkɪ′k!"—"Ya′qɪykɪn
Miti′ began to put on "Ah, ah, ah! ah, ah, ah!" — "What art thou
her boots.

ɪnña ᵉ′an i′tɪykɪn?" — "Ui′ña yɪ′nna!" Quiqɪnn·a′qu
thus art thou?" — "Not anything!" Raven-Big

Big-Raven then put on his boots. "Ah, ah, ah! ah, ah, ah!" — "And what is the matter with you? You cry now, just as I did." — "Oh, stop (talking), bring the cooked meat, heat the broth!" Miti' drank some broth, (and immediately cried out,) "It tastes of excrement, it tastes of excrement!" — "Oh, bring it here!" Then Big-Raven also cried, "It tastes of excrement, it tastes of excrement!" — "Mouse-Women have defiled us." — "I will not forgive this. I will stun them with blows. Bring me my big club!" She gave it to him, and he started to go to the Mouse-Women. "Oh, grandfather is coming. Tell him, 'Eat some pudding of stone-pine nuts!'" — "What good are those puddings of stone-pine nuts! I have no

---

gaplaitiñvo'len. "Mɪkɪkɪkɪ'k, ɪkɪkɪkɪ'k!" — "Ya'qɪykɪn
began to put on his boots. *"Ah, ah, ah! ah, ah, ah!"* — *"What art thou,*

Ɛnña'an i'tɪykɪn? A'či a'men gŭ'mkɪñ ni'wi-gi." — "Qa'nkau,
thus art thou? Now like me talking art thou." — *"Cease,*

qɪya°'thɪn noo'wgc. Mĭna'wyi. ɪpa'ña qinathɪleu'." Miti'
bring cooked meat. Let us eat! Broth make warm." Miti'

gañvo'len ɪpa'wɪk. "A°la'tve, a°la'tve!" — "Qɪya°'thɪn!"
began to drink (broth). "It tastes of it tastes of excrement!" "Bring it here!"

5 Quyqɪnn·a'qu o'pta e'wañ, "A°la'tve, a°la'tve!" — "Pipi'kča-
Raven-Big also said, "It tastes of it tastes of excrement!" "Mouse-

ña'wgutinu ganta'witkɪñau-mu'yi." — "Qaye'm ña'no,
women have defiled us (two)." — "I will not this (forgive),

mɪkɪplɪs·qewla'tɪk. Qɪya°'thɪn qolowoču'mñɪn." Gai'lɪɪn,
I will stun them with blows. Bring big club." She gave him,

ga'lqaɪin, ya'lɪñ gata'wañlen. "Qulu', qulu', qulu'k!" —
he went away, there he was moving on. "Big, big, big!" —

"Appa'nak nenenela'mɪk. Qiwla'gɪtča, 'Nɪ'klɪ-ye'lka!'" —
"By the grandfather he appears to us. Tell him, 'With stone-pine nuts pudding!'" —

teeth." — "Then have some cloud-berry-pudding." — "Yes, I will eat some of the cloud-berry-pudding." He ate of the pudding. "Grandfather, lie down on your back and have a nap!" — "Yes, I will have a nap, lying thus on my back."

He slept, and they fastened to his eyes some red shreds. "Grandfather, enough, get up!" — "All right! now I will go home." He went home; and when he was approaching, and came close to the house, he shouted all of a sudden, "Miti′, tear in twain the worst one of our sons, to appease the fire!" Without any reason she tore her son in twain. "And where is the fire? Just now you said, 'It burns.' What happened to your eyes? They have shreds fastened

---

"Ya′qkinau nı′klı-ye′lku? Ava′nnıkıl-e-gŭm." — "Yı′ttı-
"What for (those) stone-pine nut pud- Toothless am I." — "With
dings? cloudberry [1]-

ye′lka!" — "O, yı′ttı-ye′lka-van tı̆ya′yilku." Ġayı′lkulin.
pudding!" — "Yes, with cloudberry-pud- I will eat the He ate of the
ding pudding." pudding.

"Appa′, wŭ′ssiñ gayı′lqata!" — "O, wŭ′ssiñ tı̆yayı′lqatiñ."
"Grand- on your sleep!" — "Yes, on my I will sleep."
father back back

Ġayı′lqalin, gaʟamyımka′lenat. "Appa′, i′n·ač, qak-
He slept, they to his eyes attached "Grand- enough, get
(red) shreds. father,

5 ya′wgi!" — "Awwa′, a′nam-e⸰en tıyayai′tiñ." Ġa′lqaʟin
up!" — "Well, all right! I will go home." He went

yaite′tı, gayaitiñvo′len, gaʟañvo′len. "Mitei′, qanto′ge,
home, he was coming near, he was approach- "Miti′, come out,
to his home, ing.

kmi′ñın a⸰ččıñıča⸰n qanva′kyıntat qangekıplena′ñu."
son the worst (of all) tear in twain to strike the fire with."

Ata′mtım ganvakyınta′ʟin kmi′ñın. "Mannu′ki qa′ngaqan?
Vainly she tore in twain the son. "Where is the fire?

a′či ni′w-i-gi, qanga′tıykın. Ġaya′qlinat lela′t, gaʟamyım-
Now saying-wert- it burns. What happened to (your) with shreds
thou, eyes,

---

1 *Rubus chamæmorus.*

to the eyelids. The Mouse-Women have defiled you."
He said, "Hm! now at last I grew angry. Bring me my
big club. I will go there and club them."

He went there. "Oh, grandfather is coming! Say to
him, 'Have some pudding of root of *Polygonum vivipa-*
rum!'" — "What for?" — "Then have some pudding of
berries of *Rubus Arcticus*." — "Yes, I will have some
pudding of berries of *Rubus Arcticus*." He entered, and
began to eat the pudding. "Grandfather, lie down on
your side and have a nap!" — "All right! I will lie
down on my side and have a nap."

He slept, and they painted his face with charcoal.
"O grandfather! get up, the day is breaking!" — "Yes,

---

ka′lenat? Pipi′kča-ña′wgutıyık gantawitkıña′w-i-gi." E′wañ,
attached to eyes? By Mouse-Women   by them defiled-art thou."   He said,

"Ģm, wŭ^ε′tču nanñıčvına′w-ģŭm. Ǫıya^ε′thın qolowočŭ′mñın.
"Hm! just now   grew angry-I.   Bring   big club.

Mıyo^ε′onau kıpļo′nvu."
I will find them to strike them."

Ģa′lqaɩɩn.   "Ǫulu′,   qulu′,   qulu′k!" — "Appa′nak
He went away.   "Big,   big,   big!" — "By the grand-
                                                    father

5 nenenela′mık.   Ǫiwļa′gıtča, 'A′wyek-ye′ļka!'" — "Ya′q-
he appears to us.   Tell him,   'With root ¹-pudding!'" —   "What

kınau!" — "Pa′yıttı-ye′ļka." — "O, pa′yıttı-ye′ļka tïya′yiļ-
for those!" — "With berry-pudding — "Yes, with berry-pudding I will eat
               of *Rubus Arcticus*."   of *Rubus Arcticus*

kuñ." Ģaya′lqıwlin, ģañvo′len yi′ļquk. "Appa′, a′yıčña
the pud-   He entered,   he began   to eat of "Grandfather, on your
ding."   the pudding.   side

gayı′s·qata!" — "A′nam-e^ε′en, a′yıčña tïyayı′ļqatıñ."
sleep!"   —   "All right!   on my side   I will sleep."

Ģayı′ļqalin, gaļa^εwkali′lin wŭ′ļka. "Appa′, qakya′wgi,
He slept,   they painted his face with coal. "Grandfather,   get up,

10 a^εlona′nñıvoi!" — "O, e^ε′en tıyakya′wiñ." Ģakya′wlin.
daylight is coming!" — "Yes, all right! I will get up."   He awoke.

---

¹ *A′wyek*, root of *Polygonum viviparum*.

all right! I will get up." He awoke. "Grandfather,
have a drink from the river there!" — "All right! I
will drink." He went away, and came to the river. He
began to drink, and there he saw in the water his own
image. "Halloo, Painted-Woman! you there? I will drop
a stone hammer as a present for you." Oh, he dropped
it. "Halloo, Painted-Woman! I will drop down my own
body! Halloo, Painted-Woman! shall I marry you?" Oh,
he jumped down into the water. That is all.

"Appa′, ña′nɪko va′amɪk yiwgɪči′ta." — "Eᵉ′en a′nau
"Grandfather, there in the river have a drink!" — "All right!

tĭyayi′wgɪčiñ." Ga′lqaʟin, gaḷa′lin va′amɪk, gañvo′len
I will drink." He went, he came to the river, he began

i′wgɪčik, gaḷaᵉ′ulin čini′nkin vɪ′yiḷvɪyiḷ. "Mei, Ka′li-ña′ut,
to drink, he saw his own image. "Halloo, Painted-Woman!

gɪ′ssa ɛ′nki? Yɪpa′ña mɪna′yatɪn." Gek, gana′yalin.
thou there? (Stone) hammer I will drop." Oh, he dropped it.

5 "Mei, Ka′li-ña′ut, u′wik mɪna′yatɪn! Mei, Ka′li-ña′ut,
"Halloo, Painted-Woman! body I will drop. Halloo, Painted-Woman!

me′če mɪma′ta-ge?" Gek, u′wik gana′yalin. Aččo′č.
whether I shall marry thee?" Oh, body he dropped it. That is all.

3. The Mouse-Girls.[1]

Mouse-Girl said, "Let us play!" They played, and one
of them lost a tooth, the youngest one of all. They said
to her, "How did you lose this tooth?" She said, "I was

Pipi′kča-na′wgut e′wañ, "Mĭno′yɪčvaḷa." Gañvo′ḷenau
Mouse-Woman said, "Let us play!" They began

uyɪčva′tɪk guyɪčvanñivo′ḷenau. Qoḷḷa gava′nnɪntaḷen, ɪlalu′.
to play they were playing. One has lost a tooth, the youngest one.

E′wañ, "Ya′qi vannɪnta′tɪ?" — "Iᵉ′ya-Nɪpaiva′tɪnak
They said, "How didst hast lost a tooth?" — "Heavenly by the Envious-one
thou

[1] Compare W. Jochelson, The Koryak, l. c., No. 97, p. 284.

shot by the Envious-One from heaven. By his arrow I lost my tooth. Now I shall die, how can I live?" They said to her, "Do not stay outside! Let us carry you into the house!" They carried her home. Her mother said, "What has happened to you?" — "I was shot from the sky by the Envious-One with an arrow."

The mother said, "Let us call grandmother!" They called her, they brought her to the house. She began to practise shamanism (in order to find out) where the small daughter got her suffering. She said, "My breath does not fit anywhere. Then she wanted to go to the porch. Ermine-Woman said, "Halloo! I will go to the porch, I will inspect the puddings." The small girl pilfered there, and so she lost her tooth. They looked at the

---

inaḷqaina′wi, iñi′nñinɪk ma′qmita tuva′nnɪntatɪk. Tyaviᵉ′yañ,
I was shot at, from this one arrow I lost a tooth. I shall die,

me′nqañ mɪkyuḷa′tɪk?" Ɣewñɪvo′ḷen, "Ɣa′čñɪn, mi′qun.
how shall I live?" They said to her, "In the outside, indeed!

Mĭnɪnyai′taḷa-ge." Ɣek, ɣanyai′taḷen. ɪḷaᵉ′ gi′wlin, "Ya′qi
Let us bring thee home!" Oh, they brought her Mother said, "How didst
home! thou

ɛnña ᵉ′an i′tɪ?" — "Ega′ñko naḷqaine′w-gŭm ma′qmita
thus wert thou?" — "From heaven shot was I with an arrow

5 Nɪpaiva′thɪtñɪnak."
by the Envious-one."

E′wañ, "An·a′ mĭnaiña′wḷan." Ɣaiña′wlin, ɣanyai′taḷen,
She said, "Grand- let us call!" They called her, they brought her
mother to the house,

ɣañvo′ḷen aña′ñyak, mañe′nko ñawa′kak ɣaño′vaḷen.
she began to practise from where female child became suffering.
shamanism,

E′wañ, "Ui′ña wɪ′yɪwɪ apḷɪpa′tča menkei′tɪ." Ki′tañ am-
She said, "Not breath does not fit anywhere." Then

yaqaḷheñe′tɪñ taya′ñikɪn. E′wañ Imča′na-ña′wɣut, "Yawo′,
to the porch she wanted. Said the Ermine-Woman, "Halloo!

10 yaqaḷheñe′tɪñ mɪḷqa′tɪk. Yi′ḷku mɪnčĭcatɪs·qi′wnau." Qai′-
to the porch I will go. Puddings I will inspect. Small

puddings, and saw that one made of stone-pine nuts had been gnawed at. There she left a tooth. Indeed, when pilfering she lost a tooth. Ermine-Woman brought in the tooth. "Whose tooth is it?" Ermine-Woman said, "On which of the small girls shall we try this tooth?"

She said to one of the small girls, "Open your mouth!" That one opened her mouth. She applied the tooth, but it did not fit. In the same way it did not fit any of those small girls. Ermine-Woman said, "Let us try it on the little suffering girl!" She tried it, and it fitted her well. Ermine-Woman said, "She was pilfering." What should she do?

ña'wis·qat tawi'tkɪñi, iñi'nñinɪk vannɪnta'tɪ. Ǥayoᵋo̜lenau
woman did havoc, therefore she lost a tooth. They found

yi'l̜ku, ma'ñin nɪklɪ'-ye'l̜kɪye̜l, ña'nyen ga̜čĭ'čhul̜in. Ña'nɪko
the which stone-pine pudding, that one was gnawed. There
puddings, nut

va'nnɪl̜ñɪn gape'l̜al̜en. Qa̜čĭ'n ɛna'n tawi'tkɪñik gava'nnɪn-
a tooth she left. Really she pilfering has lost a

tal̜en. Imča'na-ña'wgutɪnak gana'tvɪl̜en va'nnɪl̜ñɪn. "Miko'n
tooth. By the Ermine-Woman was brought in the tooth. "Whose

5 vannɪl̜ño'n?" Imča'na-ña'wgut gi'wl̜in, "Ma'ñin-qai-ña'wis·-
tooth?" Ermine-Woman said, "To which small woman

qatɪk mɪntante'nmɪñl̜an?"
we shall apply it?"

Ɛ'wañ ñu'nin qai-ña'wis·qat, "Quwa'ñil̜at." Ña'nyen
She said to yonder small-woman, "Open your mouth!" That one

gawañil̜a'l̜en. Va'nnɪl̜ñɪn gatan·apče'pɪnl̜in, gaaqai'pal̜en.
opened. The tooth she applied it, it badly fitted in.

ɪ'mɪ ga'mga-qai-ña'wis·qat, ɪ'mɪ gaaqai'pal̜en. Ɛ'wañ
Also to every small-woman, also it badly fitted in. Said

10 Imča'na-ña'wgut, "Em-taᵋl-qai-ña'wis·qatɪk qatante'nmɪn-
Ermine-Woman, "To the suffering-small-woman apply it."

ñan." Ña'nenenak gatante'nmɪñl̜en, gaplepa'l̜in. Ɛ'wañ
To that one she applied it, it fitted in. Said

Imča'na-ña'wgut, "ɛna'n tawi'tkɪñɪk." Me'ñqañ nɪᵋtvaᵋan?
Ermine-Woman, "She did harm." How could she be?

Her mother scolded her, and said, "Go and die! Strangle yourself on a forked twig!" She (went, and very soon) came back. She said, "I could not strangle myself on a forked twig." Mother scolded her, and said again, "There, go away!" She went away, and then only she died. That is all.

ɪˌaᵉ′ gaqɪtaiña′len. Ɡi′wlin, "Quvɪᵉyas·qi′wg̣i, qulñaqa-
Mother   scolded her.   She said,   "Die,   strangle
                                                          yourself on a

tɪs·qi′wg̣i." Ɡayai′tɪḷen. E′wañ, "Tapka′vɪk oḷñaqa′tik."
forked twig!" She came home. She said, "I could not   strangle myself
                                                          on a forked twig." [1]

ɪˌaᵉ′ gaqɪtaiña′ḷen. Ɡi′wlin, "Toq, qa′lqathi." Ɡa′lqaɪ̣in,
Mother   scolded her.   She said,   "Oh,   go away!"   She went away,

wŭᵉ′tču g̣aviᵉ′yaḷen. Aččo′č.
then only   she died.   That is all.

4. How a Small Kamak was transformed into a Harpoon-Line.[2]

A small kamak said to his mother, "I am hungry." She said to him, "Go and eat something in the store-room behind the sleeping-room!" He said, "I do not want to. I want to go to Big-Raven's house." The mother said, "Do not do it! You will die. You will be

---

5 Q̣ai-ka′mak ɪˌaᵉ′ñ e′wañ, "Tɪgɪtta′tɪykɪn." Ɡi′wlin,
   Small kamak   to the   said,   "I am hungry."   She said
                 mother   to him,

"Yɪnoi′tɪ gawyis·qi′wa." E′wañ, "Qɪymeᵉ′en. Q̣oyqɪnn·a-
"To the rear (go and) eat some- He said, "I do no want to. To Raven-Big's
storeroom   thing!"

qoyɪkei′tɪn." ɪˌaᵉ′ gi′wlin, "Qɪymeᵉ′en. Q̣uyavɪᵉ′yañɪ,
(house)."   Mother said to him, "Do not do it. Thou wilt die,

---

[1] The natives believe that the mice actually commit suicide by strangling themselves in a forked willow-twig (cf. Jochelson, The Koryak, l. c., p. 285, footnote).

[2] Compare W. Jochelson, The Koryak, l. c., No. 98, p. 285.

caught in a snare." She said, "Go to the upper store-room (in the porch) and eat something!" He said, "What for? Those provisions taste of the upper storeroom." She said, "Go to the cache and eat something!" He said, "What for? Those provisions taste of the cache."

Big-Raven spread a snare close to his elevated store-house (raised on supports). The small kamak ran there, and was caught in a snare. He began to whimper; "Oh, oh, I am caught, I am caught!" Big-Raven said, "It came to my mind to go and to look at this snare." He came to it, and wanted to enter the storehouse, but stumbled over something lying in the way. "What now, what is it?" — "It is I. I am caught." The small kamak

---

nayanoga′thi." E′wañ, "Yas·qaḷkai′tiñ ḡawyis·qi′wa."
thou wilt be caught   She said,   "To the house-top   (go and) eat some-
in a snare."   thing!"

E′wañ, "Ya′qkɪnau, nɪyas·qaḷqača′čaqenau." E′wañ,
He said,   "What for?   they taste of the house-top."   She said,

"Oḷhɪwe′tɪñ ḡawyis·qi′wa." E′wañ, "Ya′qkɪnau, noḷhoča′-
"To the cache   (go and) eat some-   He said,   "What for?   they taste of
thing!"

čaqenau."
the cache."

5   Quyqɪnn·aqu′nak ena′t ḡantɪwa′ʟen ma′mik. Ñanɪkai′tiñ
Raven-Big   a snare   has spread   near the ele-   There
vated storehouse.

ḡagɪnta′wḷin, qai-ka′mak, ḡawga′ḷen ena′tɪk, ḡañvo′ḷen
he ran,   small kamak,   was caught   in the snare,   he began

qalhai′ak, "I, tu′kwak, tu′kwak." Quyqɪnn·a′qu e′wañ,
to cry,   "Oh, I am caught, I am caught!"   Raven-Big   said,

"Yawo′, ena′tpel mɪyoᵋ′an, ḷɪ′ḡɪ tɪ′tčɪn." Ḡayoᵋ′oḷen, ai′ak
"Well, now,   snare   I will visit,   to my   I had it."   He visited it, into the
mind   storehouse

ḡaya′lqɪñvoḷen, ḡeñu′ḡaḷen. "Wu′tčɪn yaq, yɪ′nna?" —
he wanted to enter,   he stumbled.   "This,   now,   what?" —

10 "Ḡŭ′mma, kɪtta′ tu′kwak." A′naqun kuḷa′kata¹ nɪmeyeyɪt-
"I,   there I am caught."   And so   with (his) fist   he was brushing

¹ Borrowed from the Russian кулакъ FIST.

was crying, and brushing away his tears with his small fist. "Stop blubbering! I will take you to Miti'." He brought the small kamak to his house, and said, "O, Miti'! dance in honor of (our) catch!" She began to dance, "We have a small kamak, we have a small kamak!" Big-Raven said, "You dance in a wrong way. Ḡa'na, step forth and dance in honor of (our) catch!" She came out and began to dance, "We have a small ma'kak, we have a small ma'kak!" Big-Raven said, "Really this is right."

They took him into the house. The house-master said, "What shall we make out of you, a cover for the roof-hole?" — "Not this. If I am made into a cover for the roof-

---

va'qen, nıqalhai'aqen. "Aqalhai'aka qitı'ykın-i'-gi. Mete'nañ
away tears,   he was crying.   "Not crying   be   thou.   To Miti'

mınyaita't·ge." Ḡanyai'taḻen. "Mitei', qai-ka'makpel qam-
I will bring thee   He brought him   "Miti',   small kamak small dance
to the house."   to the house.

ḻa'wun." Ḡek, gañvo'ḻen mı̆la'wuk, "Ḡaqqaika'makata
for his   Oh,   she began   to dance!   "With a small ka'mak
(catch)."

gana⁶'l-mu'yu, gaqqaika'makata gana⁶'l-mu'yu!" Quiqın-
became we,   with a small ka'mak   became we!   Raven-Big

5 n·a'qu e'wañ, "A'ḻvañ qamḻa'wun. Ḡa'na, qiwi'ni, gı'ssa
said,   "Wrongly   thou dancest   Ḡa'na, come out, thou
             for him.

qımḻa'we." Ḡiwi'nilin, gañvo'ḻen mı̆la'wuk, "Ḡaqqai-ma'ka-
dance!"   She came out, she began   to dance,   "With a small ma'kak

kata gana⁶'l-mu'yu, gaqqai-ma'kakata gana⁶'l-mu'yu!"
became we,   with a small ma'kak [1]   became   we!"

E'wañ Quyqınn·a'qu, "I'pa, ɛnña⁶'an."
Said   Raven-Big,   "Indeed,   thus."

Ḡana'tvıḻen, e'wañ, "Ya'qu mıntaikıḻa'-gi, tomñena'ñu?"
They carried him (the house- "Into   shall we make thee, into a cover for
in,   master) said, what   the roof-hole?"

10 E'wañ, "Qıyme⁶'en. Tomñena'ñu qinataikıḻa'tık, tıyañlan-
He said, "I do not want it. Into a cover for you shall make me, I shall feel
                 the roof-hole (if)

---

[1] Ḡa'na mixes up the sounds of the word ka'mak. Still Big-Raven finds it quite right.

hole, I shall feel smoky, I shall feel cold." The house-master said, "What shall we make out of you, a plug for the vent-hole?" — "Not this. If I am made into a plug for the vent-hole, I shall be afraid of evil spirits passing by." The house-master said, "What, then, do you wish us to make of you? Perhaps a work-bag for Miti'." He said, "Not this. I shall feel smothered." The house-master said, "We shall make you into a thong." The small kamak began to laugh and said, "Yes!"

They made him into a thong, they cut him duly, then they carried the line out and began to stretch it (tightly). Thus stretched, they (left it there). Big-Raven's people went to sleep. Frost-Man and his people said,

---

ñɪvo'ykɪn, tɪyaqatmawñɪvo'ykɪn." E'wañ, "Kulipčina'ñu
smoky, I shall feel cold." (The house-master) said, "Into a plug for the vent-hole

mintaikiḷa'-gi." E'wañ, "Qɪymeᵋ'en. Kulipčina'ñu qinatai-
we will make thee." He said, "I do not want it. Into a plug for the vent-hole if you shall

kiḷa'tɪk, tɪyayɪmgumganñɪvo'ykɪn ñenve'thɪčñɪn." E'wañ,
make me, I shall be afraid of evil spirits (pas-sing by)." (The house-master) said,

"Ya'qu-yak quwai'matɪn aᵋntai'kɪ-gi? Miti'nak čai'učhu?"
"Into what, then, thou desirest one should make thee? For Miti' into a working-bag?"

5 E'wañ, "Qɪymeᵋ'en. Tɪyapeikiḷanñɪvo'ykɪn." E'wañ,
He said, "I do not want it. I shall feel smothered." (The house-master) said,

"Ñi'ḷñu mɪntaikiḷa'-gi?" Gañvo'ḷen ačacha'tɪk, e'wan, "O!"
"Into a thong we shall make thee?" He began to laugh, he said, "Yes!"

Ñi'ḷñu gatai'kɪñvoḷen, gas·vɪñvo'ḷen, ña'čhɪnoñ gaḷa'ɪ̯en,
Into a thong they made him, they cut him (into a line) to the outside they carried it,

gañvo'ḷen tve'tɪk, ga'tveḷen. Quyqɪnn·aqu'wgi gayɪ'ḷqalinau.
they began to stretch it, they stretched it. Big-Raven's people went to sleep.

Annɪmaya'tɪyɪk gi'wlinau, "Quiqɪnn·aqu'nak qai-ka'mak
(Those) with the Frost-Man said, "By Raven-Big a small kamak

"Big-Raven has caught a small kamak. They made him into a thong. Let us go and steal it!" They found it, and began to untie it. Then it cried aloud, "Quick, get up! Already they are untying me!" Big-Raven said, "What is the matter with our small line? It wants to awaken us. Quick, let us get up!" They woke up, and said to the small kamak, "What is the matter with you? Why were you crying so loudly?" The small kamak said, "Frost-Man's people wanted to carry me away."

The people living down the coast heard (about the thing), — how Big-Raven caught a small kamak; and how they made him into a thong; and how no one succeeded in carrying it away, it was so watchful. Those people began to say, "We will go and carry it away."

---

ganu′kwalin.   Ñi′lñu   gatai′kɪlin.   Mɪntu′las·qewlan."   Ga-
they caught him.   Into a   they made him.   Let us steal it!"   They
            thong

yoᵉ′olen,   gañvo′len   yi′ssɪk.   ɛ′nki   gaku′mñalen,   "I′naᵉ,
found it,   they began   to untie it.   Then   it shouted,   "Quick,

qɪkyawla′tɪk.   Ke′nam   nassi′ñvo-gŭm."   Quyqɪnn·a′qu e′wañ,
wake up!   Already   they are untying me."   Raven-Big   said,

"Ñi′lñɪpilɪñ   ya′qñɪvoi?   Tenanɪkyo′nñɪvoi.   I′naᵉ mĭnɪkya′wla."
"Thong small   what is the   It wants to awaken us.   Quick,   let us get up!"
            matter with it?

5 Ǧakya′wlinau.   Ǧi′wlin, "Nɪya′qi-gi,   nɪpɪs·viča′ti-gi?"   E′wañ,
They woke up.   They said "What is the   Why wert thou crying   He said,
            to it,   matter with thee?   (so loud)?

"Annɪmaya′tɪyɪk   nɪtula′tɪy-gŭm."
"By Frost-Man's people they wanted to steal me."

Attaᵉ′yol-yaᵉ′mka   gava′lomlen,   Quyqɪnn·aqu′nak   qai-
By Down   people   they heard it,   by Raven-Big   small
(the coast)

ka′mak   ganu′kwalin,   ñi′lñu   gatai′kɪlin,   napkawñɪvo′ykɪn
kamak   was caught,   to a line   they made it,   they could not

tula′tɪk,   nɪlhɪkyu′qin.   Ǧewñɪvo′lenau,   "Močhɪna′n mɪntu′-
steal it,   it is quite wakeful.   They began to say,   "We   will go

10 las·qewlan."   E′wañ, "Mi′qun,   mɪssatulala′nñɪn."   Quyqɪn-
and steal it."   They said,   "Why,   we will steal it."   Raven-

They said, "Surely we will carry it away." Big-Raven's people went to sleep. The people living down the coast came and took the line. It wanted to awaken the other people, but it was unable to awaken them. "Oh, they are untying me already, they are carrying me away!" Indeed, they untied it and carried it away; they stole the line.

The others woke up, but there was no line whatever. It had been taken away. Big-Raven said, "People living down the coast have committed this theft. Indeed, they took it, nobody else." Eme'mqut said, "A very good line was taken away, still we will bring it back." Eme'mqut made a wooden whale and entered it. He went away and came to the people living down the coast. Those people were walking around. They were saying, "This

---

n·aqu'wgi ġayı'lqalinau. Ġŭ'mḷañ ġatu'las·qewlin Attaᵋ'yol·
Big's people   slept.   Again   they stole it   by Down
                                                                      (the coast)

yaᵋ'mka. Ġañvo'ḷen tenanıkyu'nka, qupka'wñunenau
people.   It began   to waken them,   it could not them

yanıkya'wñak. "Kena'm nassıtoya'ñvoi-ġŭm, natuḷa'nñıvoi-
to waken.   "Already   they untie-me,   they steal-me."

ġŭm." Ġassıtoya'ḷen, ġalla'xtaḷen, ġatu'ḷalin.
         They untied it,   they carried it   they stole it.
                            away,

5 Ġakya'wlinau, eᵋ'en· yaq ñi'ḷñın ni'tın, ġatu'ḷalin.
  (Those) woke up,   indeed   what   line   should   they stole it.
                                                     be there,

Quyqınn·a'qu e'wañ, "Attaᵋ'yol-yaᵋ'mka natuḷa'tın. Ui'ña-
Raven-Big   said,   "By Down   people   they stole it.   Not
                                         (the coast)

wan minka'kıḷa, eᵋ'en ġanka'kıḷa." Ama'mqut e'wañ,
by anybody (else),   indeed,   by those."   Eme'mqut   said,

"Tan-ñi'ḷñın natuḷa'tın, e'wun mıssaitıḷa'ñın." Amamqu'tınak
"Good-line   they stole it,   still   we will bring it   Eme'mqut
                                        (back) home."

u'ttı-yu'ñı ġatai'kılin, ġankaġeñe'tı ġaya'lqıwlin, ġa'lqaɹin,
wooden whale   he made it,   in there   he entered,   he went,

is the first time that such a whale has come near to us. It is a very good whale."

They attacked the whale, came near to it, and threw at it a harpoon with a new line. The small kamak lustily bit into the whale. Eme′mqut said to him under his breath, "Why are you biting me? I have come to fetch you home." Eme′mqut threw into the boat of the whale-hunters some berries of *Rubus Arcticus*, and they began to eat them. Meanwhile Eme′mqut fled in all haste to his house. He carried away the new line, and took it home. They ceased carrying the line out of the house. They kept it always in the inner room, so the others could not steal it. That is all.

---

gaḷa′lin. Atta‵yol-ya‵′mkɪñ galai′vɪñvoḷen. Gewñɪvo′ḷenau,
he came.   Down (the coast) people   walked around.   They were saying,

"Wŭ′tču iñi′nñin yu′ñɪ qulai′vun, mal-yu′ñɪ."
"This time   such   whale   comes (to us),   good-whale."
   only

     Gayuñyupe′nyɪḷenau, gayo‵′oḷen, tui-ñi′ḷña gata′kyɪlin,
     They attacked the whale,   they came close   with a new   they threw at it,
                to it,   (harpoon) line

qai-ka′mak yu′ñyuk gamaḷɪnai′vuḷen. Amamqu′tinak gi′wlin
small ka′mak   into the whale   well bit.   Eme′mqut   said

5 vi′n·va, "Quya′qɪñ qinei′gu? Gŭmna′n te′ttɪ-gi." Atvɪgeñe′tɪ
secretly, "What art thou   art biting   I (come to)   fetch-thee."   Into the boat
      doing   me?

Ama′mqut pa′yitta gape′wɪwaḷen. Ña′nko gana‵′linau
Eme′mqut   with berries   threw into.   Then   they were
     of *Rubus Arcticus*

pa′yittok. Ama′mqut gamaḷhɪnta′wḷen yaite′tɪñ. Gangɪn-
eating berries   Eme′mqut   well fled   to the house.   He stole
of *Rubus Arcticus*.

tawa′ʟen, ganyai′taḷen; gana′nkauḷen tɪnaḷa‵′tik. Qo′npŭ
   it,   he brought it home;   they ceased   to carry it out.   Altogether

ya′ḷku nɪnnipñɪvo′qen. Qo′npŭ ganka′wlinau tuḷa′tɪk.
  in the   they kept it.   Altogether   those ceased   to steal.
inner room

10 Aččo′č.
That is all.

5. Big-Raven and the Kamaks.

Raven-Big said, "I will slide down hill." [He slid down hill.] He went and found a mountain, which was the largest of all. From that mountain he slid down, and rolled into the porch of the house of the kamaks. There he came in. Small kamaks went to the porch, and said, "Oh, human game has come to us of its own free will!" — "I am not human game, I am a man." They took him into the house, and began to eat his body joint by joint. Still he was alive. They consumed Big-Raven. Then he came home, because he was a shaman.

He recovered his senses, and said to his wife, "Cook

Quyqɪnn·a′qu e′wañ, "Mnı′kak, myalitčus·qi′wak." Ǥa-
Raven-Big   said,   "I will do   I will slide down-hill."   He
                          something,

yalitčus·qi′wlin.   Ǥa′lqaɪin,   ma′ñin   nɪma′yɪnqin   ñai′ñai,
slid down.   He went,   which   big one   mountain,

ña′nakañqo gaya′lilin, ka′mak-yaqaḷe′tɪñ gaku′ḷaḷen, ña′nyen
from that   he slid down, to the kamak's[1] porch   he rolled in,   there

gai′pɪḷen Quyqɪnn·a′qu. Ña′nyau qai-ka′makau yaqaḷe′tɪñ
he came in   Raven-Big.   Those   small ka′maks   to the porch

5 ga′lqaɪinau gaḷa′linau. "Oyamya′ta yaᵉ′yoa ga′ntɪ-mu′yu." —
they went   they came.   "Of Man-game of his own possessed we."   —
                                                    will

"O, gŭ′mma qa′čɪk oyamyei′-gum? gŭ′mma oya′mtɪwɪḷei-
"Oh,   I   whether Man-game-am I?   I   man-am

gŭm." Ǥana′tvɪḷen, anina′wi nɪqupu′wi nanoñvo′ykɪnenau,
I."   They brought him,   his   joints   they are consuming,

vɪ′yañ ḷeḷapɪtčoñvo′ykɪn. Quyqɪnn·a′qu ganu′lin, ɪmɪñ
notwith-   he looks up.   Raven-Big   they ate him,   still
standing

gayai′tɪḷen, mi′qun, naña′nqin.
he came home,   why,   he is a shaman.

10 Ǥačɪčaña′wḷen. E′wañ, "Qita′pañ." Ǥata′pañḷen.
He recovered (his senses).   He said,   "Cook soup!"   She cooked soup.

[1] Evil spirit (cf. W. Jochelson, The Koryak, l. c., p. 27).

some soup for me!" She cooked some soup, and he ate all alone a large kettleful. Then he said to Miti', "Bring the big hammer!" She gave him the hammer, and he swallowed it. He arrived at to the house of some kamaks, and vomited through the vent-hole. (He filled the whole house) and made· them climb upward. The big kamak was standing in the middle of the house. Big-Raven struck him with the hammer. He killed him. Big-Raven came home. That is all.

Ña'nyen	kuka'-yɪčɪn·a'qu	am-ɛˤna'n	ganu'lin.	E'wañ
Then	kettle-ful big	alone he	ate.	He said

Mete'na,	"Qɪya'thin	kɪ'lvɪ-yɪpa'ña." [1]	Gai'lɪʟɪn.	Gek,
to Miti',	"Bring	(large) grooved hammer!"	She gave it to him.	Oh,

ganu'lin.	Gek,	gaḷa'lin	kamakn·aqo'yɪkɪñ	yɪnootñe'tɪ	gañ-
he ate it!	Oh,	he came	to the kamaks' (house)	into the vent-hole	he

vo'ḷen	gɪya'lɪk,	ganɪpga'wḷenau.	Kama'kn·aqu	gɪno'n-
began	to vomit,	he made them climb upward.	Ka'mak-big	in the middle

5 | čottai'nɪk-tve'tekɪn. | Ña'nyenata | kɪ'lvɪ-yɪpa'ta | gaki'pluḷen, |
|---|---|---|---|
| outer part of the house | is standing. | With that | (large) hammer groove | he struck him, |

ga'nmiḷen.	Quyqi'nn·aqu	gayai'tiḷen	ña'nyen.	A'ččič.
he killed him.	Raven-Big	went home	that one.	That is all.

6. Kĭlu' and the Bumblebees.[2]

Eme'mqut lived with his people. He married Kĭlu', but they were childless. One time Eme'mqut went into

---

ɛnñaˤ'an	Amamqu'tinu	vañvoḷai'ke.	Amamqu'tinak
Thus	Eme'mqut's people	lived.	By Eme'mqut

Kĭlu'	gama'taḷen,	ui'ña	akmi'ñɪka	gi'ʟinat.	Vaˤ'yuk
Kĭlu'	was married,	no	childless	they were (dual).	Afterwards

---

[1] A large stone hammer with a narrow groove for hafting.
[2] Compare W. Jochelson, The Koryak, *l. c.*, No 107, p. 294.

the open (country). He followed a river upstream. Then he saw numerous people. Some of them were women. Their bodies were resplendent with the reflection of light. All the men wore jackets of broadcloth, all the women wore calico overcoats. Eme′mqut hurried to them. He fell in love, and began to help those people. They were fishing with drag-nets. Very soon he married a Bumblebee-Woman. Those people were Bumblebee people. His new wife brought forth numerous children.

Then Kĭlu′ became restless, and could not sleep. She came to the river, and followed it up-stream. Then she looked around, and saw those fishermen. Eme′mqut was

---

Ama′mqut notai′tĭñ ga′ḷqaɹin, va′am-eče′tɪ ga′ɹilin, va^ε′yuk
Eme′mqut   to the (open)   went,   river-up stream he followed, afterwards
        country

ganyininiña′linau i′naḷka oya′mtɪwɪlu, ya′nya e^ε′en ña′wɪt-
appeared to him   numerous   people,   partly   women,

qatu, lɪ′gan mɪmtelhɪyaḷai′ke, qḷa′wuḷu am-palto′ḷu,[1] ña′wɪs·-
even resplendent with light,   men all in jackets of   women
                       broadcloth,

qatu am-mani′ssaḷu. Ama′mqut avi′ut gaḷa′lin, gaqalei′pɪlin,
all in calico.   Eme′mqut in haste   came,   fell in love,

5 gañvo′ḷen vɪnya′tɪk kaña′tɪla^εk. Avi′ut Yu′qya-ña′ut
began   to help   fishing with   In haste Bumblebee-Woman
               drag-nets.

gama′taḷen. Ña′nyeu qači′n Yuqyamtɪla^ε′nu. I′naḷka
he married.   Those   indeed Bumblebee-Men.   Numerous

kmi′ñu gaitoi′vɪḷenau.
children she brought forth them.

Va^ε′yuk Kĭlu′ ña′nyen gapkawñɪvo′ḷen yayɪs·qa′ññɪk.
Afterwards Kĭlu′ that one   could not   sleep.

Ga′ḷqaɹin va′amɪk eče′tɪ, va^ε′yuk gaɹapɪtčoñvo′ḷen, a′nke
She went to the river up-stream, afterwards she looked around,   there

10 gagetañvo′ḷenau kaña′tɪḷu. Ama′mqut a′nke o′maka
she saw   the fishing   Eme′mqut   there   together
         people.

---

[1] Borrowed from the Russian пальто OVERCOAT.

there with them pulling in the nets. Kĭlu′ approached them. She trampled to death Eme′mqut's new wife, who scattered around a large quantity of fly-eggs. All the eggs became Bumblebees. The fishermen also turned to Bumblebees. Eme′mqut could do nothing, so he went home. That is all.

---

kaña′tɪykɪn. Ḡayoᵋ′oḷen Kĭlu′nak. Amamqu′tɪnin ña′wɪtqat
is fishing.   She visited them   by Kĭlu′.   Eme′mqut's   woman

ḡačañčɪs·qu′lin,   ya′qam   ai′kɪpa   ḡapɪ′wyalin.   Yuqya′nu
she trampled her,   only   with fly-eggs   she scattered   Bumblebees
herself around.

ḡanaᵋ′linau, ɪmɪñ kaña′tɪḷu yuqya′nu ḡanaᵋ′linau. Ama′mqut
they became,   also   fishermen   bumblebees   became.   Eme′mqut

nɪyaqñɪvo′ykɪn. Ḡayai′tiḷen. Aččo′č.
what had he to do.   He went home.   That is all.

7. Eme′mqut's Whale-Festival.[1]

Eme′mqut and his people were living. They were hunting whales, and killed one whale. They took it home. Then they arranged a thanksgiving ceremonial. They gathered together all the reindeer-breeding people, also the Magpies (namely, Magpie-Women).

"Magpie-Woman, you dance!" — "What shall I sing

---

5   ᴇñaᵋ′an Amamqu′tinu vañvoḷai′ke. ᴇñaᵋ′an ḡavaḷaikɪ-
Thus   Eme′mqut and his   are living.   Thus   they were
people

ḷañvo′ḷen   yu′ñyuk,   ḡayuñyu′linau,   ḡanyaitanñɪvo′ḷenau.
pursuing   a whale,   they killed the whale,   they took it home.

Vaᵋ′yuk ḡenačaxčanñɪvo′ḷenau, ɪ′mɪ ča′wčuwau. Vakɪthɪm-
Afterwards   they arranged a thanksgiving   all   reindeer-breeding   all Magpie-
ceremonial,   people

tɪḷaᵋ′nu ḡanumaka′wlinau, to, Vakɪ′thi-ña′wgutinu.
People   they gathered,   oh,   Magpie-Women.

"Vakɪ′thɪ-ña′wgut, qamla′wge!" — "Ya′qin-yaq tiᵋ′wɪk?
"Magpie-Woman,   dance!"   —   "What, then, shall I say?

---

[1] Compare W. Jochelson, The Koryak, *l. c.*, No. 89, p. 266.

while dancing? I am unskilful. Vakikikikikiki′. My mother
told me, 'Do not leave anything from the other people's
wallets!' My grandmother said to me 'Leave something
from the other people's wallets!' Vakikikikikiki′!"

"So it is," said Kĭlu′. "When we come to find them,
our wallets are (half-)eaten." Magpie-Woman had nothing
to say, so she felt ashamed and flew away.

"Oh, you Fox-Woman! it is your turn to dance." She
grew excited and sang, "My brother, Pilferer, made a
knife with a well-ornamented handle. But with what shall
I eat the whale-skin? I forgot it. He wanted to strap
it to my thigh. With what shall I eat the whale-skin, eh?"

Aḷaitiḷačñei′-gŭm. Vakikikikikiki′! ıḷa^εga ini′wi, 'Tu′m-
Unskilful-am-I.   Vakikikikikiki′!   By mother I am told, 'From

ginau kawa′ssočhu annuwai′ka! An·a′nak ini′wi, 'Gan-
the other wallets   do not leave   By grand- I am told, 'Leaving
men   anything.'   mother

nuwai′a ga′nta! Vakikikikikiki′!"
something do!   Vakikikikikiki′!"

"Čemeče^εn." Kĭlu′ e′wañ, "Mıtyo^εoykınenau, kawa′s-
"So it is."   Kĭlu′ said,   "We come to find them, the

5 sočhu ganu′linau." Yı′nna nitha^εan? Ye′lı gayi′ñalin,
wallets are eaten."   What had to be done?   There she flew away,

gañekeḷa′ḷen.
she felt ashamed.

"Toq, Yayoča′mtıḷa^εn, gın-ya′q qamḷa′wge!" Gañvo′ḷen
"O, Fox-Woman![1] thy turn, dance!"   She began

yathıpa′wñık, "Kothaño′nak maḷ-kaḷ-yekoi′gu-waḷ getei′kilin.
to grow excited. "By (my brother) good-ornamented-handle-knife he made it.
       Pilferer

Ya′qa tıyıthı′ḷgu? Gantıgıva′ḷen. Assä′kı gaiqa′ntenma
With shall I eat   I forgot it.   On the arranged
what whale-skin?   thigh

10 nınayatei′kiñqin. Ya′qa tıyıthı′ḷgu, va?"
he wanted to make it.   With shall I eat ah?"
        what whale-skin,

---

[1] Literally, VULPES-HOMO. In Yay′oča-mtıḷa^εn, -mtıḷa^εn is abridged from oya′m-tlwıḷa^εn HOMO. This compound form is used more frequently for the masculine, FOX-MAN; and for the feminine, Yayo′ča-ñawgut FOX-WOMAN is used. Still the first form may refer to both sexes, but here it is used exactly for FOX-WOMAN. The same is true in all analogous cases.

The old man Big-Raven said, "Ah, ah! they are singing about their feeding at other people's expense." Still another Fox-Woman began to sing. She also grew excited. "I am she who eats hard excrements. I am she who gnaws the snowshoe-strings."

Ah, she was brought to shame by Eme'mqut. He said, "Yes, when we find them, the snowshoe-strings are gnawed through." She felt ashamed and went away.

"O, Small-Magpie-Woman! it is your turn to dance." — "What, then, shall I sing? I feel ashamed. Vakikikikikiki'! On the gables of other people's storehouses, with her running and skipping foot, the magpie is striding and

---

E, ña'nyen gani'kalin ɪ'npɪ-qḷa'wuḷ gewñɪvo'ḷen, Quyqin-
Oh, that did something old-man said Raven-

n·a·'qu, "Ann, ann, tu'mgin ɛnña͡ɛ'an yamaiñanñɪ'gɪtñɪn
Big, "Ah, ah! other people's thus growing up [1]

nanaiña'wɪykɪninau." Va'sqiñ gani'kalin, ɛ'nki gañvo'ḷen,
they are exclaiming about." Another did something, there she began,

ye'ppa yathɪpawñɪ'ykɪn. "Kɪm-a͡ɛ'ḷu-ña'wɪy-gŭm, tigi'lñu-
only she is growing excited. "Hard excrement woman am I, snowshoe-
eating strings eating

5 ña'wɪy-gŭm."
woman am I."

Če! Amamqu'tina gañekeḷa'ḷen. "Če, mɪtyo͡ɛ'oykɪnenau,
Eh! Of Eme'mqut she grew ashamed. "Eh, we find them,

tigi'lñu gačvi'tčulinau. Mɪtyo͡ʒ'oykɪnenau, tigi'lñu gačvi't-
snowshoe- are cut through. We find them, snowshoe- are cut
strings strings

čulinau." Gañekeḷa'ḷen, ga'ḷqaʟin.
through." She felt ashamed, she went away.

"Toq, Qai-Vakɪ'thɪmtɪḷa͡ɛn, gɪn-ya'q qamḷa'wge." —
"O, Small Magpie-Woman! thy turn, dance!" —

10 "Ya'qin-yaq ti͡ɛ'wik, tenanñei'kɪlñɪn! Vakikikikikiki', to'mŭk-
"What then Shall I say, my shame! Vakikikikikiki', to the other
people's

megeñe'tɪñ o'tña-kḷaw-gɪtča'ta nɪtɪñpuvaqa'tqen." — "Ann,
storehouse with a running foot she is pecking striding." — "Ah,
gables skipping

---

[1] This means, that they are exclaiming about (the fact that they are consuming what serves for) the bringing up of other people's (children).

pecking at the food." — "Ah, ah! they are singing about their feeding at other people's expense. — O, Raven-Woman! it is your turn to dance." — "Caw, caw! my cousin's shadow passes on the water." [Raven-Woman began to dance (and sing) in this manner: "My cousin's shadow passes on the water."] "Caw, caw! Oh, I like you while you pass!"

She finished her dance. Then Eme′mqut went out, and the two (Magpies) were sitting there. "O girl! use your voice! Abuse Eme′mqut!" — "He is feeding on dog's inner skin, on reindeer inner skin. (He is consuming) a reindeer-hoof!" — "Off! When have we fed on dog's inner skin? Even when wandering in the open we do not eat (reindeer) inner skin. Much less do we

---

ann, ᴇñña⁰′an tu′mgin yamaiñanñī′gɪtñɪn. — To, Va′čvɪ-
ah! thus other people's growing up. — O, Raven-

ña′wgut, gɪn-ya′q qamḷa′wge." — "Qooñ, qo′oñ, gŭ′mɪk
Woman! thy turn dance!" — "Caw, caw! By my

yeḷa′linak i′mɪḷ-tawyi′ḷñɪḷaⁿ." Va′čvɪ-ña′wgut gañvo′ḷen
cousin on the shadow is thrown." Raven-Woman began
  water

ᴇñña⁰′an mīla′wɪk, "Gŭmɪk-yeḷa′linak i′mɪḷ-tawyi′ḷñɪḷaⁿ.
thus to dance, "By my cousin on the shadow is thrown.
  water

5 Qo′oñ, qo′oñ, ᴇñña⁰′an qenanvaḷeḷña′wiñ."
Caw, caw! Thus thou art pleasing me."

E⁰′en ᴇñña⁰′an gamḷawanka′wḷen. Va⁰′yuk ᴇ′nki gan-
Then thus she ceased to dance. Afterwards then went

to′ḷen Ama′mqut. ᴇ′nki vai′ke. "Illa! qaqoḷeya′wage,
out Eme′mqut. There they are "O, girl! use your voice,
  (dual).

Ama′mqut qɪya′wa." — "Aⁿttäⁿyɪpna′, qoyayɪpna′, qoya′-
Eme′mqut (ill-)use." — "With dog's inner with reindeer reindeer
  skin inner skin,

atvagɪḷño′n!" — "Got, ti′taq mu′yu mɪtaⁿttayɪ′pnuḷa?
hoof!" — "Off, when we we on dog's inner skin
  have fed?

eat dog's inner skin." Ah! they felt ashamed and flew away.

Yini'a-ña'wgut wanted to skin a dog. "Halloo! who will hold it for me?" Raven-Woman said, "I will hold it." They went out and began to skin the dog. Raven-Woman pecked out one of its eyes. "Who pecked out this eye here?" — "I do not know." She pecked at the coccyx. "Was it here?"

Then she pierced the other eye, and the liquid squirted on Yini'a-ña'wgut. "Are you now looking for this one? What of that! I only shut my mouth." But this carcass I will lay aside." She buried it in the ground under a steep river-bank.

Qu'nam nu'tak ui'ña ane'lhɪyɪpnuka. Lɪ'gɪqai mɪna⁸tta-
Even in the no not eating inner skin. Much less we have fed
(open) country

yɪ'pnuḷa." Ye, gayi'ñalinat, gañekeḷa'ḷenat ni'ka.
on dog's Ah, they flew away they felt ashamed somehow.
inner skin." (dual), (dual)

Yini'a-ña'wgut taa⁸ttanvanña'tɪk. "Añe', maki'kɪč ne⁸e-
Yini'a-ña'wgut wanted to skin a dog. "Halloo! who there will

naa'yen?" Va'čvɪ-ña'wgut, "Gŭmma menaa'yek." Ye,
hold it for me?" Raven-Woman, "I will hold." Ah!

5 ganto'ḷenat, gañvo'ḷenat a⁸ttanvanña'tɪk, ḷeḷa'lñin gaito'ḷen.
they went out, they began to skin the dog, an eye she took out.

"Wutča'kin ḷeḷa'lñɪn mannu'qi?" — "Qo!" Čɪtča⁸'ttamik
"This here eye where is it?" — "I do not An the buttocks
know." bone

tɪnpo'ykɪnen. "Ma'či wu'tčuk?"
she pecked. "Whether here?"

Gaḷa'nvilin. Yini'a-ña'wgut gepetčaita'ʟin. "Ačhi'kin
She pierced the On Yini'a-ña'wgut it squirted. "This now
(other) eye.

nenenaye'ye-ge? Gŭmna'n tɪnpɪtča'wun, ya'qu-kɪč? Wu'ssin
seeking art thou? I gnashed my teeth, what there? This

10 gɪlhɪtva'n mɪnu'mkawɪn." Yɪñyɪmḷage'ñka guḷgu'wlin.
carcass I will lay aside." Under a steep bank she buried it.

Then they finished the thanksgiving ceremonial with the food appointed for distribution. The reindeer-breeding people loaded their sledges quite largely with sole-leather cut out from the middle, and scraped clean of hair, also with thong of the same quality. They tied up their loads (and went away). That is the end.

E´nki yu´la⁏n ḡapḷıtču´linau inačaxča´tık. Ča´wčuwau
Then that, what was they finished performing the thanks- Reindeer-
appointed for food giving ceremonial. breeders

ḡamaiñi-inaña´linau im-qu´ḷta-vı´thıya, im-i´ḷña-vı´thıya. Ḡe-
largely loaded (their sledges) with sole middle, with thong middle. They
hairless leather hairless

noma´ḷenau. A⁏ččıč na⁏ḷḷıñ.
tied it up. The end grew.

8. Eme´mqut and ıla´.[1]

Big-Raven was living with his people. Eme´mqut (his son) had no wife. Eme´mqut went out, and found outside an old man who was (busy) making ornamented (tobacco-) mortars. He said to him, "What kind of (tobacco-) mortars are you making?" The other one said, ("Go into the house.) You will find an old woman. (Tell her) to

---

Ni´ykau Quyqınnˑaqu´nu vañvoḷai´ke. Ḡek, Ama´mqut
Some Raven-Big's people are living. Oh, Eme´mqut

5 ui´ña aña´wtıñka. Ama´mqut notai´tıñ ḡa´ḷqaɹin, ḡayo⁏oḷen
not wifeless. Eme´mqut to the (open) went, he found
country

ı´npı-qḷa´wuḷ. Ta-kale´-kıpla´ñekın. Ḡek, e´wañ, "Ya´q-
old man. Making-ornamented-(tobacco) Oh, he said, "What
mortars he is.

kinau E´nyau kıpla´wi qutei´kıñınau?" Ḡek, ña´nyen e´wañ,
(kind) those (tobacco-) thou art making Oh, that one said,
mortars them?"

---

[1] Compare W. Jochelson, The Koryak, *l. c.*, No. 101, p. 289.

cook a meal for you." He entered (the house), and (the old woman) cooked a meal. When she had finished cooking, she took the meat out of the kettle, (and gave it to the guest.) He ate, and soon was through with the meal.

Then the old man went home and gave him the mortars; and he said to him, "Take these with you, haul them away, but (in doing so) take care not to look back at them!" He went away and hauled the mortars, but he did not look back; and though the mortars were heavy, he did not stop. At last he saw that a large (reindeer-) herd was passing ahead of him. Then he stopped and looked back. A (young) woman was (sitting) in a covered sledge (driving a reindeer-team). He took a seat (on the

---

"Ne′nako qɪyoᵋ′oge čača′me, aᵋnkukai′vɪ-gi." Ģek, gaya′ḷ-
"There thou wilt find old woman, let her cook for thee." Oh, he

qɪwlɪn, gañvo′ḷen kukai′vɪk, ģek, ña′nyen gapḷɪ′tčulin
entered, she began to cook, oh, that one finished

kukai′vɪk, ģek, gakuka′ñpaɹen, gawyeñvo′ḷen, gawya′n-
cooking, oh, she took (the meat) he began to eat, he refused
out of the kettle,

kawḷen.
eating.

5 Ģek, ña′nyen gayai′tɪlen, ɪ′npɪ-qḷa′wuḷa gai′ḷɪɹin kɪ′plau.
Oh, that one went home, by the old man he was given the mortars.

Ģi′wlin, "Ģaɹa′xtata wu′tčau, gāᵋa′nñɪvota. Kɪtta′ atawaḷ-
He said, "Take them these, haul them away! Take care do not
(with you)

ñiḷa′ka." Ģek, ga′ḷqaɹin, gañvo′ḷenau āᵋak, ui′ña atawaḷ-
look back!" Oh, he went away, he began them to haul, not not

ñiḷa′ka, i′nmɪq tapañañɪvo′ykɪn, ui′ña a′nvɪḷka. Ģek,
looking back in truth it was heavy, not not stopping Oh,
(he was), (he was).

ɛñãᵋ′an nekañvo′ykɪn, gačaᵋ′awlin, ñalvɪla′n·aqu ɛ′nɪk
so he did something, he looked, herd big of him

10 yanote′tɪ gaḷañvo′ykɪn. Ģek, ga′ñvɪḷen, gatawaḷñiḷa′ḷen,
ahead to pass begins. Oh, he stopped, he looked back,

same sledge). They two drove home, and lived there in joy.

Then ɪla' said, "How did you come (by all this)?" The other one then told him, "I found an old man who was working on ornamented (tobacco-)mortars." ɪla' said, "I understand." He set out and found the same (old man). Then he said (to the old man), "What kind (of mortars) are you making?" (The old man) said, "Go and find the old woman! Let her cook a meal for you!" He went to her, and she prepared a meal. Then she took (the meat) out of the kettle, and he ate. (The old man) gave him, too, the mortars, and said, "Haul them away, and take care not to look back at them!"

---

qaya'čɪku ña'wɪs·qat va'ykɪn. Ģek, ña'nqo gaña'ḷqɪwlin,
in a covered   woman   is.   Oh,   there   he sat down,
sledge

gaḷqa'ʟinat, gayai'tɪḷenat, gayennawñɪvo'ḷenat.
they (two) went, they (two) came they (two) lived in joy.
                   home,

Ģek, ña'nyen ɪla' e'wañ, "Ģɪ'ssa me'ñkañ i'tɪ?" Ģek,
Oh,   that one ɪla' said,   "Thou   how   wast?"   Oh,

ña'nyen gañvo'ḷen i'wak, "Tɪyoᵉ'an ɪ'npɪ-qḷa'wuḷ ta-kale'-
that one   began   to say, "I found   old   man   making-
                                                   ornamented-

5 kɪpla'ñɪḷaᵉn." Ña'nyen e'wañ, "Tɪye'yoḷok!" ɪla' gaḷa'lin,
(tobacco) mortars." That one said, "I understand!" ɪla' came,

assa'kin pa'nin gayoᵉ'oḷen. Ña'nyen e'wañ, "Ya'qkinau
of the other the same he found him. That one said, "What kind
day   (old man)

ᴇ'nyau qutei'kɪñɪnau?" Ģek, gi'wḷɪn, "Ñe'nɪna-čača'me
those thou art making?" Oh, he said, "That   old woman

qɪyoᵉ'ogɪn, aᵉnkukai'vɪ-gi." Ģaḷa'lin, gañvo'ḷen kukai'vik,
thou wilt find let her cook for thee." He came, she began to cook,
her,

gakuka'ñpaḷen, gawyi'lin. Ģú'mḷañ gai'lɪʟin kɪpla'wi,
she took (the meat) he ate. Again he gave him (tobacco-)
out of the kettle,   mortars,

10 gi'wlin, "Ģāᵉa'nñɪvota, kɪtta' atawaḷñɪḷa'ka."
he said, "Haul them away, take care do not look back!"

He hauled them away, and every little while he would take a rest. He moved on, and he would make one stride and then he would look back. One time a reindeer-leg appeared out of one of the mortars. But he sprang at it and struck it (in order to break the bone and get the marrow). Another time he looked back, and a (reindeer-)face appeared (out of the mortar). He sprang at it, and struck at the mortar with his knife, and chopped up the (reindeer-)face. Then he came home, and left (his sledge) with Eme'mqut. (There was nothing on it) but the tobacco-mortars. That is all.

Gañvo'len ā^aala'tık, a'mñuč pañawgiñıvo'ykın. Tawa'-
He began   to haul,   every time   he is taking rest.   He moves

ñekın, qu'n·ač vaqyı'yikın, gŭ'mlañ tawalñıla'ykın. ɛnna'n
on,   one time   he strides,   again   he looks back.   One

qo'yen gıtča'lñın kıpla'gıgiñko gače'pñıtolen, penye'kınen
of reindeer   leg   out of the mortar   peeped out,   he rushes at it

talai'vık. Gek, gata'wañlen gŭ'mlañ, gatawalñıla'len; gek,
to strike.   Oh,   he moved on   again,   he looked back;   oh,

5 gŭ'mlañ gatawalñıla'len, gŭmlañ lo^εlqal gačɛ'pñıtolen.
again   he looked back,   again   (reindeer-)face   peeped out.

Gape'nyılen vala'ta kı'plak, gaqa'yıčulin lo^εlqal, gayai'-
He rushed at it   with the   at the   he chopped small   the face,   he went
     knife   mortar,

tılen. Gapela'lenau, Amamqu'tinak gayo^εolenau. Am-
home.   He left them,   with Eme'mqut   he brought them.   Mere

kıpla'wi yıltelai'ke. Aččo'č.
mortars   are lying.   That is all.

9. How Eme'mqut became a Cannibal.[1]

Big-Raven lived with his people. Eme'mqut married

Quyqınn·aqu'wgi vañvolai'ke. Amamqu'tinak Vi^εyai
Raven-Big's people   live.   By Eme'mqut   Grass
                                                 (-Woman)

---

[1] Compare W. Jochelson, The Koryak, l. c., No. 108, p. 295.

Grass-Woman. Eme′mqut said to his wife, "Let us go out." She said, "It seems that you are going to do wrong." He said, "Why should I? This time I shall not do so." He went out into the open country and came home, having killed wild reindeer. Then he staid for a night in the open. After that he staid for two nights and very soon all the time. Grass-Woman went for a visit to her father Root-Man. She came and looked through the vent-hole, she quietly looked in and saw that just then Eme′mqut had split Root-Man in twain. He was eating his own father-in-law.

Grass-Woman went to her open-country house and

gama′taḷen. Amamqu′tinak e′wañ ña′wɪs·qatɪñ, "Mɪnnu-
he married her.   By Eme′mqut   he said   to the woman,   "Let us go

tɪḷa′tɪs·qiw." Gewñɪvo′ḷen, "Qa′yiñun quyaakuyičva′nñɪñ."
into the (open)   She said,   "It seems   you are going to do wrong."
country!"

E′wañ, "Ta⁵ya′qak? Ačhiva′n qaye′m." Notai′tɪñ qanñɪ-
He said,   "Why should I?   This time   I shall not."   To the (open)   he is
country

vo′ykɪn, ya′tikɪn, eḷvau′ ga′nmiḷenau. Va⁵′yuk gatčewñɪ-
going,   he comes,   wild   he has killed them.   Afterwards   he passed
reindeer

5 vo′ḷen ɪnña⁵′an, gek, va⁵′yuk ñee′tčɪñ, va⁵′yuk a′mñut.
a night   thus,   oh,   afterwards   twice,   afterwards   all the time.

Ña′nyen Vi⁵′yai ɪɛle′tɪ ga′ḷqaɪin, Tatkagɪtñɪ′yɪkɪñ. Gaḷa′lin,
That   Grass   to her   went,   to Root(-Man).   She came,
(-Woman)   father

gawa′s·vilin yɪnootñe′nqo, maḷe′ta gawa′s·vilin, e⁵′en ɪni′n
looked in   into the vent-hole,   quietly   looked in,   her
(father)

Tatka′gɪtñɪn gakaggu′péḷen akiḷa⁵′č Amamqu′tinak, ña′no
Root(-Man)   he split him in twain   just now   by Eme′mqut,   that one

yu′ykɪnin mata′ḷa⁵n čini′nkin.
he was eating   father-in-law   his own.
him

10 Ña′nyen Vi⁵′yai nekai′tɪ notayai′tɪñ gata′ḷqɪwlin. Ya′ḷku
That   Grass   somewhere into the (open)   entered.   In the
(-Woman)   country house   inner room

entered it. She put one small louse into the inner room, and another into the storehouse. Then she fled to Big-Raven's (house). She came to Big-Raven's, and said, "I do not know what has happened to Eme′mqut." They constructed a raised platform. Oh, Eme′mqut came to the open-country house, and he called, "Grass-Woman!" and it answered from the house, "Oh!" He came to the storehouse and called again, "Grass-Woman!" and it answered from the storehouse "Oh!" He recognized the voice of those small lice. He said, "The deuce! She is deceiving me!" He said, "Maybe I shall not be able to eat those people!" He came (to Big-Raven's house). The people were sitting on a raised platform. Eme′mqut

---

qo′ʟa qai-mɪ′mɪč, qo′ʟa ai′ak o′pta qai-mɪ′mɪč gayo′oʟen.
one   small louse,   one   in the storehouse   also   small louse   she put in.

To, ɛ′nnu Qoyqɪnn·aqoyɪkai′tɪñ gagɪ′ntawlin. Qoyqɪnn·a-
Oh,   she   to the Raven-Big's (house)   fled.   To the Raven-

qo′yɪkɪñ gaʟa′lin. E′wañ, "Ya′qikɪn, a′mu, Ama′mqut?"
Big's (house)   she came.   She said,   "What happened to,   I do not know,   Eme′mqut?"

Ǥatui′veñlinau. Ǥek, Ama′mqut nuta′yak gaʟa′lin, e′wañ,
They constructed a raised platform.   Oh,   Eme′mqut   to the (open) country house   came,   he said,

5 "Viᵋyoi′." Yayačɪkoi′tɪñ e′wañ, "A?" Aia′čɪku gaʟa′lin,
"Grass (-Woman)!"   From the house   it said,   "Ah?"   To the storehouse   he came,

gŭ′mʟañ e′wañ, "Viᵋyoi′." Aiačɪkoi′tɪñ e′wañ, "A?"
again   he said,   "Grass (-Woman)!"   From the storehouse   it said,   "Ah?"

Ñanyaiña′nu qai-mɪ′mčɪt vaʟo′meke. E′wañ, "Ñi′yuq!
Those   small lice (dual)   he heard them.   He said,   "The deuce!

tayɪñtinu′ñikin." E′wañ, "Qaye′m ña′no-van mɪnutña-
deceiving she is."   He said,   "Not   those   I shall be able

na′wge." Vaᵋ′yuk ginini′lin. Ui′veʟqak gaña′ʟqɪwlinau.
to eat them."   Afterwards   he appeared.   On the platform   they were sitting.

said, "Maybe I shall not be able to eat them, since they have constructed a platform!"

He approached, and began to lick with his tongue (the supports of the platform). Big-Raven cut at his tongue with a hatchet. He broke the edge of the hatchet; and when he examined it, it was quite jagged, like the broken gums (of an old man). (He did) the same with an axe; then he examined it, and it was also all jagged.

Big-Raven said, "Well then, Grass-Woman, give him his own offspring!" She dropped their small son into his mouth, and he spat out mere broken bones. Then Big-Raven said to him, "Well, then listen to me! Since you are like that, listen to me! Just do try and eat your own body!" Immediately he began to gnaw the points

---

E'wañ Ama'mqut, "Qaye'm ña'nu mɪnutñanau'. Čemya'q
Said   Eme'mqut,   "Not   those I shall be able to eat.   Really
gatuï'veñlinau."
they constructed a platform."

Ġaḷa'lin, čɪḷɪnmɪḷuḷa'tikɪn.   Quiqɪnn·aqu'nak   ga'thata
He came,   with tongue licked.   By Raven-Big   with hatchet
čɪ'ḷɪḷ čvitču'ykɪnin, ɪ'mɪñ čima'tikɪn ga'tte, yɪčiča'tikɪnin,
tongue he cut at it,   all he is breaking hatchet, he is examining it,
5 gaɪnnɪmčačai'vɪlin.   Va⁸'ak a⁸'aḷ o'pta gan·čiča'lin, o'pta
it is with broken gums. Afterwards axe   also   he examined,   also
ɪ'mɪñ gaɪnnɪmčačai'vɪlin.
all   it is with broken gums.

Quiqɪnn·a'qu e'wañ, "Vi⁸yoï', čini'nkin ɪni'n ya'qu-ɪ'nki."
Raven-Big   said,   "Grass   own   his   what of that."
                       (-Woman),   (child)
Ġana'yalin kmi'ñɪpil čɪkɪ'tñɪk. Ġatamtɪva'ḷen. Quyqɪnn·a-
She dropped   son small   into the   He spat out (broken) By Raven-
                           mouth.   bones.
qu'nak gewñɪvo'ḷen, "Ya'qu-e'nki, qenava'ḷom! Čini't
Big   he said to him, "What of that,   listen to me!   Since
10 ɪnña⁸'an qi'tɪ, qenava'ḷom, u'wik ve'tha-qo'nom qnu'ñvon."
so   thou   listen to me, self   just now   consume."
   wert,

of the nails of his own toes. After that he consumed his legs; then his body, arms, and shoulders. At last merely the neck was left, merely the throat. Then only did he die. After a while they burned him.

One time they were sitting in the dark. Their fire had just gone out, and Yini′a-ña′wgut said to her sister, "Let us go and stop up the smoke-hole!" They stopped up the smoke-hole; and then they began to say, "Those two are coming back! (One of them) is carrying something on his shoulders. It seems to be Eme′mqut, carrying his little son." (Indeed,) those two came and said, "Bring out the fire!" The women carried out the fire. They fed the fire (with sacrifice). Then only did the new-comers enter.

Va⁸′yuk u′wik gañvo′ḷenau va′gɪtčɪnu yu′kka. To, va⁸′yuk
Afterwards himself he began them nail-points to eat. There, afterwards
(of toes)

ɪ′mɪñ gɪtča′t uwi′kinat ganu′linat, va⁸′yuk u′wik, va⁸′yuk
all legs his own he consumed afterwards body, afterwards
them,

mɪ′ngɪt, va⁸′yuk čenpɪ′nmɪn. Va⁸′yuk am-elei⁸′neyɪ, am-
arms, afterwards shoulders. Afterwards mere neck, mere

qamatča′n ga′tčɪlin. Wǔ⁸′tču gavi⁸′lin. Ganqa′ngawlin
throat became. Then only he died. They burned him

5 tito-o′n.
after a long time.

Va⁸′yuk vos·qe′tɪ guyetvei′ñeḷenau, va⁸′yuk Yini′a-
Afterwards in the dark they were with extinct fire, afterwards Yini′a-

ña′wgutinti gewñɪvo′ḷenat, "Mɪnto′mñaḷqiw." Gatomñaḷ-
ña′wgut (and talked (dual), "Let us stop up the They stopped
her sister) smoke-hole!"

qi′wlinat, va⁸′yuk gi′wlinat, gewñɪvo′ḷenat, "Če, assa′kinat
the smoke- then they said, they talked, "Ah, those (two) of
hole, the other day

ya′tiki. Quḷumti′čitaḷat, ti′wgak, ɛnɪ′n kmi′ñɪpil gaquḷum-
are coming! They carry something it seems, his son small he carries on
on shoulders,

10 ti′lin." Va⁸′yuk gewñɪvo′ḷenat, "Miḷho′n qanaḷaga′tča."
shoulders." Then (those) said, "Fire bring out."

Gamiḷhɪna′linat, ginaḷva′linat. Wǔ⁸′tču ga′ḷqɪwlinat.
They carried out the fire, they fed the fire. They only (those) entered.

From that time on he ceased to say, "Let us go to the open country!" They staid at home all the time. They lost all desire to roam in all directions and to all places. They staid at home at the same place. That is all.

Qo'npŭ ganka'wlin i'wak, "Mɪnnutɪḷa'tɪs·qiw." Qo'npŭ
Altogether   he ceased   to say,   "Let us go to the (open)   Altogether
                                              country!"

am-ya'yak vañvoḷai'ke,. qo'npŭ ganka'wlinau ga'ḷñiḷ men-
only at home   they stay,   altogether   they ceased   in all   where-
                                                                    directions

kai'tɪ ya's·qanñık. Am-ya'yak gana⁶'linau ɛnna'niku. Aččo'č.
soever to want to walk. Only at home they became in one place. That is all.
                                              (staying)

10. Eme'mqut and Fox-Woman.[1]

Eme'mqut married Fox-Woman. He said, "I will go and get some blubber from our summer place." He arrived there. One of the flippers of his blubber-bag was gnawed at by a mouse. The mouse was dead. He found it and said, "What is it, a wolverene?"

He loaded it on his sledge and hauled it home. He came home. Then only he looked back and saw that

---

E'enač   Amamqu'tinak   Yayo'ča-ña'wgut   gama'taḷen.
One time   by Eme'mqut   Fox-Woman   he married her.

5 E'wañ "Mɪmɪ'tqantak a'ḷa-nɪmyolhe'tɪñ." Ǥaḷa'lin. Pipi'-
He said, "I will go for blubber to the summer-habitation." He came there. By a

kaḷña pu'pgan ga⁶pakoḷo'ḷen. Ǥek, gavɪ⁶'yalin ña'nyen
mouse   the blubber- was gnawed at the   Oh,   died   that
         bag   flipper.

pipi'kaḷñın. ɛ'nke gayo⁶'oḷen. "Yinna'wi, qapayn·a'qu?"
mouse.   There he found it.   "What is it,   a wolverene?"

Wuya'tik gaiña'lin gā⁶añvo'ḷen yaite'tɪñ. Ǥayai'tıḷen.
On the sledge he loaded it, he began to   home.   He came home.
                              haul it

Wŭ'tču gatawaḷñıḷa'ḷen, gagi'talin, e⁶'en qapayn·a'qu
Then only   he looked back,   he saw,   and   a wolverene

---

[1] Compare Jochelson, The Koryak, *l. c.*, No. 106, p. 294.

the mouse had turned into a wolverene. He looked into the house and said, "Mi'ti, I have killed a wolverene. Let some of you come out."

They took in the wolverene and began to beat the drum. Fox-Woman, the untidy one, was sitting with her boot-strings loose. She was looking for lice. "Oh, you Fox-Woman! it is your turn to beat the drum." The untidy woman was making leather thimbles. She began to beat the drum, "I am an unskilful one, I am an untidy one! I am eating hard excrement, left outside! I am eating strings of snowshoes in the brightness of the full moon."

Indeed, they eat them. Whenever we come to look for our snowshoes, the strings are eaten.[1]

---

gana⁸'lin. Ģačvɪ'nañlin, "Mitei', tɪqa'payuk! Ģanto'ta!"
became. He looked in, "Mi'ti, I killed a wolverene! Come out (somebody)!"

Enña⁸'anet gana'tviḷen qapayn·a'qu, gañvo'ḷenau ilu'tčuk.
Then they brought in the wolverene, they began to beat the drum.

Yayo'ča-ñawgut, vače'n·ñɪ-ñaw, pča'ggɪtñɪt ganvɪ'yiwlinau,
Fox-woman, untidy-woman, the boot-strings were loose,

miḷu'ykɪninau. "Toq, Yayo'ča-ña'wgut, gɪn-yaq qiḷu'tču."
she was looking for lice. "O, Fox-Woman! thy turn beat the drum."

5 Vače'nñɪ-ñaw ve'ḷo ya'qam ninataikɪñvo'qenau, ni'ka. Ģo,
Untidy-woman (leather) thimbles was making, somehow. Oh,

gañvo'ḷen iḷu'tčuk, "Uqu'gwai-ñaw-i-ŭm, vače'nñɪ-ña'w-i-ŭm,
she began to beat the drum "Unskilful woman am I, untidy woman am I,

nu'ta-maikina'ta, qɪm-a⁸'ḷu-ču'ču-ña'w-i-ŭm, tigi'ḷñu-ču'ču-
in the left, (open) country hard-excrement-eating woman am I, eating- showshoe- eating strings eating-

ña'w-i-ŭm e's·hɪpye-e⁸'ḷɪkɪñ."
woman am I by the full moon." shining

O⁸'nnen Enñi'ninak nenanuñvo'qenau. Nenavo⁸'ñvo-mu'yu
Indeed, by those they ate them. When we find them,

10 e⁸'en ganu'linau.
and they are eaten.

---

[1] Remark of the narrator.

She felt ashamed and went away, even with untied boot-strings. She went away, and did not come back. After some time Eme′mqut went outside and found her. A number of children were there. He said to Fox-Woman, "Whose children are these?" — "I said to myself, 'Perhaps they will keep me back somehow. I wanted to go away into the open country for my delivery. And I was delivered outside.'" — "Now, at least, stop your clamor! Let us go home!"

They went home. The thimbles which she had made before, and hung up outside, now turned somehow to clothes for her numerous children. The people were asking Eme′mqut, "From where have you brought the woman?" —

Eᵍ′en ye′ᶜ̣l gañekeḷa′ḷen, ui′ña alpini′tčalin ga′ḷqaḷin,
Then   there   she felt ashamed,   not   not tied boot-   she went
                                          strings   away,

qo′npú ga′ḷqaḷin; vaᵍ′yuk qu′lin Ama′mqut notai′tiñ ga′ḷ-
altogether she went away; then afterwards Eme′mqut to the (open)
                                                     country

qaḷin, gayoᵍ′olen. Yaya′ña ꞇ′nki va′ykın. I′naḷka vaḷai′kᴄ
went,   he found her. A house   there   is.   Numerous are

kmi′ñu. Gi′wlin Yayo′ča-ña′wgut, "Wutčai′u minka′kinau?"—
children. He said to   Fox-Woman,   "These   (are) whose?" —

5 "Gŭ′mma newñivoi′-gŭm, 'Pa′ḷa me′ñqañ nıyanñepñivoi′-
   "I   told myself,   'Perhaps in some way they will keep

gŭm. Kmeña′tınvu no′tañ nıḷai′-gŭm, ninaito′ñvoi-gŭm
me back.   For delivery to the I went away,   I was delivered
                        (open) country

nu′tak.'" — "Ačhikı′ču-ai′ñaka, mınyai′tımık."
in the (open) "At this time   do not   let us go home!"
country.'" —   then   clamor,

Gayaitınvo′ḷenau. Kmi′ñaḷvin assa′kinau veḷı′ḷñu nena-
They went home. Of her numerous recent   thimbles she
                   children

taikıñvo′qenau, ña′cñın nenanyopanñıvo′qenau, ña′nyeu
made them,   outside   she was hanging them,   those

10 i′ssu gana ᵍ′linau ni′ka. Gewñıvo′ḷen Ama′mqut, "Mañe′nqo
to the became somehow. They began to Eme′mqut, "Where from
dresses   tell

"I brought her from the open country. Long ago she went away to give birth to her children secretly outside. All those together are her children." In truth, she was a skilful seamstress, and had no reason for going away and living in secrecy.

After that they lived in joy. Eme'mqut married Kĭlu,[1] Ila' married Yini'a-ña'wgut. When so disposed, they would ascend the river and catch plenty of winter fish. Then they would return to their house-mates. They killed plenty of game. In this manner they led a happy life. What has become of them I do not know. That is all.

ña'wɪs·qat yathaᵍ'an?" — "Nuta'nqo. Ai'ñun kmi'ñu vɪ'n·va
the woman   thou hast   "From the (open). Long ago   children   secretly
             brought?"   country.

nenaitos·qewñɪvo'qenau.   Eᵍ'en   ña'nyeu   oma'ka   ɪ'ssu."
she went away to bear them.   Then   those   together   they."

In'miq ña'no awa'nñi-ñaw, atau' ña'no ɛnñaᵍ'an nɪtva'ñ-
In truth, that one seamstress-woman, vainly that one thus lived

voqen vɪ'n·va.
secretly.

5   Qo'npŭ ɡaaimɪyo'oḷenau.   Amamqu'tinak Kĭlu' ɡama'-
     Quite   they lived in joy.   Eme'mqut   Kĭlu'   married,

taḷen, Ila'nak Yini'a-ña'wgut ɡama'taḷen.   Ḡaimawḷai'ke,
        Ila'   Yini'a-ña'wgut   married.   (If) they wish,

gepiḷai'ke,   vai'amɪk,   gepɪñvoḷai'ke,   qatapñɪtɪñvoḷai'ke,
they go up-   by the river,   they begin to go   they catch winter fish,
stream,   up-stream,

vaᵍ'yuk yaya'ḷu nayoᵍñvo'ykinenau.   I'naḷka gɪ'ynik ɡa'n-
then   the house-   they are visiting.   Plenty   of game   they
       mates

mɪtčuḷen.   Vaᵍ'yuk ña'no ɡaaimɪyo'oḷenau, me'ñqañ a'nam
have killed.   Afterwards   those   were living in joy,   in what   then
                                                          manner

10 gɪ'ʟinau.   A'ččɪč.
    they became.   That is all.

---

[1] The narrator seems to have forgotten the marriage of Eme'mqut with Fox-Woman, and their subsequent reconciliation.

11. Ermine-People. — I.

Ermine-People were living. One Ermine-Man came home, and said, "You are asked to live with Big-Raven's people." He was telling lies. Nothing of the sort was said to him. They came to that house, and wanted to enter. Then they were beaten severely. They went away, and said, "We are rejected here." They came home and began to talk, "Let us go and live in a cave!" They went and lived in a cave. Afterwards they were caught by a flood. They had to climb upwards. That is all.

Imčanamtılaᵋnu vañvoḷai′ke. Ɠek, ña′nyen Imčana′m-
Ermine-Men   are living.   Oh,   that   Ermine-Man

tılaᵋn ɠayai′tıḷen, gi′wlin, "Quyqınnꞏaqu′nak qıyaipıḷa′tık."
came home,   he said,   "With Raven-Big's (people)   live together."

Ña′no nıtınma′tqen. Ui′ña i′nmiq i′wka ga′ntıḷen. Ɠaḷa′-
That one   is telling lies.   Not   indeed   not told   he was by   They
                                             them.

linau, gañvo′ḷenau yaḷqı′wık, gañvo′ḷenau ki′pḷık. Ña′nyeu
came,   they began   to enter,   those began them to strike.   Those

5 ganto′ḷenau, gi′wlinau, "A′nku naḷñıḷaikıne′mık." Ɠayai′-
   went out,   they said,   "To refusal   we are put to."   They

tiḷenau, gewñıvo′ḷenau, "Agêñe′ti mǐnıḷqaḷa′mık." Ɠaḷqa′-
came home,   they said,   "To a cave   let us go!"   They

ʟinau, gaḷa′linau. Ña′nako agi′ñka vañvoḷai′ke. Vaᵋ′yuk
went,   they came.   There   in a cave   they staid.   Afterwards

gatañvo′ḷenau, gati′pgaḷenau. A′ččič.
they were flooded,   they climbed upward.   That is all.

12. Ermine-People. — II.

Imčanamtıḷa′nu vañvoḷai′ke. Va‛yuk ni′ka Imčanamtı-
la‛nin ña′wıs·qat ǥakmi′ñaḷen. Imčana′mtıḷa‛n e′wañ,
"Canalo‛-ña′wıs·qat kmiña′ti." E′wañ, "Ya′qa mıččakıḷıs·-
vıḷa′ñın?" — "Tıke′nvıyık a‛aḷ va′ykın." — "Tıkei′, a‛aḷ
5 tu′yık va′ykın?" — "Ui′ña."

A′nam Aıgınvı′yıkıñ ǥaḷa′lin, "Amei′, a‛aḷ wu′tčuk
va′ykın?" — "Ui′ña. A′nam Aıgıḷe′yık va′ykın." Aıgı-
ḷe′yıkıñ ǥaḷa′lin. "Aıgıḷei′, a‛aḷ wu′tčuk va′ykın?" —
"Wuttınno′!"
10 A‛aḷ ǥa′kmiḷin, ǥayai′tıḷen, wŭ‛tču ña′nyen ki′ḷkiḷ
ǥu′ptılin. Ǥañvo′ḷenau takno′ñık, Imča′nala‛n ǥapa′ḷın.
Ǥewñıvo′ḷenau, "Qoyqınn·aqoyıkai′tıñ qaivıḷaḷa′tık." Ǥai-

12. Ermine-People. — II.

Ermine-People lived. After some time Ermine-Woman
brought forth a son. Ermine-Man said, "Ermine-Woman
has brought forth a son. [He said,] With what shall we
cut the navel-string?" — "With-Smell-Pusher-Away has
an axe." — "O Smell-Pusher! have you an axe?" — "No,
(I have not.)"

Then he came to With-Odor-Pusher-Away. "Halloo!
Have you an axe?" — "No, (I have not,) but With-Odor-
Averter has one." He came to With-Odor-Averter. O
Odor-Averter! have you an axe?" — "Here it is!"

He took the axe, came home, and only then did they
sever the navel-string. They began to arrange the birth-
feast. They cooked for this one Ermine-Man. The master
said, "Carry some meat to Big-Raven's people!" They

vıḷa′ḷenau. Ǧa′ḷqaᴌin, gaḷa′lin, gi′wlin, "Ya′qañ ya′ti?" —
"ıḷḷaᵉ′ kmiña′ti." Ǧewñıvo′ḷen, "Ya′qañ ya′ti? Qaᵉ′ḷatči."

Aᵉtte′tıñ gani′nḷalin, am-kama′ñı gai′ḷıᴌin, gŭ′mḷañ ga-
yai′tıḷen, gi′wḷin, "Amei′, am-Miti′nak yu′nin, ui′ña ı′npı-
5 qḷa′wuḷa." — "Yaivače′ñın ı′npı-qḷa′wuḷ. Ǧŭ′mḷañ ñai′añ
qaivıḷa′gi." Ǧaivıḷa′ḷen, gewñıvo′ḷen, "Ya′qañ ya′ti?"
Ǧu′mḷañ Quyqınn·aqu′nak a′wun-qama′ma gani′nḷalin
ñas·hınoi′tıñ.

Ǧas·s·aḷvıye′lin vıᵉya′tvık, vaᵉak ya′wač gayai′tıḷen.
10 "Me′ñqañ i′ti yu′ḷaq?" — "Amamqu′tinak am-a′yetvata,
'Awnu′p maḷ-ñawa′kak.'" Mi′qun Ama′mqut e′wañ, 'Qı-
yaipıḷa′tık, qıya′ᴌatık.'" — "Iñe′! Ǧŭ′mma gŭ′mḷañ ga-
tuyıkımiña′t-i-gŭm." — "A′mḷıñ anñe′nyi-emte′ta."

Ye′ḷıñ gata′wañḷenau, gaḷa′linau. "Imča′naḷu ya′qkinau
15 aᵉḷa′tčıgınkinau." Ǧaḷa′linau, gañvo′ḷenau yaya′s·qıwñık,
gañvo′ḷenau kı′pḷık. "A′nku naḷñıḷaikıne′mık." — "Ǧı′nku
naḷñıḷaikıne′tık. Ñai′añ ma′ma nıya′nutıñ." Ǧŭ′mḷañ
Quyqınn·aqu′nak u′ttä gañvo′ḷen kı′pḷık.

E′wañ ñawa′kak, "Ǧŭ′mma mıya′nutık. Eñi′, ı′npı-
20 qḷa′wuḷ qinaya′qı qinangınkıḷa′wı? Čini′n tıya′teuḷañ."
Ǧanka′wḷenau, ga′ḷqaᴌinau. Vaᵉyuk, "Meñkeito′ mǐnı′ḷ-
qaḷa? Ačıñeto′ mǐnı′ḷqaḷa."

Ǧamıčñoḷa′ñetıñ ga′ḷqaᴌinau. E′nmık gaya′lelin, gavıᵉ′-
yalin. "Mai, nıma′ḷqin, nikawi′čaqin, nıma′ḷqin." Ǧata′k-
25 yalinau agi′ñkı, gayı′ḷqalinau, gan·kiača′s·qiwlin, ɛ′nki ayi′yai

carried some meat. (One girl) went and came there They said, "Why did you come?" — "The mother brought forth (a child)." They said, "Why did you come? You smell of excrement!"

They threw the meat to the dogs, and gave her back the empty dish. She went home again and said, "Oh, oh! Miti' ate it all herself, (she gave) nothing to the old man." — "Poor thing, that old man! Carry again some more meat there." She carried the meat; and they said to her, "Why did you come?" and again Big-Raven threw her out of the house, together with her dish.

She remained there in a swoon the whole day, only then she came home. "Why did you stay there so long?" — "Eme'mqut held me back all the time, (saying, 'This is a) very good girl.' Moreover, Eme'mqut said, 'Go there, live together!'" — "Oh, but I have just now given birth to a child!" — "Have no care. I will carry it wrapped in a coverlet."

They set off, and arrived there. "Why have those Ermine-People come? They smell of excrement." They arrived there, and wanted to enter, but the others began to strike them. "Oh, they reject us!" — "(No,) they bid you welcome. Let mamma enter first!" Again Big-Raven began to strike them with a stick.

The daughter said, "I will go first. Eh, old man, why are you bidding me such a welcome? I can shake (my coat) myself." They were rejected, and went away. After that they said, "Where shall we go? We will go to a cave."

They went to a place rich in edible seaweed. (Ermine-Man) fell down from a cliff and fell in a swoon. (Then he came to, and said,) "Oh, it is a good (cliff), it makes you motionless with pleasure, a very good (place)!" They descended into a cave, and slept there. (Ermine-Man) went out in the night-time to pass water; and there (on

mi'mḷa gata'ḷen. "Mei, Gɪwɪ ̣ ̣ e',[1] mañɪ'n·ač i'ti?" Gaya'ḷ-
kɪwlin. "Ma'ki ninanɪmgumga'w-i-gi?" E'wañ, "'Gɪwɪ ̣ e',
mañɪ'n·ač nɪče'ḷpoqen?' E'wañ, 'Mal-kɪčo'l!'" E'wañ,
"Qai'ḷɪm mɪna ̆ ᵋso'ñvoḷa."

5   Gayɪ'ḷqalinau, va ̆ ᵋyuk añqa'ta gatañvo'ḷenau. "Gɪ'ssa
galu'tai-gi." E'wañ, "I'pa a'nam gɪ'ssa galu'tai-gi. Gani'-
kalinau, gi'wlinau, "Añqa'ta nataḷaikɪne'mɪk. Gañvo'ḷenau
e'nmɪk yatɪpga'nñɪk, ɪ'mɪñ kɪmi'ñu nanimtilɪñtatɪ'ykɪninau;
gatɪ'pgalinau. Gaya'nuḷen tɪpga'tɪk, gei ̆ ᵋññalin ñɪto'ḷñɪn,
10 guptɪnta'lin.

     Gatɪ'pgalinau, "Qakokaivɪḷa'tɪk." Gi'wlin, "Minka'kin
wu'ssɪn?" E'wañ, "Tanño ²   nɪgaḷa'qenau, wo'tto ñɪto'ḷñɪn
nape'ḷan." Gañvo'ḷen ɪpa'tik. Aki'nna ̆ ᵋt gapgupgaññivo'ḷen,
gañvo'ḷen ta ̆ ᵋḷɪk. Ña'wɪs·qata gi'wlin, "Ya'qɪykɪn?" E'wañ,
15 "Tɪta ̆ ᵋḷɪykɪn." Ganu'lin, gavɪ ̆ ᵋyalin.

     Ña'wɪs·qata gača ̆ ᵋulin, ñɪto'ḷñɪn ᴇni'n ui'ña. "ᴇni'n a'mu
ñɪto'ḷñɪn mɪtnu'ḷan. Meñkeito' mínɪ'ḷqaḷa? Ga'mga-oḷgɪ-
we'tɪñ, tə'mɪk-oḷgɪwe'tɪñ." Imčanaḷa'wge qo'npú gana ̆ ᵋli-
nau. Aččo'č.

13. Eme'mqut and the Kamaks.[3]

20   Amamqu'tinu vañvoḷai'ke, va ̆ ᵋyuk notai'tɪ ga'ḷqaṇin,
yaya'ña gayo ̆ ᵋoḷen. ᴇ'nki gi'wlin, "Mai, Ḷa'wa, gɪ'ssa?"

¹ Gɪwɪ ̣ e' STONE-FACE. Standing columns of natural rock frequent on the shore
cliffs and mountains of these countries, also the large bowlders lying about are
considered by the natives to be human-like beings, petrified, but still leading a
mysterious life of their own (cf. Bogoras, The Chukchee, Publications of the Jesup
North Pacific Expedition, vol. vii, p. 285). Ermine-Man pretends to have seen one
of these beings catching fish in the sea; but it was only a standing block of ice,
too unstable to be considered as a living bring.

the sea), upright blocks of ice were submerged in the water. "O Stone-Face! what success have you had in catching fish)?" He went back into the house, "With whom have you been talking?" He said, "(I inquired) what success Stone-Face has had catching fish with a small drag-net; and they answered, 'All right!'" She said, "Now we shall eat some cooked fish."

They went to sleep, and in a little while the sea-water came to them. "You have passed water." The other one said, "It is you who have passed water." They looked around, and said, "We are caught by water." They began to climb up the cliff. (Ermine-Woman dragged up) all the children. Even all the straps were snapped (in two). They climbed up. He climbed first; then one of his sides fell down detached.

The others climbed up. "Cook (this meat)!" (Ermine-Woman) said, "Where does it come from?" He said, "The Chukchee passed by and left it." They began to cook it. As soon as the (water in the) kettle began to boil, he felt unwell. The woman said, "What is the matter with you?" He said, "I am unwell." They ate the meat, and he died.

The woman saw that one of his sides was missing. (She exclaimed,) "We have eaten one of his sides without knowing it! Where shall we go! To every cache, to other people's caches." They turned into real ermine. That is all.

13. Eme'mqut and the Kamaks.[3]

Eme'mqut lived with his family. One time he went into the open and found there a house. (A voice from)

---

[2] The Reindeer Koryak and the Reindeer Chukchee call each other mutually by the same name, Ta'nñïtan (cf. The Chukchee, l. c., p. 11).

[3] Compare W. Jochelson, The Koryak, l. c., No. 102, p. 290.

E′wañ, "La̭′wa, mañi′n·ač oya′myañ?"[1] E′wañ, "O, mɪtaḻ-voḻa′mɪk.[2] Ame′yaq ña′wɪs·qat?" E′wañ, "O kmi′ñɪn yɪto′nen. Qu′nam mu′yi am-ya′yak oya′myañ mɪtɪ′nmɪn. La̭′wa, qaña′ñya!" — "Mannu′qi ya′yay." — "Me′ñqañ
5 i′tɪykɪn? Ña′no vɪ′yañ kɪsva′čɪk va′ykɪn."

Ganvo′ḻen aña′ñyak. Gatann·as·qa′nḻenat ka′maw-ña′w-gutɪnte gaqḻa′wuḻa. Ña′nyen gana′yulin. Amamqu′tinak gagɪnta′wlinat nɪki′ta. Gan·kiačačas·qi′wlinat, ganto′ḻenat. "Kmi′ñɪn gina′tvilin. Ya′qatqi? Ñi′yaq vi′nvɪt, ya ya′ḻñ,
10 ya qoi′ñ?"

Gaya′ḻqɪwlinat, gŭ′mḻañ gayɪ′ḻqalinat. I′pa kmi′ñɪn La̭′wa ga·aḻin. "Mai, La̭′wa, ya′ti? Wo′tto ya′ti, gŭ′mḻañ a′čhi ya′ti." — "Ti′ta gŭ′mma tra′tɪk. Wŭ᷎′tču tra′tɪk."[3] — "A′me mañi′n·ač ɪ′ḻvui?" — "Uï′ña, mɪtpiḻhaḻai′kɪn." —
15 "Toq, La̭′wa, qaña′ñya." Ya′yay ga′kmiḻin, oya′mtɪwiḻen ḻo᷎′oḻ-pɪne′t. Ganvo′ḻen aña′ñyak. "Trai, tɪ́roi, trai!"[4] Ña′nyen nɪquliḻa′tqin.

Amamqu′tɪyɪk ña′nyen gann̄awtɪña′ḻin, ča′wčuwen. Qo′npŭ gaaimɪyo′oḻenau, gatvañvo′ḻenau qo′npŭ. Aččo′č.

---

[1] Oya′myañ HUMAN GAME is a word used only by the spirits.
[2] Here a man is spoken of as a "wild reindeer." In other tales a man is spoken of as a "little seal."
[3] These words are supposed to be in the language of the kamak. They differ,

there said, "Halloo, La′wa! is that you? How are you getting along with your human game?" He said, "Well, we two have killed some wild reindeer. How is (my) wife?" — "She has just been delivered of a son. And even we two, staying here at home, have killed one man. Now, La′wa, call to the spirits!" — "And where is the drum?" — "[What is the matter with you?] (Don't you know?) Of course, it is there on the cross-pole."

Eme′mqut called to the spirits. He put them to sleep, — the kamak-woman, together with her husband. He revived the other man. They fled in the night-time, together with Eme′mqut. In the middle of the night those sleepers wanted to pass water. They came out, and said, "Our son has become quite light of foot. And how is it? There are two foot-tracks, — one to this side, and the other to that side.

They entered, and again went to sleep. Then their real son, La′wa, came home. "Halloo, La′wa! have you come? Not long ago you were here, and now you come back another time." — "When have I been at home? I have arrived just now." — "How is your reindeer hunt?" — "Nothing killed. We were famishing." — "There, La′wa, call to the spirits!" He took the drum. (It was made of pieces of) skin of women's breasts sewed together. He began to call to the spirits, "Trai, Tiroi, trai!" Thus was he singing.

The other man lived with Eme′mqut's family, and married a daughter of a reindeer-breeder. They lived quite happily. They staid there. That is all.

---

however, from the ordinary Koryak of the western branch by the repeated use of *r* instead of *y*. This makes them similar to the eastern Koryak dialect, and to the Chukchee.

4 Compare the preceding footnote.

14. Eme'mqut and Shellfish-Girl.

Quyqɪnn·aqu'nui vañvolai'ke. Ġek, Ama'mqut gas·hɪn-tɪlɪ'lin, va⁸yuk ġayo⁸'olinau kɪ'lkakau, kɪ'lkakil ġu'ptɪlin, ġek, ġañvo'len qalhai'ak, e'wañ, "Igigɪ'." E'wañ ña'nyen, "Qanka'wgi qalhai'ak. Aia'ñač qas·wugɪgeñe'tɪñ yɪ'nna
5 ġɪni'n lɪpyuɪ' nu'ptɪn."

Ġek, ġani'kalin, ġača⁸'awlin, ɛ'nki yaya'pilɪñ ġato'mwalen. Ġaya'lqɪwlin, a'čhikin ġama'talen. Ġek, ña'nyen ġanyai'-taɭin. Ña'nako vañvolai'ke. A'ččɪč.

15. Eme'mqut and the Perches.[1]

Ama'mqut notai'tɪñ ġa'lqaɭin, ġayo⁸'olen nɪmyɪ'ssa⁸n.
10 ɛnke' qatapñɪtɪlai'ke qaña'tɪla-ġɪ'niw am titiča pela'qa. ɛnqa'ta ġassa'len qata'p-vai'am, ñanako tamka'ln·aqu ġa-yɪ'ssalin, ġatai'kilin. ɪna'n-awi'wut taiki'ykɪninau ta'mkalu'ttu.

Qo'ɭa ɛnña⁸'nač Yayo'ča-ñawgut ġai'lɪɭin, ġanña'wtɪñaɭin.
15 Tɪ'tič-a'wulpel-peɭa'qɪt ġanyaitanñɪvo'lenat ɛnñ·a⁸'anet ġa-yai'tɪlanat e⁸'en tamka'ln·aqu ġai'pɪlen.

Tɪ'tič-a'wulpel-peɭa'qɪt ġanunñɪvo'lenat, ɛnña⁸'nvot ġani'-kalinau va⁸'yuk, qla'wulpelɪt ġana⁸'linat. E'wañ, "Mɪ'kna-mu'yi kmɪ'ñɪ-mu'yi?" — "Ġi'wa, 'Amamqu'tina-mu'yi
20 kmɪ'ñɪ-mu'yi.'"

ɛnña⁸'anet patta⁸'la mani'ti ġayɪ'ssalinat am-ġa'nmač ġayɪssalinat ñanka'kenat ña'wɪs·qatɪt. Pɪɭvɪ'ntɪ-ya'nya-a'tvɪla⁸t ġa'lqaɭinat. Ġanyai'talenat ña'nyaqɪt ña'wɪs·qatɪt. Ya'qɪt a'mu ġatomwa'lenat, ġumaka'linat, as·ka'čɪkɪlinat.

---

[1] *Acerina cernua*. This tale was told by a young girl. It seems to be a frag-ment of longer and more coherent tale.

14. Eme'mqut and Shellfish-Girl.

Big-Raven lived with his people. Oh, Eme'mqut walked along the seashore, and found some shellfish. He detached one shellfish, and it began to whimper, "Igigi'!" He said, "Cease your crying! Yonder among the stone-pine bushes (lies) your detached hood."

Oh, he went and looked for it! It had turned into a small house. He entered the house and married that Shellfish-Girl. Then he brought her home. They lived there. That is all.

15. Eme'mqut and the Perches.

Eme'mqut went into the open and found a village. They were catching winter fish with drag-nets. The fish were small perches. He dragged a net along that fishing-river, and filled with fish a set of drying-poles. He made such a set. Very quickly he constructed those drying-poles.

After a while they gave him Fox-Woman, and made him marry her. He brought home two small dried perch-tails. These he brought home, and hung them on the drying-pole.

They were going to eat these small dried perch-tails, and all at once something happened. (These small tails) turned into small men. They said, "Whose sons are we?" — "Say, 'We are sons of Eme'mqut.'"

Then the (two) girls of this place filled with dried meat two bags; one for each [they filled]. They went away in iron canoes, and took the girls along. What has become of them I do not know. They went together, (both of them), headlong.

ɛñãᵉʼan genačɪxčanñɪvoʼḷenat, ḷawtɪḷñu gaipɪñvoʼḷenau.
 Genˑačɪxčatpaañvoʼḷenat, Amamquʼtinti genˑačɪxčatpaañvoʼ-
ḷenat. Ñankaʼkɪḷu ganãᵉʼlinat, gaaimɪyoʼoḷenat. Aʼma-qliʼka-
kmiʼña gakmeñanñɪvoḷenau Yayoʼča-ñaʼwguta.

5   Laqlañyoʼykin, gaʼḷ̃iḷ tiḷaivɪñvoḷaiʼke. Nanyemkɪčɪwñɪ-
voʼykɪnenau vaʼčaq. Aččoʼč.

16. Mitiʼ and Magpie-Man.[1]

Quyqɪnnˑaquʼnu vañvoḷaiʼke. Gek, Quyqɪnnˑaʼqu eʼwañ,
"Muwɪčñaʼḷik." Gek, ñaʼnyen Mitiʼ qaiʼ-aᵉʼttu yawyetɪs-
qiwñɪvoʼykɪnenau. Vakɪthɪʼmtɪḷaᵉʼn ñaʼnɪko awyeñyoʼykɪn.
10 Ñaʼnyen Mitiʼnen iʼñɪñpɪk iʼñuiʼñɪn yɪčemawñɪvoʼykɪnen.

Gek, ñaʼnyen yaiʼtekɪn. Mitiʼ Quiqɪnnˑaquʼnak ewñɪ-
voʼykɪnen, "Gayaʼqlin iʼñuiʼñɪn gatɪʼnpɪčulin?" Eʼwañ,
"Aᵉʼttaʼya oʼpɪtčɪnɪk am-iᵉʼña iʼyɪk, ɛñãᵉʼan iʼtɪ." Gek,
Quyqɪnnˑaquʼnak ɪʼmɪñ aᵉʼttaʼya oʼpɪtčɪnu ɪʼmɪñ čuwiʼykininat.
15 Gek, gúʼmlañ ñaʼnyen wɪčñaʼḷɪykɪn. Ñaʼnyen Mitiʼ ñɪtoʼ-
ykɪn aᵉʼttaʼyalqak vagaʼḷekɪn, ñɪvoʼykɪn gɪyaʼpčak, "Moʼol-
qele!"

Vaᵉʼyuk Vakɪthɪʼmtɪḷaᵉʼn gayaʼʟin, giʼwlin, "Mɪnyaʼlqɪw
yaʼlku." Quyqɪnnˑaʼqu qayeʼm iʼnˑa nɪyaʼtin. Qayeʼm
20 enaḷhaʼlmɪk."

Ganaʼtvɪḷen. Kiʼkič gayaʼḷqɪwḷin ineyegeñeʼtɪ̃, ñaʼnɪko
gagɪnñɪčanñɪvoʼḷenat, vaᵉʼyuk Quyqɪnnˑaʼqu gayaʼʟin ga-
kuʼmñalin, "Miteiʼ, qetɪgoʼn vɪᵉʼy-ɪʼmɪt." Gek, eʼwañ Miʼti,
"Ikḷayoʼk aneʼtɪn. Gúʼmma taᵉʼptɪʼykɪn." Eʼwañ, "Ginaʼn

Those (i. e., Eme'mqut and his wife) were sent away
by the people, and were given (reindeer with) halters of
grass. Then the people ceased to send them away. They
ceased to send away Eme'mqut and his wife. They
became as natives, and lived in joy. Fox-Woman now
was bringing forth mere male children.

Winter came, they were wandering in all directions.
At times they visited their neighbors. That is all.

16. Miti' and Magpie-Man.[1]

Big-Raven lived with his family. Oh, Big-Raven said,
"I will (go and) fetch some willow-bark." Oh, Miti' went
to feed the little puppies. Magpie-Man came to eat there.
He pecked at Miti''s face (to indicate his love), and her
whole nose was covered with scratches.

Oh, that one (Big-Raven) comes home! He said to
Miti', "What has happened to you? Your nose is
scratched all over." She said, "By hitting with my nose
against the sharp ends of the dog-shed corner I was
scratched thus." Oh, Big-Raven cut away all the ends
of the dog-shed corners. Then again he went for willow-
bark. Miti' went out, perched on the top of the dog-shed,
and began to sing, "I am walking along the cross beam!"

Then Magpie-Man came, and said, "Let us enter the
sleeping-room! Big-Raven will not come back soon. He
will not catch us."

She took him into (the house). Just as soon as they
entered the sleeping-room and began to make love there,
then Big-Raven came back, and called out, "Miti', take
this load of willow!" Miti' said, "Let the I'kla[2] bring it
down! I am busy trampling a half-scraped skin with my
feet." — "Nay," said Big-Raven, "I want you to take it

---

[2] Small wooden charms of human shape (cf. Jochelson, The Koryak, l. c., p. 42).

a'ḷımıñ qeti'gin." To, Miti'nak gai'tıḷen, gaktı'nveḷen, gana'tvıḷen.

Ña'nyen Quyqınn·a'qu gaya'lqıwlin, gañḷo'yıḷen. Ġǔ'mḷañ yıno'gıtñın gato'mñaḷen, ku'lipčina gato'mñaḷen, gañḷı'ḷ-
5 qawlen. Ini'yıgıñ gavakıthaiñıñvo'ḷen. Ña'nyen Va'kıthın mal·ki't ganto'ḷen, čınko'nañ-vethñe'tı ganto'ḷen.

Va'kıtha naya'q-gǔm?" Ġek, ña'nyen Va'kıthın gayai'-tıḷen. Miti' gañvo'ḷen vamya'tvak. Ġek, lilipila'qut vaᵉ'yuk gaito'ḷenat ña'nyaqıt. Vaᵉ'yuk gamaiñanñıvo'ḷenat. Ġek,
10 ña'nyat Quyqınn·aqu'nak u'nmi yaiva'čı yıssıñvoi'kınenat.

Quyqınn·aqu'nu gatai'ñat nomkawñıvo'ḷenau. Ñaye'yıt nı'wqinat, "Ma'ma, mıtqugıta't." E'wañ, "Qanto'tık, ta'tana qı'wgutık, 'Mıtqugıta't.'" Ġek, ganto'ḷenat, gai'ḷınat o'pta am-ya'tıt. Ġek, gaya'lqıwlinat gačı's·hulinat. Ġǔ'mḷañ
15 gi'wlinat, "Mitqugıta't." E'wañ Miti'nak, "Qanto'tık, ta'tana qwañla'tık."

Ganto'ḷenat. "Tato'! mıtqugıta't!" — "Qu'nam qun gi'wa, "Tula'-va'kıthınat." Kmi'ñıt ñaye'yıt gaqalhaiañvo'-ḷenat. "Igi', nanaᵉyıva'wmık." Miti'nak gi'wlinat, "Qanto-
20 to'tık, qı'wgutča, 'I'pa lı'ge-ta'ta ñe'nako qoyaḷa'tekın." Ġaya'lqıwlinat, Miti'nak mani'gık gayo'ḷenat, ga'mgave'ḷoqaḷık. Ġa'ḷqaṛin, gaḷa'lin. Vakıthıntıḷa'yıkıñ, gaktıne'ñıḷenat.

E'wañ ña'nyen Quyqınn·a'qu, "Tıpaivaka'nñıvok, Mêtě'-
25 yıkıñ mı'ḷqatık." Ga'ḷqaṛin, gaḷa'lin. "Mitei', qanto'ge! ı'npı-qḷa'wuḷ ya'tti." Miti' e'wañ, "ᴇna'n-ve agıtca'kᴇḷen? Čini'n yayaḷqıwı'ykın." Ġaya'lqıwlin, gaqamı'tvaḷen, gañvo'ḷen a'wyik, gaqa'qḷaḷen, ñačınoi'tıñ gagı'ntawlin.

Miti'nak nenaaiñawñıvo'qen, e'wañ, "Quqe'!" — "Oi!"

down." Oh, Miti' took it, and with a violent pull drew it into the house.

Then Big-Raven entered the house and made a smouldering fire. He also stopped up the entrance-hole and the smoke-hole, so that the sleeping-room was full of smoke. Then a Magpie's voice was heard from the sleeping-room. That Magpie came out. He escaped through a narrow crack.

"(See) what (this) Magpie has done to me!" The Magpie, however, went home. Miti' was with child. After some time she brought forth two small eggs. (The two children) grew rapidly, and Big-Raven had a great love for them.

Big-Raven's people were storing their catch of fish. Those two said, "Mamma, we are hungry." She said, "Go out and say to daddy, 'We are hungry.'" They went out, and were given two whole dried salmon. They entered, and nibbled up (the fish). Then they said again, "We are hungry." Miti' said to them, "Go out and ask daddy (for more)."

They went out. "Daddy, we are hungry!" — "No wonder! Two thievish magpies!" Those two sons began to weep. "Oh, he is reproaching us!" Miti' said to them, "Go out and tell him, 'Our real daddy is herding reindeer (with the wealthy reindeer-breeders).'" (After that) they entered again, and Miti' put them into a grass bag, (placing) each in one of the (lower) corners. She went away, and came to Magpie-Man and flung (her bag right in).

Big-Raven said, "I feel lonely. I will go to Miti'." He went and came there. (The people said,) "Miti', come out! Your old man has come to you." Miti' said, "Has he no legs? Let him enter of his own accord!" He entered, and she gave him food. He began to eat, and was choking. Then he ran out of the house.

Miti' called to him. She said, "Big-Raven!" — "Oi!"

Pŭkawñɪvo'ykɪn. Ģaktɪkomña'ḻen, e'wañ, "Oi!" Ña'nyen yaḻu'yičan egɪtñei'tɪñ gačɪnkaita'ḻen. Quyqɪnn·a'qu ña'nyen gayai'tɪḻen. Aččo'č.

17. How Big-Raven's Daughter was swallowed by a Kamak.[1]

Quyqɪnn·aqu'wgi vañvoḻai'ke. Ñawa'kak mɪ'mḻa nɪnu'qin.
5 Qalñe'-key gate'wḻaḻen, qai-mɪ'mɪč gaito'ḻen ɪnna'n. E'wañ ña'wɪs·qatɪñ, "Ya'qu mɪntai'kɪr?" Ģi'wlin ña'wɪs·qata, "Ya'qu mi'qun qatai'kɪgɪn? Ya'nmɪñin." E'wañ, "Yaya'yu mɪntai'kɪn."

Yaya'yu gatai'kɪlin. E'wañ gača⁸'ulin, e'wañ yaya'yu
10 gato'mwaḻen qai-mɪ'mɪč. Quyqɪnn·a'qu qo'npŭ gañvo'ḻen aña'ñyak. Ģes·hɪpa'ḻin e'wḻañ ga'mga-nɪme'tɪ, gewñɪvo'-ḻenau, "Quyqɪnn·a'qu qo'npŭ qañañya'ñvoñ. Ģapa'lqaḻin ui'ña aña'ñyakɪḻen. Ya'qin a'mu gatai'kɪlin ya'yay?"

Quyqɪnn·aqu'nin ñawa'kak vɪ'n·va vañvo'ykɪn. Ui'ña
15 o'ya a'tvaka. ɪ'mɪñ-nɪ'myɪsu giwi'nilinau ñawɪnyo'nvu. Ģi'wlin, "Mi'kinak ya'qin ya'yay yanyɪ'wñɪnin, ña'nyenena ñawa'kak tɪyei'ḻɪñɪn. ɪ'mɪñ-gi'ynik añqa'ken nanyɪwñɪvo'-ykɪn. "Yu'ñyun." E'wañ, "Aḻva'lin." ɪ'mɪñ i⁸'gin, qo'yen, ɪ'mɪñ-qun iču'ču. E'wañ, "Aḻva'lin." Napkawñɪvoi'kɪn
20 yanyi'wñɪk.

Va⁸'yuk mêḻhe'ñko gače'pñɪtoḻen ñenve'thɪčñɪn, ake'ykɪ-ḻa⁸n, vɪ'yañ gapanqai'pɪḻen. "Ģumna'n myanyɪ'wñɪn, ya'yay ya'qin gatai'kɪlin. Ača'ḻun gatai'kɪlin." — "Aḻva'lin." —

1 Compare Jochelson, The Koryak, l. c., No. 103, p. 291.

Then he could not help himself, and shouted, "Oi!" The piece that choked him flew out (of his mouth, and fell down) at a great distance. Then Big-Raven went home. That is all.

17. How Big-Raven's Daughter was swallowed by a Kamak.[1]

Big-Raven was living with his people. One of his daughters was (almost) eaten by lice. They shook her combination suit, and found there one small louse. (Big-Raven) said to his wife, "What shall we do with it?" The woman said, "What will you do? Why, you will kill it." He said, "(No,) we will make it into a drum."

They made it into a drum. They looked at it, and the small louse turned into a drum. Big-Raven immediately began to act as a shaman. The news of this was carried everywhere, to all the villages; and the people began to talk, (and say,) "Big-Raven has become quite a shaman, but he has grown old without having any spirits. What unknown kind of drum has he made?"

Big-Raven's daughter was living in secrecy. She did not appear openly. All the neighbors gathered as suitors. He said, "Whosoever can state rightly the material of which my drum is made, to him I shall give my daughter." They named all kinds of sea-game. One said, "Of whale;" but Big-Raven said, "Not of that." Others also said it was of wolf-skin, of reindeer-skin. They named every living thing; but he said, "Not of that." They could not describe it properly.

Then from the fire crept out an evil spirit, with no clothes on, with only a cap (on his head). "I can tell of what your drum is made. It is made of a chamber-vessel." — "Not of that." — "It is made of a kettle." —

"Kuka′kin gatai′kɪlin." "Aḷva′lin." — "A′nam qai-mɪ′mčin." Miti′nak gewñɪvo′ḷen. "ɛñaᵋ′an! Ñawa′kak mɪssai′ḷɪ̃ɪn kama′kɪ̃."

Ǥaito′ḷen ñawa′kak, gañvo′ḷen yɪtañatawa′tɪk. Wūᵋtču
5 galaᵋuñvo′ḷen. Ǥañvo′ḷen qaḷhai′ak ñawa′kak. Mu′u-yiḷ gatai′kɪ̃voḷen, ya yu′ñyun, ya qo′yen, ya yi′yin, ɪ′mɪ̃-kɪyuḷaᵋ′ḷu. Koro′wapel[1] gaito′ḷen ya′waḷañqaḷ. Ña′nako ñawa′kak gaña′ḷqɪwlin, va′ḷa gava′xgɪᴛin ñawakka′ta, qo′ḷḷa pi′pip karma′nɪk[2] gayo′oḷen. Ǥata′wanḷenau. Qo′npü ña-
10 wa′kak nɪqaḷhaiañvo′qen.

Ǥaḷa′linau kama′kɪ̃, kama′kau ganto′ḷenau, qoya′wge ɪ′mɪ̃ ganuñvo′ḷenau, "N·am, n·am, n·am." ɛnna′n koro′-wapel ganaᵋ′lin. Vaḷa′ta ganmɪtčoñvo′ḷenau kama′kau. Vaᵋ′yuk ɛnna′n ganaᵋ′lin wotta′kin ake′ykɪḷaᵋn. Vaᵋ′yuk
15 pi′pip gani′ñḷalin, ña′nkalqak gaña′ḷqɪwlin. Vaᵋ′yuk ga-pka′wḷen yatɪpga′nñɪk, gapka′wḷen yanu′ñka ñenve′thɪčña.

E′wañ, "Qa′wun pani′ta mi′kinak nayamata′ge, ñêya′nɪ̃-kmê′ñɪ̃ yanaᵋ′lɪ̃, ɛ′nki tɪyanu′wgi." Ña′nyen ñênvê′thɪčɪ̃n ga′lqa′ᴛin. Čawčuwa′ta gama′talen. Vaᵋ′yuk kmi′ñɪn
20 gaito′ḷen, vaᵋ′yuk va′sqɪ̃ gaito′ḷen, gū′mḷañ gañvo′ḷen qaḷhai′ak. E′wañ, "Kama′kata naya′nuw-gŭm."

Vaᵋ′yuk qḷa′wuḷ ga′lqaᴛin notai′tɪ̃, ka′mak ga′yaᴛin, ganu′lin. Yanu′ñkɪ pa′quḷ ganu′mkawlin, pa′quḷa qaḷa′ḷvɪn ganči′mawlin. Ñenve′thɪčɪ̃n gaviᵋ′yalin, ganto′ḷen. Miti′w
25 gakya′wlin, e′wañ veta′tekɪn. E′wañ, "Mi′kinai′-gi?" — "Ai′gewe tɪnu′wgi."[3]

---

[1] Borrowed from the Russian корова, THE COW; -pel is the suffix of the diminutive.
[2] Borrowed from the Russian карманъ THE POCKET.
[3] The ka′mak turned into an ordinary human being; namely, into a woman, who was assisting them in their work.

"Not of that." — "Then of a small louse." Miti′ said, "That is right! Now we must give our daughter to the Kamak."

They brought out the daughter, and began to prepare her for the journey. Then only, for the first time, was she seen. The daughter began to cry. They arranged for her three lines of sledges. One was hauled by whales; another, by reindeer; the third one, by white whales. All three kinds were alive. In the end they brought a small cow. The girl mounted it. She put on a large knife in a bandoleer, and also put a comb into her pocket. They set off. The girl was crying very hard.

They came to the kamak's house, and the other kamaks went out and ate all the reindeer, "N·am, n·am, n·am!" Only that cow was left. Then the girl began to kill the kamaks with her knife. At last only one was left, — the first one, with no clothes. Then she threw down the comb, (and it grew quite large.) She climbed to the top of it; but he could not climb it, and so the evil spirit could not eat her.

He said, "Though at a future time you will marry a certain man and have two children by him, just then I shall eat you." Then the evil spirit went away. She married a reindeer-breeder. After a while she brought forth a child, and then another. Again she began to cry. She said, "The kamak is going to eat me!"

One time her husband had gone out, and then the kamak came and ate her. She had concealed about her at this very moment her woman's knife, and with that knife she ripped open his body (insides). The evil spirit died, and she came out. The next morning, when they awoke, a woman was busying herself around their house. (The mistress) said, "Who are you?" — "I (am the one who) ate you yesterday."

Oya′mtıwılu ganaᵉ′linau gŭ′mḷañ kmi′ñu. Kmi′ña gama′-
taḷen. Oḷa′wuḷ gaya′ʟin wŭᵉ′tču. Qoyqınnˑaqoyikei′tı gaˑ′l-
qaʟınau. Kmi′ñın gŭ′mḷañ gaña′wtıñḷen. Qoyqınnˑaqoyı-
kei′tñ gaḷa′linau. Ǵi′wlin, "Ñawako′k nayato′n." E′wañ,
5 "Ñenve′thıčña naḷḷa′xtatın. Yaq-ña′wısˑqat ni′tın?" Ga-
wa′sˑvılin. "Wutınnaḷai′-gŭm, tıya′tık." Ganto′ḷenau, gaya′l-
qıwlinau. ᴇnna′niku gatvañvo′ḷenau, gapıttuña′wḷenau.
Aččo′č.

18. The Kamak and his Wife.[1]

Ni′ka, ma′kiw a′mu vañvoḷai′ke. Vaᵉ′yuk ñenve′thıčñıt
10 gawa′sˑvılinat. E′wañ, "Mai, ui′ña ava′ḷeika?" — "Uḷgu′vık
vaḷai′ke." Uḷhu′vıñ gaḷa′linat, gañvo′ḷenat va′ḷuk. "Čo-
pro′tka vaḷu′tka!"[2] Ǵŭ′mḷañ miti′w. "Mai, ui′ña ava′ḷeika?"
— "Yaqa′ḷık vaḷai′ke." — "Čopro′tka vaḷu′tka! Ava′ḷeika
yanaᵉḷa′ntık, miti′w to′čhın-ya′q mıssanusˑqiwḷa′ntık."

15 Ǵagınta′wlınau nıki′ta gıčhoḷai′tı. Ma′qım gani′nḷalin,
vinvınˑa′qu gato′mwaḷen. Ñanekai′tñ gagınta′wlinau.

Ǵaya′ʟinau. "Mai, ui′ña ava′ḷeika?" Ui′ña. "Mınyaḷ-
qıwičña′nau! A′mu ᴇ′nnu gapı′sˑqalinau." A′wun gaya′l-
qıwlinau, ı′mı ga′nčılinau kıčva′ču. Ui′ña yı′nna.

20 E′wañ, "Mınanˑačo′mık."[3] Ǵanvaqyiḷa′wḷen. Ača′gcıñın

---

[1] Compare Jochelson, The Koryak, l. c., No. 105, p. 293.

[2] Compare p. 68, footnote 3.

[3] *Mınanˑačo′mik*, literally LET US ACT WITH THE GRANDMOTHER. The word *a′na*
(GRANDMOTHER) is used also for DIVINING-STONE (cf. W. Jochelson. The Koryak, l. c.,
p. 44).

Meanwhile her sons became (grown) men. One son married that woman. Just then her husband came. They went to Big-Raven's people. Another son also married. They came to Big-Raven's people. The people said (to Big-Raven), "Your daughter is being [brought] here!" He said, "The evil spirit took her away. What (kind of a) daughter may come from there?" She looked into the house. "I am here, I have come!" They went out (to meet her), and all entered. From that time they lived together and grew rich. That is all.

18. The Kamak and his Wife.

Some people lived in a certain place. One day a kamak and his wife looked down (through the entrance-hole). They said, "Halloo! have you not some blubber?" — "There is some in the cache." They entered the cache, and began to eat blubber. Then they sang, "It tastes well. We are eating blubber." The next morning it was the same. "Halloo! have you not some blubber?" — "There is some in the porch." — "It tastes well. We are eating blubber; but when you have no more blubber, [to-morrow] we shall eat you."

They fled upwards in the night-time. They threw an arrow (upwards), and it became a road. They fled along this road.

Those came again. "Halloo! have you not some blubber?" But there was no answer. "Let us jump in! They are hidden somewhere." They entered, and searched in all the corners. There was nothing.

They said, "Let us try the divining-stone!" [3] (The

The reason is probably that divination with stones is chiefly practised by women, and that the divining-stone, though usually a round pebble or a piece of bone ornamented with beads and tassels, represents a female guardian of the family.

an·a′nu nı′lñıqen. "Ečhathıčñe′tı yagıntawḷa′ñe, mıssaya-
waḷa′nñınau. Voḷqıgeñe′tı yagıntawḷa′ñe, mıssayawaḷa′nñı-
nau. Añqai′tı ı′mı mıssayawaḷa′nñınau. Gıčholai′tı yagın-
tawḷa′ñe, mi′qun? Aña′ña aḷai′tıñ na′ntımık. Me′ñqañ
5 mınya′waḷat?"

Gañvo′ḷen lo′lo i′luk. "Añei′kıḷka panenai′tı mínınto′-
mık?[1] Yaqaḷnawıčñe′tı mínınto′mık." Kama′w-ña′ut, "Qina-
quḷuimti′gi." Emtei′pıḷen. "Qinanpiykaḷa′wı." Vaḷeḷei′tı
gai′pıḷen. "Gına′n qun nıta′witkıñi-gi."

10 Vaᵋ′yuk gaviᵋ′yalinat. ɛnña′an gayıḷteḷñıvo′ḷenat. Vaḷe-
ḷei′tı ḷa′wut gana′lilin. Vaᵋ′yuk ña′nyeu gewñıvo′ḷenau.
"Mınyoᵋ′oḷan yaya′ña." Gayoᵋ′oḷen, pıḷvı′ntı-ča′yinaña
ga′nvılin ḷa′wut, a′wun im-ḷa′wtalin.

"Qe′e!" Voḷqageñe′tı gani′ñḷalinat. Gatvañvo′ḷenau,
15 gaaimıyoᵋ′oḷenau, añenve′thıčñıka ganaᵋ′linau. Ačňo′č.

19. Gull-Woman and Cormorant-Woman.[1]

Niyka′wgi ya′qyaq-ña′wutu ña′nyaqat gañaw-yiḷa′ḷñı-
to′mga yagınñıvo′yke. Ivva′lu-ña′wgut e′wañ, "Aya′tka
ageñe′tıñ, mıḷñitatis·ki′wık." Ña′nyen kama′kn·aqu e′wañ,
"Mas·hı′ntıḷık." Gas·hıntıḷeñvo′ḷen, vaᵋ′yuk ñe′nin e′wañ,
20 "Yınna′qi e′lhı-peye′ykın?"

[1] Compare Jochelson, The Koryak, l. c., No. 99, p. 287.

kamak-woman) made (her husband) stand with his legs apart. She used his penis as a divining-stone. "If they have fled to the morning dawn, we shall follow them. If they have fled to the sunset, we shall follow them. To the seaside also we shall follow them. If they have fled upwards, what then? God would not treat us very pleasantly. How can we follow them?"

He began to sway his penis. "Shall we go out through the same opening without any fear.[1] Let us go out through the vent-hole in the roof of the porch!" The kamak-woman said, "Take me on your shoulders!" He took her on his back. "Oh, you are strangling me!" (His head) thrust itself into her anus. "Oh, you are playing mischief!"

Finally they both died, and lay there. His head slipped into her anus. After a while (the fugitives) said, "Let us visit the house!" They visited it, and dragged out his head with an iron hook, and his head had become (quite) hairless.

"Oh, oh?" They threw them into the direction of the sunset. Then they lived and were happy. They were not (molested) by spirits. That is all.

19. Gull-Woman and Cormorant-Woman.

Gull-Woman lived with a companion, who was her female cousin. They sat sewing. Cormorant-Woman (i. e., the cousin in question) said, "While no one comes to the cave, I will go and prepare my sinew-thread." At the same time Big-Kamak said, "I will walk along the shore." He walked along the shore. Then he said, "What is there, that shows so white?"

---

[1] Literally, WITHOUT SHAME. SHAME for FEAR is used also in the Chukchee (Publications of the Jesup North Pacific Expedition, vol. viii, No. 10, p. 63, footnote 1).

Ģayoᵋʹoḷen: yaʹqyaq. Qaʹčɪn uiʹña anaʹḷuka gatɪʹtkaḷen.
Ňaʹnyen Kamaʹknᵃaqu gayaiʹtɪḷen, eʹwañ, "Tɪtaᵋʹḷɪykɪn."
Ģayaiʹtɪḷen, kiʹkit gayɪʹḷteḷen, gek ñaneʹninak Yaʹqyaq-
ñaʹwtinak paʹquḷa qaḷaʹḷvun yɪčimaʹwɪykɪnin. Ģek, ñaʹwɪs·-
5 qatɪk eʹwañ, "Qenanyaikɪniʹ-gi." — "Eʹnnu-koroʹtka, gek,
eñvaʹratka!" [1]

Kamaʹknᵃaqu gavɪᵋʹyalin. Ňaʹnyen Yaʹqyaq-ñaʹwut gan-
toʹḷen. Ģañvoʹḷen čotčɪḷqeʹtɪñ pinkuḷaʹtɪk. Pŭkaʹwekɪn
yayɪñaʹñka. ᴇnaʹn kɪtčaʹta geneiʹmaklin. Ģayiʹñalin, ga-
10 kuḷaʹlin, gañaikapɪʹtkalin. Ňaʹnyeninen ñaʹwɪs·qat kɪnmaʹ-
čɪku ñaʹnako gapɪʹs·qalin. Ģek, gŭʹmlañ yaqaiʹqun gayiʹ-
ñalin, yaʹsqaḷqak giʹḷin.

Ģayaiʹtɪḷen, giʹwlin, "Kamaknᵃaquʹnak inaʹnui, kĭmaʹk
tɪvɪᵋʹyak." Ňaʹnyen Ivvaʹlu-ñaʹwgut, "Oʹpta mniʹkak.
15 Tiʹta oʹpta ninanuvaᵋʹan." Eʹwañ qutiʹninak, "Qɪymeᵋʹen,
apaʹquḷkeḷ-eʹ-ge." — Gŭmniʹn vai vain·aquʹwgi, vaᵋʹga
tyančɪmaʹwɪkɪniñɪn, ḷuʹgu iʹwka mañɪnmɪḷaʹtɪykɪn."

Ňaʹnyen gaaʹḷaḷen, gapkaʹwḷen iʹwak. Ageʹñɪñ gaḷaʹlin,
gatvañvoʹḷen. Ňaʹnyen Kaʹmak-ñawgut qaiʹgut gaḷaḷanñɪ-
20 voʹykɪn. Uiʹña aḷaᵋʹuka. Ňaʹnyen tayyeñɪvoʹykɪn, ewñɪ-
voʹykɪn, "Wutɪssaiʹ-gŭm." Meʹnqañ miʹqun uʹka aᵋḷaᵋʹwun?

Eʹwañ, "Qageʹ, wutɪnnaḷaiʹ-gŭm, qinaʹnu!" Pukawñɪ-
voʹykɪn ḷuᵋk. Qaiʹgut čančɪs·qonvoʹykɪnen. "Mannuʹqi?"
Ģek, gaḷaᵋʹulin. Eʹwañ, "Tɪyanuʹwgi!" Eʹwañ "Qina-
25 nuʹwgi!" Ģanuʹlin, uiʹña oʹpta anaʹḷuka gatɪʹtkaḷen. Ģek,
ñaʹnyen gayaiʹtɪḷen. Ģek, gŭʹmlañ eʹwañ, "Tɪtaᵋʹḷɪykɪn."
Qḷaʹwuḷɪñ eʹwañ, "Qenanyaikɪniʹ-gi." — "Eʹnnu-koroʹtka,
eñvaʹratka!"

---

[1] Compare p. 68, footnote 3.

He came (nearer, and it was) a Gull; and, [even] without chewing, he swallowed her. Then Big-Kamak came home, and said, "I am unwell." [He came home,] and as soon as he lay down (to rest), that Gull-Woman, with her woman's knife, ripped open his body (from the inside). Oh, he said to his wife, "Cheer me up (by some means)!" — "Without collar-string, without nostrils!"

Big-Kamak died. That Gull-Woman came out (of his insides). She began to jump up on the cross-pole above his pillow; but she could not fly up, because she was all covered with slime. She flew up again, and fell down and thudded against the ground. His wife lay flat in the corner (from sheer fright). Nevertheless she flew up again, and was on the house-top.

She came home, and said, "Big-Kamak swallowed me, I nearly died." That one, Cormorant-Woman, said, "I also will make something. Let him also swallow me!" The other one said, "Don't do it! You have no woman's knife." — "Here are my nails. I will rip him open with my nails. If it were done, I should feel elated."

That one (Kamak-Woman) passed by, but she could not talk to her. She went to the cave and staid there. That Ka'mak-Woman, indeed, was often passing by, but she could not see her. That Cormorant-Woman began to cough, and to say, "Here I am!" but how could she see her in the dark?

She said, "Here I am! Swallow me!" But she could not find her. Indeed, she almost stepped over her. "Where is she?" Oh, she found her! She said, "I will swallow you!" The other one said, "Do swallow me!" She swallowed her, also, without chewing, gulped her down. Oh, she came home. And again she said, "I feel unwell!" She said to her husband, "Cheer me up!" — "Without collar-string, without nostrils!"

Gŭ′mḷañ ga′nmiḷen, pa′ninau vača′pgɪčñu va⁵′ga vagɪt-
ču′ykɪninau.¹ Ña′nyen gavɪ⁵′yalin. Gŭ′mḷañ ganto′ḷen.
Ivva′lu-ña′wgut ganto′ḷen, ta⁵y-a′mu gavetho′ḷenau a⁵′ḷmuḷqu.

Gek, gayai′tɪḷen. Ña′nyen gi′wlin, "Gŭmma vai panet-
5 čɪnai′tɪ tĭyaa′nkawɪñ." Uwi′kiu gangɪḷa′wḷenau; ageñe′tɪ
tḷai′vɪk qo′npŭ ganka′wḷenau. A′ččɪč.

20. Yini′a-ñawgut and Kĭlu′s Marriage with Fish-Man.³

E⁵′en Quyqɪnn·aqu′nu vañvoḷai′ke. Kĭlu′ e′wañ Yini′a-
ña′wgutina, "Minno′tantaḷa." No′tañ gaḷa′linau, ᴇ′nnɪ-ḷa′wut
inu′nu ga′kmiḷɪn. Gaḷa′linat, gañvo′ḷenat a′wyik. Gaḷqai-
10 ña′wlin ᴇ′nnɪ-aḷpɪ′ttama. Gagi′ntawlin, "Kama′kanu Yi′ni
na⁵′llɪñ." E′wañ, "Ui′ña kama′kanu ana⁵′ḷka." — "I′n·ač,
mi′qun, kama′kanu na⁵′llɪñ."

Gañvo′ḷen yanaqmɪtkatu′yawñik, gapka′wḷen, gayɪ′ḷqalin.
E′wañ Kĭlu′, ña′nyen gayai′tɪḷen, gi′wlin, "Ma′nnu-yaq
15 Yi′ni?" — Kama′kanu na⁵′llɪñ." Ña′nyen Yini′a-ña′wgut
gaqya′wlin. ᴇ′nki ᴇnnɪ′mtɪla⁵n pipi′tčuykɪn. ᴇ′nki qata′p-
e′mat va′ykɪn.

Gewñɪvo′ḷen, "I′n·ač, qaqya′wgi!" Gaqya′wlin. Gek,
gama′taḷen, ᴇnke′ gatvañvo′ḷenau, gamaiñɪtaiña′linau.
20 Va⁵′yuk gayai′tɪḷenat Qoiqɪnn·aqoyɪkai′tɪñ. "Ñawa′kak
naya′tɪn!" — "Yaq ñawa′kak ni′tɪn. Mu′čhin kama′kanu
gana⁵′ʟin." — "Wuttɪsaḷai′-gŭm, tɪya⁵′tɪk."

---

¹ The respective rôles of Big-Kamak and his wife are evidently confused in this
tale. Thus the husband, killed not long ago, would seem to be alive again. Similar
confusion is met in several other tales, Chukchee and Koryak (cf. for instance,
Bogoras, Chukchee Mythology, Publications of the Jesup North Pacific Expedition,
vol. viii, part ii, No. 1, pp. 15, 19).

She killed her again, and tore the old scars[1] with her nails. This one died. Again she came out. [Cormorant-Woman came out,] and cut her way through several mounds of drifted snow.

Oh, she came home. (The kamak) said, "I have enough of these [former] doings." They have punished their own bodies, and ceased to walk along the stone.[2] That is all.

20. Yini′a-ñawgut and Kīlu′s Marriage with Fish-Man.[3]

Big-Raven lived with his family. Kīlu′ said to Yini′a-ña′wgut, "Let us go for a walk!" They went out walking, and they took a fish-head for (travelling-)provisions. They came to a certain place and began to eat. (Kīlu′) threw at her (cousin) the cheek-bone of a fish. She sped away, and said, "Yi′ni has become a kamak." That one said, "I have not become a kamak." — "Enough, indeed, you have become a kamak!"

She tried to detach it, but could not do it, so she fell asleep. Kīlu′ said, (when) she came home, and they said to her, "Where is Yi′ni?" (She said, "Yi′ni) became a kamak." Then Yini′a-ña′wgut awoke. There was Fish-Man combing his hair, and a load of winter-fish was (there also).

He said to her, "Enough, wake up!" She got up. He married her. They lived there, and caught plenty of fish. After some time they came home to Big-Raven's house. "They brought your daughter." — "Which daughter may come here? Our daughter became a kamak." — "Here I am! I came."

---

2 Both Kamaks seem to have revived after having been killed.
3 Compare Jochelson, The Koryak, No. 109, p. 296.

ɛnnɪmtɪlaᵋ'na Kĭlu' gakenanñɪvo·'l̥en. "Yinei'! me'ñqañ
gɪ'tča i'tɪ?" — "Ǥɪna'n ɛnñaᵋ'an ina'ntɪ." — "Ǥini'n to
q!a'wul nɪma'l̥qin."

"Čan·ai', mɪnno'tanta!" Ga'lqaᴌinat, gal̥a'linat no'tañ,
5 gañvo'l̥enat a'wyik. O'pta l̥a'wut ga'kmiᴌin inu'nu. "Čan·ai',
qina'l̥qaiñaw." Ǥewñɪvo'l̥en, "Qɪymeᵋ'en mil̥qaiña'wgi."
E'wañ, "Am-mu'yu mɪnpɪttuñawl̥ai'ke."

Ǥal̥qaiña'wlin. Ui'ña aqmɪ'tkatča. Ǥa'kmiᴌin, vɪᴌɪᵋ'yña
gañaᵋ'ᴌin. Vaᵋ'yuk mal̥-ki't gañaᵋ'ᴌin. "Toq, Čan·ai', qena'-
10 pel̥a." Ǥape'l̥alen. "Čan·ai', ui'ña kama'kanu anaᵋ'l̥ka."
Ǥŭ'ml̥añ gaᴌa'xtɪlin. E'wañ, "Qena'pel̥a. Ǥayai'ta, gi'wa,
'Kama'kanu naᵋ'ᴌiñ.'"

Ǥewñɪvo'l̥en Quyqɪnn·a'qu, "ɛnɪ'k anñena'ta, me'ñqañ
ni'tɪykɪn." Kĭlu' a'wgi tɪ'nmɪ-qal̥haiañvo'ykɪn, gayɪ'l̥qalin.
15 O'pta gakyawñɪvo'l̥en, ɛnke' ɛnnɪ'mtɪlaᵋn. Ǥi'wlin, "I'n·ač,
gɪna'n ewgupa'tik." Ǥakya'wlin, ɛnnɪmtɪl̥aᵋ'nak o'pta
gama'tal̥en. ɛ'nki gatvañvo'l̥enat gamaiñɪtaiña'linat.

Vaᵋ'yuk gayai'tɪl̥enat Qoyqɪnn·aqoyɪkai'tɪñ. Ǥi'wlinau,
"Kĭlu' naya'tɪn." — "Mu'čhin Kĭlu' kama'kanu gana ᵋ'ᴌin."
20 E'wañ, "Wuttɪnal̥ai'-gŭm, tiya'tɪk. ɛnnɪmtɪl̥aᵋ'nak enama'tai."
ɛ'nki gatvañvo'l̥enat, nalñɪqa'tvuqinet yatai'ñanñɪk. Yini'a-
ña'wgutinti kmeñanñɪvo'ykɪnat. Qu'ttu q!a'wul̥u naitoñ-
vo'ykɪnenau. Aččo'č.

Kílu′ began to envy (her cousin on account of) her Fish husband. (She said,) "Yi′ni, how did it happen to you?" — "You did this thing to me." — "But your husband is a good one."

"Čan·ai′, let us go out for a walk!" They went out, came to a place, and began to eat. They also took a (fish-)head for (all) provisions. "Čan·ai′, throw a bone at me!" The other one said, "I will not [throw]." (Kílu′) said, "(Do it!). We shall gain much by it."

She threw the bone at her, but it did not stick (to her face). She took it and glued it on with her saliva. At last it was (sticking) all right. "O Čan·ai′! leave me (alone)!" She left her (and went away). "Čan·ai′, I did not become a kamak." (The other one) again came back. She said again, "Leave me (alone)! Go home and say, 'She has become a kamak!'"

Big-Raven said, "It is her own mind. Let her be (wherever she desires)." Kílu′ [falsely] pretended to be crying, then she fell asleep. She also woke up; and there was Fish-Man. He said, "Enough, it is all your pretensions." She got up, and Fish-Man married her. They also staid there and caught plenty of fish.

After some time they went home, to Big-Raven's house. People said, "They have brought Kílu′." — "Our Kílu′ became a kamak." She said, "I am here, I came! Fish-Man married me." There (both Fish-Men) lived. They were quite successful in catching fish. Yini′a-ña′wgut and her cousin brought forth sons. They bore some male children. That is all.

21. Big-Raven and Fox.

Dialect of Pa′llan.[1]

Qutkı′nnaxu gergiñe′lqılin, vi′tvitpi ġayoᵋ′oḷen, gı′vlin, "Qa′iñun meḷ-gı′rniku, ya′vač ata′ḷıñka." Ġa′ateḷin, a′ñqak geni′reḷin. Ḷıgı′mmen gewge′ḷin, keli′laᵋn ġayoᵋ′oḷen, ḷıgı′mmen ᴇ′nkıta gı′vlin, "Qa′iñun meḷ-gı′rniku, ya′vač
5 ata′ḷıñka." Ġa′ateḷin a′ñqak.

Me′mıl ġayoᵋ′oḷen, ga′ateḷin a′ñqak. Riri′ñe ġayoᵋ′oḷen, geni′reḷin. Yu′ñiy ġayoᵋ′oḷen, va′sqın ye′pluq nımei′ñäqin yu′ñiy, att′ı′yuḷ geni′reḷin. Ḷıgı′mmen gewge′ḷin, va′sqın ġayoᵋ′oḷen gekeli′lin yu′ñiy. "Vai-i′ yu′ñiy!"

10 A′ttı nı′mnımu gakıtaiñe′lqılin. A′ttı Ta′nñın-i′rrıt ġa-yuñpe′ntaḷen vaḷa′ta gepi′riḷqıḷa. A′ttı givi′niḷqıḷa, gaḷaᵋ′ulin, ᴇna′nna a′ttı gečeñ′ače′ñıḷqılin. A′ttı rıkrı′ñık gere′lqılin, ᴇ′nki genaḷpuño′lqılin mı′tqa. Ġemeiñeyı′nmılin, a′ttı gathai′tıḷen, geti′ñemyılin.

15 Ta′tolata[2] gaḷaᵋ′ulin. "Me′nqut ku′rıtkın?" — "Umyu′m!" I′vıtkın, "Tı′nna?" I′vıtkın, "Tumyu′m!" Ḷıgı′mmen e′wın, "Tı′nna?" E′wın, "Yuñyu′ñ!"[3] Mı′tqamıt get′e′lin ᴇnı′kkı tā′n'aw.

"Qai′ḷım, tetemı′tqañın." A′ttı ku′m'ukum gelpi′rtelin
20 aᵋ′tta-qa′meñ. Qutkı′nnaxu getemi′tqanlin ne′m'ek. A′ttı-yaq tato′lape getei′kılin mesqa′ven, a′ttı gerı′yalin, genñi-ve′lin Qutkınnaxu′nak. A′ttı ᴇnñi′n rıya′-vi′ḷa ᴇnñi′n ga′nmıḷen. Tenma′vıḷaᵋn.

See p. 6.
[2] The fox, in the Koryak and Chukchee, is usually a female, Fox-Woman.

21. Big-Raven and Fox.[1]

Big-Raven walked along the sand-spit, and found a small ringed-seal. He said, "It seems that if it were a good catch, it would not lie so far (from the water)." He kicked it, and threw it into the sea. He walked farther on, and found a spotted seal. He said as before, "It seems that if it were a good catch, it would not lie so far (from the water)." He kicked it into the sea.

Then he found a thong-seal, and kicked it into the sea. He found a white-whale, and threw it into the water. He found a whale, and another whale, quite big (bowhead whale), and he threw it in still farther. He walked on, and found a striped whale. (Then he said,) "Here is a good whale!"

Then he called aloud to the neighboring people. A number of Chukchee rushed for the whale, knife in hand. They were approaching. He looked on them and felt frightened. So he entered the mouth of the whale. There he began to suck in the whale-oil. He filled his mouth full, then he jumped out and flew away.

A fox[2] saw him. "Where do you come from?" — "From the whale." She says, "What?" He says, "From the whale." She said again, "What?" — "From the whale!"[3] Then the oil dropped down directly on her (back).

"That is good. I gathered some oil." She wrung out her coat in a dogs'trough. Big-Raven also gathered oil (for himself). Then the small fox prepared a cake of (berries and other) vegetable material, and sent it to Big-Raven to show her gratitude. With these return-payments, however, she killed him.[4] It is finished.

---

[3] The first two answers are given by Big-Raven with mouth closed; the third, with mouth open. They are also imitative of the cry of the raven.

[4] Evidently by poison mixed with the berries.

22. Eme'mqut and Envious-One.

Dialect of Paren.[1]

Nɪpaivatɪ'čñin miti'w Ememqu'tinak luᵋ'nin, i'wnin, "Me'nnu luᵋ'wan, mɪnyoᵋoga'ᵋan. Ģŭ'mlɪñ vus nayoᵋoga'ᵋan niwga'ᵋan "Toq, yawo' eḷekɪ'mkɪn mɪpaḷausqa'wa." Ña'nɪ-yax Ememqu'tinak peḷa'nen Nɪpaivatɪ'čñin.

5 Ñɪvoi' eḷekɪ'mkɪmɪk, ine'ñeyik, pḷɪ'tkui. Yäqqai'-qun qati'. Vaᵋ'yuk ni'tkinek mel-ñe'wɪs·qat ñe'wänu ḷɪ'ñnin. Ñane'nɪnak Nɪpaiva'tɪčñinak pe'nin qun ɪm Uwe'ñpilɪñ nanyaita'tɪnat. Ti'tequn niwga'ᵋan, "Ọle'gi. Ñe'wɪs·qätit mɪnɪntenčɪte'wnet!"

10 Ña'nɪ-yax Nɪpaivatɪ'čñin, "Yawo', čɪčeʟe'ñɪn!" A'mḷɪñ-van kɪtve'-lɪ'ga penči'ykɪn, ñe'wɪs·qät pêḷhɪnolñɪ'toḷa yi'san gattai'ḷen. Čɪtavaña'nnen. Če'tɪk va'čañ äče'aḷa êḷhɪtaw-ñu'tkinen čɪmoʟɪtawɪtkoñu'tkɪnen.

Vaᵋ'yuk yetha'as ña'nɪ-yax. Ememqu'tina ñe'wɪs·qat 15 nenčɪmpetha'ᵋan. Nanatvuga'ᵋan. Ñe'nin Nɪpaiva'tɪčñinin nenewuyetha'ᵋan, oma'ka yu'ñyu-veli'ta. "Ñe'wɪs·qätɪt mɪnɪntenčɪte'wnet!"

Naitoga'ᵋan "Awe'n, ewliḷashɪla'n·aqu ewloiñila'n·aqu." Exune'če penčɪ'tkɪnen ñe'wɪs·qät talñathɪsñɪ'nvɵ. "E'wun-20 van ya'ḷvuñnen." To, ñe'nin Ememqu'tinin ñe'wɪs·qät naitoga'ᵋan. Nɪpaivatɪ'čñin viᵋgi.

Oma'ka yu'ñyu-veli'ta poxḷa'nñui. Nenumke'wɪn. Čɪgɪ-čeñe'wgi. E'wañ, "geyɪ'ḷqat-gŭm." Mu'qun yɪshɪ'ykineu čo'nñonenau ɪni'neu qaḷaḷvɪnɪ'ñqo ganto'ḷenau. Ģŭ'mḷɪñ

---

[1] See p. 6. This is evidently a fragment of a larger tale, but the narrator knew no more.

22. Eme'mqut and Envious-One.[1]

The next morning Eme'mqut saw Envious-One, and he said to him, "Where did you see him? Let us go and visit him." Again they visited him, and said to him. "Oh, wait! we are going to roast the omasum on a flat stone." Then Eme'mqut left Envious-One.

He began to busy himself with the omasum, and to roast it. He finished this. Then he went away. After some time he took a fine girl for a wife. Envious-One brought to his home his former (wife) Little U'weñ. After a long time they said to each other. "Come here! Let us compare the beauty of our wives!"

Envious-One said, "All right! I will bring her." After that every time again he rushes at his wife. She had an overcoat fringed with reindeer-mane. He took her along. While on the way, he washed her quite frequently, with (liquid from) the chamber-vessel, and (by rubbing) forced the blood into her face.

Then those two came. Eme'mqut's wife was hidden. They were going to bring the wives. Envious-One fed his wife sumptuously, giving her plenty of whale-blubber. "Let us compare the beauty of our wives!"

They brought them in. "Ah, but she has long lashes! She has large buttocks!" All the time he kept jumping over to his wife and re-arranging the parting of her hair. "Oh, surely she will came out the victor!" Then they brought forth Eme'mqut's wife. Envious-One swooned at the first look.

He had a diarrhea from that whale-blubber.[2] They took away the woman. Then he recovered his senses. He said, "I have slept." And really he began to eat

---

2 It seems that he had eaten some whale-blubber with his wife.

naitogaᵋ′an.   Viᵋ′ɡi.   Yıshı′ykineu   ɡenu′lineu   ɡu̇′mlɪñ
yıto′nenau.

Gu̇′mlɪñ   nenu′mkewın.   Čıɡı̆čeñe′wɡi,   ču′nineu   yısɡı′-
ykineu   qalalvını′ñqo   ɡanto′ļenau.   Vaᵋ′yuk,   "Qime′ñen,

5   qaļqathı′tık.   Tıpa′aaᵋk."   O′pta.

again the matter vomited from his insides. They brought
in the woman again. He swooned.

That vomited matter, which he tried to swallow came
out again. They took her away. He recovered his senses,
and ate again that matter vomited from his insides. Then
(he said), "I do not want it. Go away! I have had
enough!" The end.

23. Big-Raven and Fish-Woman.[1]

(*In Six Dialects.*)

Big-Raven lived with his family. They had nothing to
eat. He went to the sea, and found there Fish-Woman.[2]
He brought her home. She cast forth spawn and they
ate it. Then Big-Raven married Fish-Woman. Miti′ grew
jealous. Big-Raven went into the open. Then Miti′ struck
Fish-Woman and killed her. She cooked her flesh and
ate of it. Some of it she left for her husband.

Then Big-Raven came home. "Fish-Woman, come out."
Then that one who was just cooked, stepped forth from
the rear storeroom. He came in and she gave him food.
Then she said to him, "Just now Miti′ has killed me,
and cooked my flesh." The next day he went away again.
Miti′ again attacked Fish-Woman. She wrung her neck
(and thought,) "This time I have killed her." Big-Raven
came back and she revived again and gave him food.

---

[1] Compare Jochelson, The Koryak, *l. c.*, No. 104, p. 292.

[2] Literally, Pıscıs-Homo. More frequently used for the masculine (cf. No. 20,
line 16).

After that Fish-Woman went away. (She said,) "Miti′ some day will make an end of me." Big-Raven came back, but she was not there. He came to the sea-shore and called out, "Fish-Woman, come here." — "I shall not come. Miti′ will try to kill me again." So he could not call her out. That is all.

Chukchee.

Ku′rkɪlɪnti [1] nɪtva′qēnat, nɪgitte′tqinet. Añqa′-gêlê′ê, ᴇn·qa′m ᴇ′nnin ora′wêʟan luᵋ′nin, rɪrai′tannên. Le′lhä gêčhêtɪ′tkoññoi, ᴇnqa′n nano′ññoaᵋn. ᴇn·qam Ku′rkɪlinä ma′tanên. Miti′ ᴇ′nɪkɪ kɪña′tɪñoi. ᴇn·qam Ku′rkɪl nota′gtɪ 5 qäti′. Miti′nä kɪ′plɪnên, tɪmnên, ɪpa′nnên, ru′nin. Čɪ′mqŭk uwaᵋqočê′gtɪ pêla′nên. ᴇn·qa′m Ku′rkɪl pŭki′rgiᵋ. "ᴇ′nni-ñe′ut, qanto′gêᵋ!" Yañai′pŭ ñɪtoi′, gɪnmɪ′lkin ɪpa′jo. Res·qi′wkwiᵋ, teqeme′ñgiᵋ, iu′nin, "Gɪ′nmɪl Miti′nä gêna′n-mɪlên úm, gêna′paʟên." Ne′me ɪrga′tɪk ewkwe′tyiᵋ, ne′me 10 Miti′nä pê′nrɪnên. Le′ut rɪka′wraunên. "I′gɪt tɪ′nmɪn." Ku′rkɪl ge·eʟin, ne′me čɪkeye′wkwiᵋ, ne′me teqeme′gnin.

  ᴇn·qa′m ᴇ′nni-ñe′ut ra′gtiêᵋ. "Miti′nä quli′nikek rênan-qo′npŭñaw." Ku′rkɪl ye′ttiᵋ, e′un ui′ñä. Añqa′gtɪ ge′lqäʟin, vañêi′pŭñoêᵋ, "Qɪye′tyiᵋ, ᴇ′nni-ñe′w-i-gɪr!" — "Qarê′m 15 mɪye′tɪk! Miti′nä-m ne′me rêna′nmɪ." Qo′npŭ eiñe′uk luwau′ñên. Erre′č.

Koryak, Kamenskoye.

Quyqɪnn·aqu′nu vañvoļai′ke, peļhannɪvoļai′ke. Añqai′tɪñ ga′lqaʟin, vaᵋ′yuk ᴇnnɪ′mtɪļaᵋn gayoᵋ′oļen, ganyai′taļen. Ļa′ļña gapewyañvo′ļen, ñanena′ta gawyeñvo′ļenau. Vaᵋ′yuk

---

[1] Aqan·qau′, the Maritime Chukchee man, who made for me the Chukchee translation of this tale, though a native of the Pacific coast, pronounced not Ku′rkɪl, but Ku′rkɪl as do the people on the Kolyma (cf. Bogoras, Chukchee Mythology, *l. c.*, vol. vii, p. 315, footnote 2).

Qūyqɪnn·aqu′nak gama′taḷen.   Miti′ ña′nyen gaqanññɪtčoñ-
vo′ḷen.   Va^ɛyuk Qūyqɪnn·a′qu notai′tɪñ ga′ḷqaɪ̯in.   Miti′nak
gata′ḷaḷen, ga′nmɪḷen, gapa′ɪ̯en, ganu′lin.   Čŭ′mkup qḷa′-
wuḷɪñ gape′ḷaḷen.   Va^ɛyuk Qūyqɪnn·a′qu gaa′ɪ̯in.   "ɛ′nni-
ña′wgut, qanto′ge!"   Yɪno′ñqo ganto′ḷen, wotta′ken apa′-
tassa^ɛn.   Gaya′ḷqɪwlin, gaqamɪ′tvaḷen, e′wañ, "Wo′tto
Miti′nak ena′nme, enapa′te."   Gŭ′mḷañ miti′w ga′ḷqaɪ̯in,
gŭ′mḷañ Miti′nak gape′nyɪḷen.   Gaḷa′wtɪntɪlin.   "Wo^ɛtvañ
tɪ′nmɪn."   Qūyqɪnn·a′qu gaa′ɪ̯in, gŭ′mḷañ gačhičaña′wlin,
gŭ′mḷañ gaqamɪ′tvaḷen.

Va^ɛyuk ɛ′nni-ña′wgut gayai′tɪḷen.   "Miti′nak va^ɛyuk
yenanqonpŭña′wɪ."   Qūyqɪnn·a′qu gaa′ɪ̯in, a′wun ui′ña.
Añqai′tɪñ ga′ḷqaɪ̯in, gañvo′ḷen aiña′wɪk, "Qɪya′the, ɛ′nni-
ñawgo′t!" — "Qayo′m mɪḷa′k!   Miti′nak gŭ′mḷañ yêna′nmɪ."
Qo′npŭ aiña′wɪk gapka′wḷen.   Aččo′č.

Koryak, Qare′ñɪn.

Qūyqɪnn·aqu′nu i′tɪḷkɪlɪ, pilhe′tɪḷkɪlɪ.   Inu′ñkɪ ge′ḷqaɪ̯in,
ora′wŭcak ɛnnɪ′mtɪḷa^ɛn gayo^ɛ′olen, ganrai′taḷen.   Le′ḷñä
gapi′wteḷkɪḷ(in), ɛnnina′ta gewye′ḷkɪḷɪ.   Ora′wŭcak Qūyqɪn-
n·aqu′nak gaña′wtɪnlin.   Miti′ ɛnni′n gakinca′tɪḷkɪḷi(n).
Ora′wŭcak Qūyqɪnn·a′qu no′tañ ge′ḷqaɪ̯i(n).   Miti′nak
ga′tkŭpḷiḷen, ga′nmɪḷen, gekukei′vulin, genu′lin.   Čŭ′mkup
oia′kocik gegnu′lin.   O′raw Qūyqɪnn·a′qu geye′ɪ̯in.   "ɛ′nni-
ñe′wut, qanto′ge!"   Ti′nuk ge′tkurḷi ganto′len, yanu′tken
gakukei′vulin.   Gere′ḷkɪlin, to′ḷkaḷ gantova′ɪ̯en, gi′wlin,
"Ya′nut Miti′nak ena′nme, inekukei′vi."   I′nnɪk mete′w
ge′ḷqaɪ̯i, i′nnɪk Miti′nak gape′ntɪḷen.   Geḷe′wtɪntɪlin.   "E′chi-
van tɪ′nmɪn."   Qūyqɪnn·a′qu geye′ɪ̯i, i′nnɪk gachicaña′wḷi,
i′nnɪk gaqamɪ′tvaḷi.

Ora′wŭcak ɛ′nnɪ-ñe′wut garai′tɪḷkaḷi.   "Miti′nak ora′wŭcak
tenanqo′npŭñaw."   Qūyqɪnn·a′qu geye′ɪ̯i, e′wun i′tka.   Inu′ñkɪ
ge′ḷqaɪ̯i, gañvo′ḷi qoqḷaḷha′tɪk, "Qɪye′thi, ɛ′nnɪ-ñe′wut!" —

"Igu′t mɪ̆le′k! Miti′nak i′nnɪk tena′nmŭñe." Qo′npŭ qo′qḷak gapka′wlɪ. Tenma′wɪḷen.

Koryak, Lesna.

Qutkɪnn·axu′nu i′tɪḷkɪlin, peḷhaḷa′tkɪ. A′ñqañ ge′lqaʟin, ora′wač ɛnnɪ′mtɪḷan gayoᵋ′oḷen, ganrai′taḷen. Ḷe′ḷña gepi′-
5 vivelin, ɛnñi′nat gewye′ḷkɪlɪn. Ora′wač Qutkɪnn·axu′nak gaña′wtɪnlin. Miti′ ɛnñi′n gači′ntawḷen. Ora′wač Qutkɪn-n·a′xu no′tañ ge′lqaʟin. Miti′nak ga′tkɪpḷiḷen, ga′nmɪḷen, gekukei′vɪlin, genu′lin. Čɪ′mkup uia′qucita gape′ḷaḷen. Ora′wač Qutkɪnn·a′xu geye′ʟin. "e′nnɪ-ñe′wut, qanto′ge !"
10 Tĭ′nuk ge′tkurḷɪ ganto′ḷen, yanu′tken gekukei′vɪlin. Gere′ḷ-kɪlin, gaqamɪ′tvaḷen, gi′vlin, "Ya′nut Miti′nak ena′nme, inekukei′vi." Ḷɪgɪ′mmen miti′w ge′lqaʟin, ḷɪgɪ′mmen Miti′-nak gape′ntɪḷen. Gele′wtɪntɪlin. "E′čhi-van tɪ′nmɪn." Qutkɪnn·a′xu geye′ʟin, ḷɪgɪ′mmen gečhɪ̆ceñe′wlin, ḷɪgɪ′mmen
15 gaqamɪ′tvaḷen.

Ora′wač ɛ′nnɪ-ñe′wut garai′tɪḷen. "Miti′nak ora′wač tenanqo′npŭnaw." Qutkɪnn·a′xu geye′ʟin, e′wun e′ʟe. A′ñqañ ge′lqaʟin, gañvo′ḷen aiñe′wɪtkuk, "Qɪye′thi, ɛ′nnɪ-ñe′wut !" — "Qate′nmɪ mɪ̆ḷe′kkɪ ! Miti′nak ḷɪgɪ′mmen
20 tena′nmɪ." Qo′npŭ aiñe′wɪtkuk gapka′vḷen. Tenma′vɪḷaᵋn.

Kamchadal.[2]

K!u′txeᵋn k!č!amjanḷ′aᵋn kcu′nl‘kajukñɪn, kpilhe′tkajukñɪn.
Ku′txen qč!a′mjanḷ‘an   junčči̯ᵋn,   pi′ḷheskɪs.
<small>Raven-Big's   people   are living,   they are hungry.</small>
Këx·a′nke ki′lkajukñɪn,   x·ū́   ŭ′nč!in k!č!a′mjanl‘ kɪ̆čki′kñɪn,
Kex·a′nke   pi′kikñɪn,   x·u′xan ni′nčin qč!a′mjanl‘ kɪ̆čki′kñɪn
<small>To the sea   he went,   then   Fish-Person   he found</small>
kɪntxɪḷa′kñɪn a′tɪnoke.   Ñe′ḷ‘ñaḷ ki′pctuin, nu′whel knu′-
kɪntxɪḷa′kñɪn a′tnok.   Ñe′nñaḷ ki′pctuin, i′nuwhel knu′-
<small>he brought her home.   With roe   she threw it out, with that   they</small>

---

2 The first line of text is Kamchadal of coast; the second line, that of Sedanka.

7—PUBL. AMER. ETHN. SOC. VOL. V.

kajukñın.　　X·ū　K!utx kña′lxkıñın (nu′whenk.)
kä̆jukñın.　L'i′l'i-ha′nxañ· Kutx kña′lxkıñan (i′nuwhenkı.)
were feeding.　Then　Raven-Big　he married her　(on her.)

Miti′ nu′whenk kxĕkanl'ka′jukñın.　Te′naq K!utx sö′nke
Miti′ i′nuwhenkı kxĕkanl'kä′jukñın.　Te′naq Kutx zö′nke
Miti′　with her　grew jealous.　Then　Raven-Big to the
　　　　　　　　　　　　　　　　　　　　　　　　　　(open) country

ki′lkıñın.　Miti′ nuᵉ ñimcx ku′jiḷın, kl'a′m'an, kı̆kuke′jın,
pi′kikñın.　Miti′ enu′ himcx ku′jiḷın, kl'a′man kı̆koka′jon,
went.　By Miti′ this　woman she struck her, she killed her, she cooked her

kıtxaᵋ′'ḷın.　Kå̊′coñ qınja′nanke kı′nftıliᵋn.　Te′naq K!u′tx
kıtxaᵋ′l'ın.　K'a′con qınja′nanke ka′nıjın.　Te′naq Kutx
she ate her.　Some　to (her) husband　she left.　Then Raved-Big.

5　kk!ö′l'kıñın.　"Ü′nč!in ñimcx, kı̆qu′mctıxıč!"　Ku′tık ¹
q!ö′l'kıñın.　"Ni′nč!in himcx, kı̆qu′mctıxč!"　Ku′texil
came.　"Fish-Woman,　come out!"　From the
　　　　　　　　　　　　　　　　　　　　　　　　rear storeroom

kı̆qu′mctıkñın, qla′′nan kı′nclin.　Kı̆če′kñın, no′num kı′n-
qu′mctıkñın, qla′′nan kı′nclin.　Kı̆č!e′kñın, no′num kın-
she came out,　that one　cooked one.　She entered,　she brought
　　　　　　　　　　　　　　　　　　　　　　　　recently

č!ıhiin, kl'o′an, "Qlank Miti′nk l'a′mhŭmnen, kokajo′-
txıḷa′kñın, klo′an, "Qlank Miti′nk l'a′mhŭmnen, kokajo′-
the food,　she said, "Not long ago by Miti′　she killed me,　she

hŭmnen."　Te′naq ku′ḷan kl'xå̊′lenk ki′lkıñın, te′naq Miti′
hŭmnen."　Te′naq ku′ḷan kl'xa′lenk pi′kikñın, o′net ¹ Miti′
cooked me."　Again　to-morrow　he went,　again by Miti′

ᴇna′nke kpe′nckıñın.　Ktxın　kli′pil'in.　"Ne′nı ven
ᴇna′nke gape′nclin.¹　K!o′mtkaḷ ganka′vravḷen.¹　"Ne′nı ven
she　attacked her.　Her (neck) [head]　she wrung.　"This　time

10　tl'a′mhın."　K!utx kk!ö′l'kıñın, te′naq kuña′′nokñan, te′naq
tl'a′mhın."　Kutx q!ö′l'kıñın, te′naq ke′cx·likñın, te′naq
I killed her."　Raven-Big　came,　again　she recovered her　again
　　　　　　　　　　　　　　　　　　　　　　　　senses,

no′num ki′nč!ıhiin.
no′num kıntxıḷa′kñın.
she brought the food.

---

¹ All these words and forms are borrowed from the neighboring Koryak (eastern branch).

Nuᵉn ü′nč!in ñimcx a′tɪnoke ki′lkɪñɪn.   "Miti′nk lhi
inu′   ni′nč!in himcx a′tnok pi′kikñin.   "Miti′nk l‘i′l‘i
Then   Fish-Woman   went   home.   "By Miti′   after a
                                                          while

l‘ɪ′mha′lhŭmnen."   K!utx kk!ö′l‘kɪñɪn, e′wun kɪme′čkɪñɪn.
l‘ɪmha′lhŭmnen."   Kutx q!ö′l‘kɪñɪn, e′wun ktsxa′l̥kɪñɪn.
she will kill me."   Raven-Big   came,   and   (there is) nothing.

Këx·a′nke ki′lkajukñɪn, kĭke′lkajukñɪn, "K!ö′lxč, ü′nč!in
Kex·a′nk pi′kikñɪn,   keḷka′jukñɪn,   "Q!ö′lxč, ni′nč!in
To the sea   he went,   he began to call,   "Come (here),   Fish-

ñimcx." — "X·ënč mk!ö′l‘kɪčɪn! Miti′nk te′naq l‘ɪmha′l-
himcx." — "Hënčɪ mq!ö′l‘k!   Miti′nk te′naq l‘ɪmha′l-
Woman!" — "I will not   come!   By Miti′   again   she will

5 hŭmnen." Hälč! o′č!kɪ ku′tuin.   Tp!ɪ′nlxun.
  hŭm."   Halč! o′č!alel ku′tuin. Tpɪ′nlxun.
  kill me."   Altogether to call her he could not.   That is all.

24. Kĭlu′ and Monster-Man.

(In Three Dialects.)

Yini′a-ña′wgut and her sister went out for a walk.
Yini′a-ña′wgut looked ahead and espied something. "What
is there? Look at it!" Kĭlu′ looked, and it fell down.
"Just now you said, 'What is coming there?'" And it
fell down again."

They came home and made a fire. Then there was
a clattering at the entrance, Monster-Being came there.
He sat down on Kĭlu′'s side. Oh, she pushed her cousin
toward him. "You saw him first! Then be at his side!"
As soon as her cousin went to sleep (with him), Kĭlu′
ran away out of the house. Even all her clothes were
torn to shreds. They caught on the trees, and she pulled
at them with violence. So, when she came to the river,
she had on no clothes at all. The trees were catching
even at her eyes. She pulled with violence, and even
bled from the nostrils.

Then she came to the village, and the people laughed at her. "What has happened to you?" — "Indeed a kamak came and devoured my cousin. It was she who saw him first." — "Let us go and look at her!" They set off and moved on. They came and saw those two walking together. (The new-comer was) a very good young man. They said to Kīlu', "If you had not run away, he would have married you."

Then Kīlu' began to boast, "The suitor came first to me!" though it was not true at all. She envied Yini'a-ña'wgut because of her husband. He entered, (and proved to be) a very good young man, and Kīlu' envied her sister to a great extent. Her cousin was married, (and not she). Oh, that is all.

Koryak, Kamenskoye.

Enñä⁵'an wu'ssɪnau Yini'a-ña'wgutinti notantaga'e. Ña'nyen ḷeḷa'pɪtčoñvoi Yini'a-ña'wgut va⁵'yuk yo⁵'onen. "Ña'no yɪ'nna ᴇ'nki qɪgitaykɪni'gɪn!" Gŭ'mḷañ ña'nyen Kīlu' ḷeḷa'pekɪn, inña'tikɪn. "A'či ni'w-i-gi, 'Ña'no yɪ'nna 5 ya'tɪykɪn?' Me, gŭ'mḷañ inña'ti."

Yaite'tɪ qatha'ai, oyeḷannivo'ai, va⁵'ak tɪ'ʟɪ-wus·his·he'tɪ. Am ᴇnñä⁵'an Ye'ñtɪñ-I'taḷa⁵n ya'ti. Inya'wut Kīlu'nɪkqaḷ va'gaḷe. Ña'nyen Kīlu'nak ña-w-yiḷa'ḷñɪ-tu'mgɪn ñanɪkañ- qaḷai'tɪñ upɪna⁵'ḷɪ'nin. "Gɪ'ssa nɪḷa'pɪtčui-gi. Čei'mɪk qat- 10 vaykɪne'-ge." Ki'čič ña-w-yiḷa'ḷñɪ-tu'mgɪn yɪḷqa'tɪ, a'wwi ñatñɪnoi'tɪñ maḷ-gɪnta'wi. Va⁵'yuk kimi'tau neka'ñvoḷai qo'ñvoḷai, u'ttɪk gɪvaḷai'ke, kɪtɪnve'tɪtkɪnen. Va'amɪ tɪḷai', ui'ña yɪ'nna. Gaṟa'ma u'ttɪk gɪvaḷai'ke, kɪtɪnve'tɪtkɪnen. Moṟata'ñvoḷai a'wun e'ñveḷma.

15 Va⁵'yuk tɪḷai', ata's·hu natčɪga⁵'an "Quyaxḷa'ntɪk?" — "I'pa a'nam ña'nyen kama'kata nanu'va⁵an. ᴇna'n ḷeḷa'- pɪtčuḷa⁵n." — "Ña'añ mɪnyo⁵'oḷan." Ga'ḷqaṟɪnau, tawa'ñḷai

gaḷañvo'ḷenau, ñêyas·hei'tɪ tɪḷai'vikɪ, o'nmɪ-maḷ-oya'ček. Kɪ́lu' newñɪvo'an, "Ai'geve agɪnta'wka, gɪ'ssa hanaᵉ-mata'-gê."

Ña'nyen Kɪ́lu' maḷ-taitɪñɪča'nñɪvoi. "Ya'not," e'wañ, Gŭ'mkɪñ gaya'ɩ.in ñawɪndu'ḷaᵉn." I'nmɪq ña'no ui'ña. Yini'a-ña'wgut ñane'ninak aki'nu ga'ḷñɪlin. Gaya'ḷqɪwlin o'nmɪ-maḷ-oya'ček. Toq, ña'nyen Kɪ́lu' maḷ-akena'nñɪvoi. Ñaw-yiḷa'ḷñɪ-tu'mgɪn nama'tan. Toq, o'pta.

Koryak, Paren.

Enñaᵉ'a wusa'nau Yini'a-ñe'wgutinti notantaga'as. Ñe'nin ḷeḷa'pɪtkonñoi. Yini'a-ñe'wgut vaᵉ'yuk yoᵉ'onen. "Ñe'no yɪ'nna ᴇ'nki qɪgitetkɪni'gɪn!" Gŭ'mḷɪñ ñe'nin Kɪ́lu' liḷe'pɪt-kɪn, inñe'etɪtkɪn. "Yɪ'shi ni'w-i-gɪs, 'Ne'no yɪ'nna ya'tɪtkɪn?' Ve, gŭ'mḷɪñ inñe'ti."

Yaite'tɪ qatha'as, oyeḷanñɪño'vas, vaᵉ'yuk tɪluus·hɪs·he'tɪ. Am enñai' Če'ntɪñ-I'taḷan ye'ti. Ečča'x-amei' Kɪ́lu'nanqaḷ vaga'ḷe. Ñe'nin Kɪ́lu'nak ñew-yiḷa'ḷñɪ-tu'mgɪn ñanikañqa-ḷai'tɪñ upɪnaᵉḷɪ'nin. "Gɪ́tča nɪḷe'pɪtkui-gɪs. Qa'ča qatva't-kɪnen." Ki'tkis ñew-gi'ḷaᵉ yɪlqe'tɪ, e'wčem ñas·hɪnoi'tɪñ mel-gɪnte'wi. Vaᵉ'yuk kimi'teu nika'nñuḷas qo'nñoḷas, u'ttɪk gɪvaḷa'tkɪs, kɪtɪnve'tɪtkɪnen. Vaia'mɪ tɪḷei', ui'ña yɪ'nna. Gaɩ.a'ma u'ttik gɪvaḷa'tkɪs, kɪtɪnve'tɪtkɪnen. Mo'ḷita'nñoḷas e'wun ge'ñveḷma.

Vaᵉ'yuk tɪḷei', te'nñu netčɪgaᵉ'an. Čaxḷatkɪne'tɪk?" — "I'pa a'nam ñe'nin kama'kata nenu'waᵉn. ᴇna'n liḷe'pɪt-kuḷaᵉn." Ñe'čɪ mɪnyoᵉ'oḷa." Ge'ḷqaɩ.inau, tawa'ñḷas gaḷan-ño'ḷenau, ñečɪshei'tɪ tɪḷei'vɪtkɪs, o'nmɪ-mal-oya'ček. Kɪ́lu' newñɪño'gan, "Ai'geve egɪnte'wka, gɪ'tča nanaᵉmata'-gɪs."

Ñe'nin Kɪ́lu' maḷ-taitɪñisa'nñɪvoi. "Yat," e'wañ, "Gŭ'mkɪñ geye'ɩ.in ñewɪnn'u'ḷaᵉn." I'nmɪx ñe'no e'ɩ.e. Yini'a-ñe'wgut ñeni'ninak aqi'nu ge'ḷñɪlin. Geye'ḷqɪwlin o'nmɪ-mal-oya'ček To, ñe'nin Kɪ́lu' maḷ-aqine'nñɪvoi. New-gi'ḷaᵉn nama'tan. To, o'pta.

Koryak, Qare′ñɪn.

Enn·a^ɛ′an wuti′nau Yiñe′a-ñe′wgutɪnti ganotanta′ɭkɪɭat. Ña′nɪ lile′piɭki. Yiñe′a-ñe′wgut o′raw yo^ɛ′onen. "Ña′nɪ tɪ′nnaq, ña′nɪ qɪgite′tkɪnɪ!" I′nnɪk ña′nɪ Kĭlu′ lile′pɪtkɪn, iñǹe′tkɪn. "Eshi i′vɪtkɪn, 'Na′nɪ tɪ′nna ye′tkɪn?' Mei, 5 i′nnɪk iñǹe′ti."

Rai′tɪɭkɪɭat ye′tɪɭkɪɭat, uyiɭa′tɪɭkɪɭat, o′raw tɪ′ʟɪ-wurgɪrge′tɪ. E′n·kɪ Te′ntɪñ-I′tɪɭän ye′ti. Amei′, Kĭlu′nañqaɭ vaga′ɭe. Ña′nɪ Kĭlu′nak ñaw-yiɭa′ɭñɪ-tu′mgɪn ña′nenqač upɪn·aɭɪ′nin. "Gɪt nɪɭe′pɪtkui-gɪt. Nura′′a qi′tkɪnin." Ki′tkit ñaw-yiɭa′ɭñɪ- 10 tu′mgɪn yɪ′ɭqäɭkɪ, eut ga′rgɪnok mel-gɪnte′wi. O′raw kimi′teu neka′lkɪɭat qu′ɭkɪɭat, u′ttɪk gɪva′tkuk kɪtɪnve′tɪt- kɪnen. Vaia′mɪ tɪɭei′, e′ɭe tɪ′nna. Gaɭa′ma u′ttik gɪva′t- kuk kɪtɪnve′tɪtkɪnen. Muʟi′tɪɭkɪɭat gagi′n·kiɭama.

O′raw tɪɭei′, kri′ru ne′ssɪn. "Taxɭatkɪne′tkɪ?" — "I′pa 15 tɪ′nna ña′nɪ kama′kat ne′nun. Ena′n lile′pĭlin." — "Na′ttañ mɪnyo^ɛ′oɭa." Geɭqaɭe′ñi, ta′vɭat geɭeɭkiɭe′ñi, ñiterge′ta tɪɭai′vɪɭkɪɭat, nime′lqin ora′cek. Kĭlu′ ni′vɪɭkɪn, "Ai′geves eginte′wka, gɪt nana^ɛmata′-gɪt.

Na′nɪ Kĭlu′ mal-taqli′nñɪɭkɪ. "Ya′nut," e′wun, "Gū′m- 20 mŭkɪñ geye′ʟɪ ñewɪnyu′la^ɛn. Em ña′ni i′tka. Yiñe′a- ñe′wgut ñane′ninak aqi′nu ge′ɭñilin. Gere′ɭqɪwlin nɪmɪ′sax- ora′cek Toq, ña′nɪ Kĭlu′ mal-aqine′tɪɭkɪ. Naw-yiɭa′ɭñi-tu′mgɪn nama′tan. To, tenma′vɪɭen.

APPENDIX I.

Songs.[1]

1.

It seems that I am going to sing of Qutx and his family. I have a wife Aḷñatvaʹgaḷ I will sing of the people of Yeʹḷmeḷ.

2.

I shall recover my senses, I shall have rest. Simply with fly-agaric (I have stunned myself). I shall recover my senses, then I will simply run to my sweetheart. I will sing of my bad children.

1.

Qayiñuʹn ñaʹno eʹwañ.   Qoʹtxɪñinu mɪnaiʹñawnau.   Gŭʹmma
It seems   there   he says.   Qutx and his   I will call of them.   I
                             family

gaḷñatvagaḷñaʹwlen.   Gŭʹmma Yeḷmeʹḷinu mɪnaiʹñawnau.
with a wife Aḷñatvaʹgaḷ   I   the people of   I will call of them.
(Strongly-Sitting-One).   Yeʹḷmeḷ

2.

Mɪčhɪčañaʹurkɪn,   tɪmtɪneʹurkɪn,   aʹttau wapaʹqata.   Mɪčhɪča-
I shall recover my   I shall have rest,   simply   with fly-agaric.   I shall
   senses,

ñaʹurkɪn   am-vɪʹnʹva-ñawêʹtɪ.   Gumniʹn aʹččɪñ kɪ̃iʹñɪt
recover my   mere   to the secret wife.   My   bad   children
senses

mɪnaiʹñawnau.
I will call of them.

---

[1] These two songs were written down from the phonographic records of Mr. Jochelson (No. 2 and No. 7 on his list). The first is in Koryak of Kamenskoye; the second is Chukchee in grammar and phonetics, and Koryak in vocabulary. It was obtained from an old Reindeer Chukchee of Parapolski Dol, who had lived for a long time among the Reindeer Koryak.

APPENDIX II.

CONSTELLATIONS.

NOTE. — In the lists given below, the numbers in parentheses indicate different dialects, as follows:

(1) Chukchee.
(2) Koryak of Paren, according to Jochelson.[1]
(3) Koryak of Kamenskoye.

(4) Koryak of Qare'ñın.
(5) Koryak of Lesna.
(6) Kamchadal of the coast.

POLAR STAR.

  (1) Ilu'k-e'ñer (= motionless star).
    Aᵉlqe'p-e'ñer (= nail-star).
  (2) Ačka'p-aña'y (= nail-star).
  (3) Alqa'p-a'ñay (= nail-star).
  (4) ᴇlke'p-e'ñer (= nail-star).
  (5) ᴇḷka'p-e'ñer (= nail-star).

URSA MAJOR.

  (1) wıyotkıña'ulıt (= sling-throwers).
  (2) elwe'-kyeñ (= wild reindeer-buck).
    elwe'-eñe'y (= wild-reindeer star).
  (3) ıḷva'-kyıñ (= wild reindeer-buck).
    ıḷva'-a'ñay (= wild-reindeer star).
  (4) ıḷva'-kı'rıñ (= wild reindeer-buck).
  (5) mai'ñı-kı'rıñ (= large reindeer-buck).
  (6) kı'rıñ (= reindeer-buck).

---

[1] Judging by the transcription, the names of constellations given by Jochelson are of Paren origin. They all have *e* instead of the *a* of Kamenskoye. *Ačka'p-añai'*, however, is either a Kamenskoye form, or, in Paren dialect, a second form of the stem used in oblique cases (cf. p. 4). I have also corrected some evident errors (cf. Jochelson, The Koryak, *l. c.*, vol. vi, p. 123); namely, *eñe'y* instead of *eñen*, *Ǝnan'venañ* instead of *Ǝna'nvenanāña*, *Yekeñeḷa'tılın* (or also *Yekeñeḷaᵋn*) instead of *Yeke'ñeḷaqlın*, *Ulve'-iy-i'mtiḷaᵋn* instead of *Ulveiyinitilaᵋn*.

[104]

PLEIADES.

    (1) ñaus·qajo′mkɪn (= group of women [2]).

    (2) ke′tmet (= little sieve).

    (3) ka′tmač (= sieve).

    (4) ke′rmes (= (sieve).

       ɪḷva′u (= wild reindeer [pl.]).

    (5) ke′rmes· (= sieve).

    (6) nö′jicx (= string).

CASSIOPEIA.

    (1) ɪlve′t (= wild reindeer [pl.]).

    (3) ñawɪs·qatɪ′mkɪn [1] (= group of women [2]).

    (5) qai-kɪ′rɪñ (= small reindeer-buck).

    (6) x·ai′hene (= wolf).

ORION.

    (1) rulte′nnin (= crooked one).

    (3) yu′ḷt-a′ñay (= crooked star).

    (4) ruḷte′yet (= crooked one).

       woḷva′kɪ-r-i′mtiḷaᵋn (= crosswise-bow carrier).

    (5) ruḷte′yɪlɪn (= crooked one).

BELT OF ORION.

    (2) ena′nvenañ [3] (= handle of scraper).

       ulve′-iy-i′mtiḷaᵋn (= crosswise-bow carier).

    (3) vu′ḷvɪ-iy-i′mtɪḷaᵋn (= crosswise-bow carrier)

    (6) kantc (= long scraper).

---

[2] "Group of women" is the name of the Pleiades among the Chukchee, and of Cassiopeia among the Koryak of Kamenskoye. One of these women is called by the Koryak of Kamenskoye Yini′a-ña′wgut, and another Kĭlu′.

[3] Among the Chukchee, the Belt of Orion is considered the crooked back of the archer Rulte′nnin. It became crooked because his wife struck at it with her tailoring-board, or, according to another version, with the wooden handle of her scraper. Among the Reindeer Koryak, the Belt of Orion is called Kĭlu′-ena′nvenañ ("Kĭlu′'s handle of scraper"). The Koryak archer, who carries his bow crosswise, is evidently identical with the Chukchee archer with the crooked back.

Milky Way.

    (1) čigei′-ve′em (pebbly river).

    (2) yaᵋ′-ve′yem (= clay river).

    (3) čẹgai′-va′am (= pebbly river).

        yaᵋ-va′am (= clay river).

    (5) a′r′u-vei′em (= muddy river).

    (6) kīx· (= river).

Corona Borealis.

    (1) omqa′-ya′gɪlhɪn (= polar bear's paw).

    (3) kawa′t-oi′pɪn (= fish-heads stuck in).

    (4) Kĭlu′-pḷa′kɪḷn̂ɪn (Kĭlu′'s boot).

Aldebaran.

    (1) čê′ʟo-maᵋ′qɪn (= copper arrow-head).

    (3) čɪčɪ′ḷo-xmä′-ḷa′wut (= copper arrow-head).

Altair and Tarared.

    (1) pegɪ′ttɪn.

    (3) pagɪ′ttɪn.[1]

Capella.

    (1) čŭ′mn̂ɪ (= reindeer-buck).

    (2) yekeñeḷa′tɪlɪn (= driving with reindeer).

    (3) g̣aka′n̂ɪḷaᵋn (= one driving with reindeer).

    (5) g̣eke′n̂ɪlɪn (= one driving with reindeer).

Wagoner.

    (1) čŭmña′-nlete′tɪlɪn [2] (= reindeer-buck carrier).

---

[1] According to Mr. Jochelson, Pege′ten ("suspended breath") is the name of the Morning Star. I was unable to ascertain the derivation of this word.

    Some stars in the constellation Wagoner are also called g̣eke′n̂ɪlɪt "reindeer-drivers"); cf. Bogoras, The Chukchee, l. c., vol. vii, p. 308.

VOCABULARY.

A circle under a letter indicates that the stem is strong (see p. 4).

Ch. Chukchee.	P Paren.	A Active (transitive).
K Kamenskoye.	Pal. Pallan.	M Medial (intransitive).
Les. Lesna	Qar. Qarenin.	

KORYAK–ENGLISH.

Stems.

ıṃ (used only in compounds), all
i′mın-, i′mıñ-, i′mı- (Ch. ım-, ımılo′),
all 76.15

ınp, old
ınpı- (Ch. ınpı-), old
nınpıqin, he is old 47.1

ıñ, glue
ı′ña (Ch. ı′ñıñ), glue
iña′tekın (Ch. iña′arkın), to glue 88.9

ıla, proper name (male) 52.3

ılalu′ (term of endearment), the youngest
one 32.8

ılñıtat, sinew thread
ılñıta′tikın M, to prepare sinew thread
82.18

ılla′! (used only among females), O girl!
O woman! 48.7 (cf. Ch. ña′ul! O
woman!)

ıḷv-. See eḷv

ıḷ, ęl, mother
ıḷaᵋ′, ęlaᵋ (Ch. ęla′), mother 33.3

ıḷa′nyọ, youngest
ıḷa′ñi (Ch. ęle′ñi), the youngest brother
or sister 23.7

eᴄh, they (cf. aᴄh)
ę′ᴄᴄi (Ch. ę′rri), they (absolute form
subject intransitive) 12.1 (cf. a′ᴄᴄi)

ᴇn, he
ᴇ′nnu, a′nnu, he, that one 19.1
ᴇ′nık (Ch. ᴇnı′k), possessive
ᴇna′n (Ch. ᴇna′n), subjective form
20.8
ᴇni′n, ani′n (Ch. ᴇni′n), his

ᴇnin-, that one
ᴇni′n, ᴇna′n (Ch. ᴇ′nqan), that one
17 6
ᴇ′nkı (Ch. ᴇ′n·kı), there 12.6
ᴇnke′ (with accent of exclamation on
the last vowel) 13.7
ᴇ′ñkı 13.5
ᴇ′nkıta Pal., likewise 90.4
ᴇñaᵋ′an (Ch. ᴇn·ñi′n), thus 13.1
ᴇñi′n·aᴄ̌, this much, to such degree

ᴇnkaya
ᴇnkaya′ykın M, to snore 28.4

ᴇnn, fish
ᴇnnā′n (Ch. ᴇnnē′n), fish
ᴇnnı′mtılaᵋn, Fish-Man 88.1
ᴇ′nni-ña′wgut, Fish-Woman 96.4

ᴇnnan K, ᴇnnen· P, one
ᴇnna′n K, ᴇnne′n· P (Ch. ᴇnne′n·), one
ᴇnna′niku, in the same place 80.7

ęḷ, father
ᴇḷi′n (Ch. ᴇḷi′gın), father 54.6

ęḷ. See ıḷ

[107]

aate,　kick

aa'tetkın Pal. (A),　to kick 90.6

ayıw,　blame

ayı'wikın M, to use bad language

yayıwa'wikın A,　to blame somebody 74.19

ayıčña,　lying on side

a'yıčña (Ch. a'rıčhʌ),　lying on side 31.8

ayıcñatva'ykın (Ch. arıčhatva'rkın), to lie upon side

ayat,　fall

aya'tikın M (Ch. ere'erkın),　to fall down

yaya'tikın M (Ch. rere'erkın),　to make something fall down 56.8

ayiyai

ayi'yai,　upright blocks of ice on the frozen sea 64.25

ayi'kvan,　nevertheless, at least 18.1

ayu,　revive

ayu'ykın M (Ch. eiu'rkın),　to revive

yayu'ykın A (Ch. reiu'rkın),　to revive somebody 61.7

aia,　storehouse

ai'an,　storehouse 36.8

aia'ñač,　since, as long as 70.4

aiv,　alms

aiva'ai (Ch. ei'veei),　present, alms (in victuals)

aivilai'kın A (Ch. eive'erkın),　to give some meat to neighbors as a present or alms 63.11

aim,　water

ai'mekın (Ch. ai'mırkın),　to fetch water 17.7

ai'mınañ (Ch. ai'mır),　watering-place, ice-hole

aimak,　cover

aima'kikın A,　to wrap up, to cover all around 84.9

aig,　odor

aiga'ai (Ch. eige'ei),　odor coming with the wind 63.6

aige'tı tıͅe'ykın (Ch. aigê'tı tıle'rkın), he moves on, crossing the wind

Ai' gıͅı,　With-Odor-Averter 63.7

Ai'gınvın, With-Odor-Pusher-Away, 63.6

ai'gewe (Ch. ai'vᴇ),　yesterday 78.26

ai'kıp,　fly-eggs 45.2

aiñaw,　call

aiña'wikın M, A (Ch. eiñe'urkın),　to call 33.6; 47.3

ai'ñun,　long ago 61.1

awa-nñi

a'wa-,　in a good manner

awanñi'ykın M,　to sew well

awa'nñi-ñaw,　seamstress 25.2; 61.13

awyi

awyi'ykın M,　to eat 12.5; 20.7

yawya'tıykın (y-awya'tıykın) A,　to feed, to make eat 72.8

a'wun (Ch. e'un),　but 96.12

awwa',　well, all right 30.5

a'wwi K, e'wčem P,　immediately, just then 100.10

awnu'p,　quite, very 64.11

a'wyͅek, a'wyik,

a'wyek (Ch. ê'êkêlhın, i'ik),　root of *Polygonum viviparum* 31.5

awi'wut.　See avi'ut

awulpel,　fish-tail

a'wulpel-pel,　diminutive 70.15

ap

a'pikın M (Ch. ı'pırkın),　to be fastened 19.3

apaͅ

apa'tekın M, A (Ch. üpaa'rkın),　to cook 63.11; 96.3

apa'ña, ipa'ña (Ch. üpa'ñı),　broth, boiled water 28.6

tapa'ñekın (t-apa'-ñ-ekın),　to make soup 42.10

appa,　father, grandfather 24.9

apt

apti'ykın M (Ch. e'ptırkın),　to kick with one's feet, to trample half-scraped skin 72.24

avi′ut, awi′wut, quickly, in haste

ınan awi′wut, most quickly 70.12

am, all

am- (Ch. em-), whole, exclusive, all, mere, only

am-qaiu′iu-na′l̥hın (Ch. em-qaiũ′-ne′l̥-hın), mere fawn-skins 22.10

am-ga′nmač, one to each (of the two) 70.21

-am (Ch. -am), particle 45.2

Amamqut K, Eme′mqut P, proper name 41.6

am

a′mu (Ch. -tgê′me), I do not know

ta ′y a′mu, I do not know, how much 55.3

a′ml̥iñ, do not care, do not mind 64.13

a′ml̥iñ-van K and P, from this time on 92.10

a′mñuč, every time, all the time 53.1

amei′. See mai

ame′yaq (= a′me-yaq), how is he? 68.2

atau′ (Ch. atau′), vainly, without reason 61.3

atau′-qun (Ch. atau′-qun), well, now; all right 14.8

atas·h

ata′s·hu yıtči′ykın, to make a laughing-stock of 100.15 (cf. Ch. ata′rge ne′-lırkın, to make a noise, to make a racket)

atv, boot

a′tva t (Ch. ä ′ttwet), boot 41.5

atvai, hoof

atva′gil̥ñın, hoof 48.8

a′ttı Pal., then 90.10

atta yol̥

atta ′yol̥, down river, down the coast 39.7 (cf. Ch. a ′tto′ol, in front)

atta m, a m, bone

a′tta m (Ch. a ′ttım), bone

atta mtıva′ykın, to spit out bones 56.8

a m-yat, the backbone of a fish, chiefly dog-salmon, dried with some meat

on it, while the upper layer is cut off for drying apart 74.14

ass, since

a′ssa, as·s·o′ (adv.), since, of the other day 18.5

assa′kin, that the other day, recent 52.6

assa, thigh

assäl̥ñın, thigh 46.9

as·ka′čıkılin, heedless, headlong (evidently a negative form, but the positive is unknown) 70.24

ač, ača, fat

a′čan, a′čın (Ch. e′čın), fat substantive) 15.4

ača′pil, little piece of fat 14.8

gača′lin (Ch. e′čılin), fat one

ača

ača′ykın M (Ch. eče′rkın), to pass water 14.2; 64.25

ačage′ñın, penis (literally, instrument for passing water) 80.20

ača′al K, äčeal P, snow soaked with urine 92.12

ača′l̥u (Ch. eču′nl̥hın), chamber-vessel 76.24

ačačhat, laugh

a′čacha′tekın, to laugh 19.2

a′ččıč (Ch. erre′č), only this, it is the end 23.2

ačh, they

a′čči (Ch. ɛ′rrı), they (absolute form subject intransitive)

a′čhin, their

ačhi (Ch. i′git), now. See yıshı

ačhi′kin, this here now 49.8

ačhiva′n (= a′čhi-van), from this time on 20.5; 54.3

ačhıñ, as·hıñ, seashore 23.2; 64.22

a′nau, all right 32.1

a′naqun (Ch. a′nı vai, a′nı ñan), and so 36.10

anya, praise, cheer

anya′ykın A (Ch. anya′rkın), to praise, to cheer up 84.5

ann, ah 47.2

annɪm, frost

   annima′ykɪn M, to freeze

   Annı′mayat, Frost-Man 38.9

ankaw

   anka′wekɪn M (Ch. ᴇnkäe′rkɪn), to cease, to deny 41.9

   a′nku ʟ̣ıñı′ykin A, to refuse 64.11

anñen, anger

   anñenai′pekɪn (Ch. anñenai′pŭrkɪn), to be angry

   anñičvɪna′wekɪn, to become angry 31.2

anñen, mind

   a′nñen, mind, common sense

   ᴇnı′k anñena′ta, it is her own mind 88.13

an·a

   an·a′, grandmother, also the divining-stone 33.6

   an·a′čoykɪn, to practise divination with the divining-stone 80.20

a′kyeḷ, also 28.6

akin K, aqin P, envy

   aki′nu ʟ̣ıñı′ykin K (A), aqi′nu ḷı′ñɪtkɪn P (A), to envy 101.6, 29

   akina′tikɪn K, aqine′tikɪn P (M), to envy 88.1; 101.7, 30

akuyičva′tikɪn M (probably aq-uyičva′-tikɪn, to make bad play), to do wrong 54.2

akiḷaᵋ′č, just now 54.8

akmit

   akmi′t-ikɪn A (Ch. eimi′irkɪn), to take 14.8

akmitkat

   akmɪtka′tikɪn, akmɪs·qa′tikɪn (Ch. eimis·qäe′rkɪn), to stick 88.8

   akmɪtka-tu′yaykɪn, to detach (literally, sticking-take off)

   y-akmɪtka-tu′ya-w-ñ-ikɪn, to want to detach 86.13

aqɪt-aiña

   aqɪtaiña′ykɪn M (probably aqɪt, blame;

aina′ykɪn, to call), to scold 35.1 (see also kitaiña)

aqa, bad

   aᵋ′cciñ (Ch. e′tqi), he is bad 22.6

   aqa′-qla′wuḷ (Ch. aqa′-qla′ul), bad man

   aqä′-liña′tikɪn (Ch. äqä′-liñe′erkɪn), to be afraid (literally, to be of bad heart)

   aᵋ′ččɪñɪčaᵋn, the worst 30.7

aqačñ, dirt

   aqačñuña′wekɪn M, to grow dirty, to soil itself

aqann·

   aqa′nn·u yɪččı′ykɪn A, to hate, to feel hatred for 15.10

aquna′ča. See exune′če

aqɪm, bag 28.5

aqɪnñɪ, love

   aqɪ′nñikɪn M, to make love 72.23

aqiñ, cave 62.6

aᵋal

   aᵋ′aḷ (Ch. aᵋlha′ttᴇ [= aᵋl-ha′ttᴇ]), axe 63.4

aᵋya

   aᵋ′yaykɪn A, to haul 51.7

aᵋpa

   aᵋpa′ḷñɪn, flipper 58.6

aᵋm. See attaᵋm

aᵋtt, dog

   Aᵋ′ttaᵋn (Ch. aᵋ′ttɪn), dog 48.8

   ñaw-aᵋttan (Ch. ñeu′ttɪn), she-dog

   a′ttaᵋlaᵋn (Ch. aᵋ′ttɪlɪn), a man driving with dogs

   attaᵋ′waw, dog's carrion 12.6

   aᵋ′ttai (Ch. aᵋttᴇ′s·qän), fringe of dog-skin; any other fringe

   ɡattai′len K and P, fringed 92.13

   aᵋtta′yan, dog-shed (literally, dog-house) 72.14

aᵋs

   aᵋ′saᵋn, cooked fish

   aᵋso′ykɪn, to eat cooked fish 66.4

aᵋḷ

   aᵋ′laᵋḷ, aḷaᵋ′al (Ch. äᵋ′ʟäᵋ′l), excrement 12.5; 47.4

aᵋḷa′tvekɪn M, to taste of excrement 29.4

aᵋḷakɪ′mkɪm K, eḷekɪ′mkɪn P (Ch. ele′m-kɪn), *omasum* (literally, excrement-net) 92.3

aᵋḷo

aᵋḷona′tekin, aᵋḷoña′tekin M, daylight is coming 31.10 (cf. Ch. aᵋlo′ñêt, the whole daytime)

aᵋlm, snow

aᵋlme′kɪn M, to shovel snow 15.9

aᵋ′ḷmuḷqan, snowdrift 86.3

añɪnmɪḷat

añɪnmɪḷa′tikɪn M, to feel elated 84.17

añạikạ

nañai′qaqen, awful

añai′qa-pɪ′tkekɪn, to thud awfully (against the ground) 84.10 (see (pɪ′tkekɪn)

añañ

a′ñañ (Ch. e′ñeñ), shaman's assisting spirit, God (Christian)

naña′nqin, full of shaman's inspiration 42.9

aña′ñiḷaᵋn (Ch. eñe′ñiḷɪn), shaman

añañya′ykɪn, to practise shamanism 33.7

añe′, halloo! 49.3 (cf. Ch. a′nɪ, there you!)

añqa, sea

a′ñqa, a′ñqan (Ch. a′ñqɪ), sea 13.3; 82.3

añq-o′ttoot (Ch. añq-ɵttoot), floating wood

añqa′ken (Ch. añqa′kên), belonging to the sea 76.17

a′ḷɪmɪñ (Ch. a′ḷɪmɪñ), nay; oh, well! 21.2; 74.1

aḷa, summer

aḷa′aḷ K, eḷe′eḷ P (Ch. e′leel), summer

aḷa′k (Ch. ele′k), in summer-time

aḷa′kin (Ch. ele′kin), adj. summer-

aḷa′ñit (Ch. ele′ñit), summer-time, summer season 31.10

aḷa′ñetɪna (Ch. ala′ñêtɪn), place of summer habitation

aḷaio′ykɪn (Ch. eleru′rkɪn), summer is coming 16.5

aḷa′-nɪmyo′lhɪn, summer habitation 58.4

aḷait

nɪḷai′tɪqin (Ch. nɪle′gtaqin), awkward 46.1

aḷai′tɪñ, awkwardly, not very pleasantly 82.4

aḷp, cheek

aḷpi′ʟɪñin (Ch. elpi′ʟɪñɪn), cheek

aḷpɪ′ttam, cheek-bone 88.10

a′ḷva, another

aḷva′lin (Ch. elve′lin), another one 76.19

a′ḷva (Ch. a′lva), on another place 18.6

aḷña, stingy

na′ḷñaqin, stingy

aḷña′wikɪn, to be stingy 17.1

aḷhaḷ

aḷha′ḷikɪn A, to catch at something 72.20

yɪyiw (*initial*), -nyiw (*medial*), -nn·iw (*medial*)

yɪyi′wikɪn A, nom. past gann·i′wlin, to state, to define 76.16

yɪyɪḷpat, yɪyɪmpat

čɪčɪḷpe′tikɪn, čɪčɪɪmpe′tikɪn P (A), yɪyɪḷ-pa′tikɪn, yɪyɪmpa′tikɪn K, to hide 92.15

yɪp

yɪpe′kɪn A (Ch. yɪpɪ′rkɪn), nom. past gai′pɪḷen (Ch. gai′pɪlên), to put on 18.1; 70.16

yɪp

yɪpi′kɪn A (Ch. yɪpɪ′rkɪn), nom. past gai′pilin (Ch. gei′pilin), to stop up, to bar 14.10

yɪpɪykaḷa (*initial*), -npɪykaḷa (*medial*)

yɪpɪykaḷa′wekɪn A, nom. past ganpɪy-kaḷa′wḷen, to strangle 82.7

yɪpɪtčav

yɪpɪtča′vikɪn M, to gnash (one's teeth) 49.8

ya'waḷañqaḷ, by the rear side 78.7

yawaḷa'tekɪn A (Ch. yaala'arkɪn), to follow 82.1

yawya'tɪykɪn. See awyi

yawo'. See wayo'

yamk, people

ya'mkɪn, yaᵋ'mkɪn (Ch. re'mkɪn), people 39.7

yamkɪčɪ, visit

yamkɪčɪ'ykɪn M (Ch. remkɪčɪ'rkɪn), to visit, to come as guest 72.6

yat

ya'tikɪn A (Ch. re'tɪrkɪn), to bring, to fetch 41.5; 61.1

yaḷa'tikɪn A, increase of action

tya'ḷañɪn K, čičeʟe'ñɪn P, I will bring it 92.10

yatv, -nạtv

ya'tvekɪn A (Ch. ra'tvu'rkɪn), to bring in 34.4

yanya, separately

ya'nya (Ch. ya'nřa), separately, asunder 44.2

ya'nya-qḷa'wuḷ (Ch. ya'nřa-qḷa'uḷ), bachelor (literally, separate man)

yanọt, fore

ya'notɪ (Ch. ya'nθt), at first 20.9

ya'not- (Ch. ya'nθt-), fore-

ya'not-gɪtca'lñɪn (Ch. ya'nθt-gɪtka'lhɪn), foreleg

yano'tekɪn M (Ch. yano'orkɪn), to be in the front 64.17

yaq, what

yɪ'nna (Ch. räᵋ'nut), what

ya'qa (Ch. re'qä), with what

ya'xpil (Ch. rä'nutqäi), small thing, trifle

yaqɪ'ykɪn (Ch. re'qärkɪn), what art thou doing? 18.10

ya'qkin, of what kind 64.14

ya'qkinki (= ya'qkin-ki), of what sort is he there? 26.10

ya'qu-ɛ'nki, what of that 56.7

-yaq (Ch. -raq), now (only with the pers. pron.)

gɪn-yaq, thou now, thy turn 14.4; 47.8

yaq, ya'qam (yaq-am), but still 45.2

-yaq K, -yax P, particle of weakly concessive meaning, like German *doch* 14.4; 92.10

yaqai'-qun (Ch. yaqai'qun), nevertheless 84.11

yaq — yaq. See ya — ya

yaqañ, driving

yaqa'ñ- (Ch. geke'ñ-), driving

yaqa'ñɪlaᵋn (Ch. gekeñɪlɪn), a man driving reindeer

yaqa'n-uya'tik, driving-sledge 22.10

yạqyạq, gull

ya'qyaq (Ch. ya'yaq), gull 84.16

yaqui. See yekui

yagɪt

yagɪ'tikɪn M, to sew 82.17

yaᵋ'yoa, of one's own will 42.5

yali

yali'ykɪn M (Ch. reli'rkɪn), to move on, to slide 42.1

yaḷu, naḷu, cud

yaḷu'ykɪn M (Ch. relu'rkɪn), to chew

yaḷu'yičan (Ch. relu'p), quid 76.1

yaḷu'p (Ch. relu'p), quid

yaḷu'pikɪn A, to take (it) for a quid 16.7

yaḷq

yaḷki'wikɪn M (Ch. res·qi'urkɪn), to enter (mostly the sleeping-house) 13.9

ya'ḷku (Ch. re'lku), in the sleeping-room 41.9

-yya, -ssa

yɪya'ykɪn, yɪsa'ykɪn A (Ch. rɪra'rkɪn); nom. past gayya'ḷen, gassa'ḷen (Ch. garra'lên), to split lengthwise, to follow (some road) in full length 70.22

-yyip. See gɪyip

yiyi

yiyi'ña, white whale 78.6

yiyk, soft

nɪyi'ykaqin (Ch. nii'rkäqin), soft

yiykuḷa'tikɪn M, to feel easy, 26.7

yičami

yiča'myi-tu'mgɪn (Ch. yiče'mit-tu'mgɪn), brother 20.6

Yini'a-ña'wgut, proper name 18.3

yinnaw

yinna'wikɪn M, to live in joy 52.2

yinḷa (= ninḷa)

yinḷa'ykɪn A (Ch. ri'ntɪrkɪn), to throw 14.11; 15.7

yiña

yiña'-ykin M (Ch. riñe'rkin), to fly, to soar 14.9; 15.6

yiḷ, moon

yiᵉ'lhɪn (Ch. yiᵉ'lhɪn), month, moon 59.8

yiḷ. See čɪḷ

yiḷk

yiḷkɪyiḷ, pudding 34.2 (cf. Ch. ri'lqäil, the contents of the reindeer stomach used for making pudding)

yeyoḷ, -yoḷ

yeyoḷe'kɪn A (Ch. yuule'erkɪn), to know, to understand 52.5

yep, still, only

ye'ppa (Ch. yep), still, only 47.4

ye'ppa i'čhi (Ch. yep-e'čhi), not as yet·

ye'pluq Pal., actually 90.7

yent K, čent P, monstrous

ye'ntɪñ K, če'ntiñ P, te'ntiñ Qar., something awful, monster

ye'ntiñ-itaḷaᵉn K, če'ntiñ-itaḷan P, te'ntiñ-i'tɪḷän Qar., monster-being 100.7; 101.15; 102.7

yekui, yaqui, handle

yekui'gɪn, yaqui'gin (Ch. yäqui'gɪn), handle 46.8

yeḷh

yeḷa'aḷ, yeḷa'ḷñɪ-to'mgɪn (Ch. yêᵉ'lhɪ-tɵ'mgɪn), cousin 48.3

ñaw-yeḷa'aḷ (Ch. ñaw-gêᵉ'lo, ñawgê'lhɪ-tɵ'mgɪn), female cousin

ye'lɪñ, to this side, there 19.9

yu (nu)

yu'-ykɪn A, nom. past ga-nu'-lin (Ch.

ru'rkɪn, genu'lin), to eat, to consume 13.6; 42.8

yumkaw, -numkaw

yumka'wikɪn A (Ch. rumke'urkɪn), to store, to stow 49.10, 74.11

yuqy

yu'qya (Ch. ro'qɪr), bumblebee 45.2

Yu'qya-ña'ut, Bumblebee-Woman 44.5

yuñ

yu'ñi, pl. yuñyu'wgi, whale 41.2

yopat

yopa'tekɪn A, to hang upon 60.9

yoᵉo

yoᵉ'oykɪn A (Ch. yoᵉ'rkɪn), to visit him 20.7

yp (*initial*), -np (*medial*)

yɪpe'kɪn A (Ch. rɪpi'rkɪn), nom. past ga'npɪlin (Ch. ge'npɪlin), to drive in, to thrust 15.7

-ykɪḷ

° kḷa'wekɪn (Ch. kɪla'urkɪn), nom. past gai'kɪḷawḷen (Ch. garkɪlau'lên), to run 47.11

yqu (*initial*), -nqu (*medial*)

yɪqu'ykɪn, nom. past ganqu'lin, the wind pushes it inward 15.2

iy

i'yekɪn M, (Ch. i'rɪrkɪn), to touch, to hit 26.4; 72.13

iyaᵉ, heaven

i'yaᵉn (Ch. ye'yeq K, e'en A), heaven 14.3

iyaᵉ'kin (Ch. ee'kin), of heaven 14.10

iw

i'wikɪn A, M (Ch. i'urkɪn), to say 74.20

e'wañ, says he 12.3

ti'wgak (Ch. ti'wkwäᵉk), it seems, apparently, 57.9

iwini

iwini'ykɪn M, to come out, to appear 37.5; 76.15 (cf. Ch. igini'rkɪn, to come to the sea from inland for hunting seals). See inini'ykɪn

iwgiči, drink
  iwgiči'ykɪn M (Ch. iwkuči'rkɪn), to
    drink 32.1
iwḷ
  iwḷa'tɪykɪn (Ch. inle'erkɪn), iwḷɪtvi'ykɪn
    (Ch. inlɪtvi'rkɪn), it becomes longer
  ni'wḷaqin *adj.* (Ch. niu'läqin), long
  iwḷa'vɪk *adv.* (Ch. niuleu'kɪ), long
  yu'ḷaq *adv.*, for a long time 16.2
i'pa (Ch. i'pe), real, actual, really,
  indeed 21.10
ipa'ña, broth 28.6 (see apa'ña)
ivvalu
  ivva'ḷun, cormorant 82.17
im, hairless
  im- (Ch. im-), hairless
  im-ḷa'wtɪḷaᶜn (Ch. im-le'wtɪlɪn, im-ḷa'w-
    talin), bald-headed 82.13
imti
  imti'ykin A (Ch. imti'rkɪn), to carry 17.5
  emtei'pikɪn A (Ch. êmtêi'pɪrkɪn), to
    take it on the back 17.4
  imti'ḷñɪn, strap for carrying something
    66.8
imča, ermine
  emčačoka'ḷñin (Ch. êmčačoka'ḷhɪn),
    ermine
  Imčana'mtɪḷaᶜn (abbrev. Ča'naḷaᶜn),
    Ermine-Man 62.1; 63.3
imḷ. See mimḷ
it, to be
  itɪ'ykin (Ch. i'rkin), to be (auxiliary) 21.2
  enñɪvo'ykɪn, inchoative 16.1
itča
  itča'ykɪn A (Ch. i'tkerkɪn), to take away
    by force, to rob of something 26.10
ithɪlh, whale-skin
  ithɪ'ḷhɪn (Ch. iti'ḷhɪn), whale-skin
  ithɪḷhu'ykɪn M, to eat whale-skin 46.9
isv, ičv, sharp
  ni'svaqin, ni'čvaqin (Ch. ni'rwuqin),
    sharp, pointed
  isvɪḷa'tikɪn M, to be pricked by some-
    thing sharp 26.4

iss, ič, dress
  issan, i'čan (Ch. i'rɪn), dress 60.10
iskuḷa'tikɪn M, to be cold 26.2
ič. See iss
iču. See iḷu
ičv. See isv
ičh. See -ečhe'tɪ
is·h, loud
  is·himḷavaiñawekɪn (= ɪs·hɪ-mḷav-aiña'-
    wekɪn), loudly-dancing-shouts (he)
  ni's·hiqin, loud 24.6
in
  in- Ch. in-), light of foot
  ni'naqin (Ch. ni'näqin), he is light of foot
  inatvi'ykɪn M (Ch. inetvi'rkin), to
    become light of foot 68.9
i'naᶜ, i'n·a (Ch. i'nē), quick, soon, early
  39.2; 72.19
inay, roast
  i'nay K, i'ney P (Ch. i'ner), roast 92.5
inačɪxčat
  inačɪxča'tikɪn, inačaxca'tikɪn M (Ch.
    inetči'rkɪn), to arrange a thanks-
    giving ceremonial, to "send away"
    the spirits of killed game by this
    ceremonial 45.7; 72.1
i'n·ač (*adv.*), enough 16.3
i'naḷka (immut.), many, numerous 44.2
i'nañ (Ch. i'ne), sledge-load 50.2
inaḷvat
  inaḷva'tikɪn M, to feed the fire (with
    sacrifice) 57.11
iniyi
  ini'yi, sleeping-tent 72.21 (cf. Ch.
    ini'rgi, coverlet, counterpane)
  anñ-ene'ye, coverlet 64.13
inini
  inini'ykɪn M (Ch. inini'ykɪn), to ap-
    pear 55.9 (cf. iwini'ykɪn)
inu
  i'nuin, i'nuñ, travelling-provisions 86.4
    (cf. Ch. i'nuun, sirloin)
  tinu'ñikin (= t-inu-ñ-ikin) M, A, to
    make provision 13.4

inya'wut, then, in that time 16.5; 100.7

i'nmi-qu'nŭm, truly, indeed, I consent 28.1

    i'nmɪq, in truth 51.8

i'nnɪk Qar., again 96.25

inñat K, inñet P

    inña'tikɪn K, inñe'etɪtkɪn P, inñe'tkɪn Qar. (M), to fall down 66.9; 100.4; 101.12; 102.4

ikḷañ

    i'kḷa, small wooden charm 72.4

igu't Qar. (particle of negation), (I will) not 97.1

iᵉy

    iᵉ'yekɪn M (Ch. iᵉ'rɪrkɪn), to pass over (the sea, the river, the abyss, the cliff)

    iᵉyɪg, e'gɪḷñɪn (Ch. 'iᵉ'nɪ), wolf 12.8

(l)inn, -liᵉnn

    iᵉ'nnɪiᵉn (Ch. 'iᵉ'tɪn), neck 57.3

    eᵉ'nnɪqol, collar-string 84.5

    eᵉ'nnɪčñɪn (Ch. êᵉ'nnɪčhɪn), necklace, small crucifix worn on the neck

    gaḷeᵉnnɪ'čhaḷen, having a necklace, a crucifix band, one baptized

iᵉñ

    iᵉ'ñiñ (Ch. 'iᵉ'ñiñ), nose

    iᵉ'ñittam (Ch. 'iᵉñɪtɪm), point

    iñui'ñɪn, big nose 72.12

    iñiñpi'kɪn M, to peck, to touch with the nose 72.10

-ȋña. See yɪña

iñi'nñin, such a one 33.1

    iñi'nñinɪk (adv.), therefore 14.3

iñei', well, now! 20.6

iḷu, iču

    iḷu'ykin M (Ch. iḷuḷe'erkɪn), to move, to stir

    iču'ča ᵉn, living thing 76.19

iḷutču

    iḷutču'ykɪn M, (Ch. iḷutku'rkɪn), to beat the drum 59.2

iḷuᵉp

    iḷuᵉ'p, shaman's stick

    iḷuᵉ'piḷiñ, diminutive 27.7

i'ḷñɪn, hairless thong 50.3

iḷh

    ni'ḷhaqin (Ch. ni'ḷhäqin), white 92.12

e'enač (Ch. e'nmen), one time 58.4

e'wañ, he said (somewhat like English "says he") 12.3; 68.1; 70.3 (see also i'wikɪn, to say)

ewgupat

    ewgupa'tekɪn M, to pretend, to force one's self on 88.16

e'wḷañ, everywhere 76.12

epetčayta

    epetčayta'tekɪn A, to squirt upon something 49.8

Eme'mqut. See Amamqut

-(y)et

    ete'kɪn A (Ch. yɪtɪ'rkɪn), to get, to fetch 72.23; 41.5

eshipat, news

    eshɪpa'tekɪn M (Ch. ergɪpa'arkɪn), to bring news 76.11

ečh, es·h, bright

    eča'tekɪn M, it grows bright, it dawns 19.4 (cf. Ch. ᴇrgɪro'rkin)

    es·hiḷa'tekɪn M, it grows bright (see qes·h)

    eča'thɪčñɪn, ečhathe'ñɪn, morning dawn 82.1 (see qes·h)

    es·hɪpye'ykɪn, it shines fully 59.7

e'čhivan Les., e'chivan Qar., this time 97.13 (cf. a'čhi-van K)

-eče'tɪ (from ič place?), vaam-eče'ti, river upstream 44.1

es·he'ḷvɪñ (probably ᴇs·he'ḷvɪñ, from ᴇs·h = ačh, they), between themselves 26.1

enaaye

    enaaye'ykɪn M (Ch. inenre'erkɪn), to hold 49.4 (see yɪnn·i'ykɪn)

enayey

    enaye'yekɪn M (Ch. ênarê'rɪrkɪn), to seek, to look for 49.9 (cf. also Ch. qäri'rɪrkɪn, to look for) enat, snare 36.5

   enogaʹtekın A, to catch in a snare 36.1

enomat

   enomaʹykın A (Ch. enomaʹarkın), to tie the load on the sledge 50.2

ęnm

   eʹnˑmeem, eʹnmeen (Ch. eʹnmeem), cliff 13.6; 64.23

ęg

   eʹgıtñın, a far-off distance 76.2

eᵋn (Ch. eʹur), indeed, and indeed 20.8; 40.5

eᵋn, oh, there! oh, well!

exuneʹče P, aqunaʹča K (Ch. aʹmqunäčä), all the time 92.19

eñyeiʹña (adv.), close to 15.11

eʹñval, nostril 84.6 (cf. iᵋñıñ, nose)

eʹrgiñ Pal., sand-spit

   ergiñeʹtkın, to walk along the sand-spit 90.1

ęlekıʹmkın P. See aᵋlakıʹmkım, under aᵋl

ęlv, ılv

   ęlhuʹlu, ılhuʹlu (Ch. ılvıluʹ), wild reindeer, caribou

   ąlvuʹykın, ılvuʹykın (Ch. ılvuʹrkın), to kill wild reindeer 68.1, 14

ęlhı-taw

   ęlhitaʹwekın K, P (A) (Ch. ilhıteʹurkın), to wash (literally, to make white), 92.12 (see niʹlhaqin)

aᵋl

   äᵋläl (Ch. äᵋLel), snow 15.8

wıʹyen. See vıʹyañ

wayoʹ, yawoʹ (Ch. yagoʹ), halloo! 33.8

wapıs·qa, slime

   wapıʹs·qaʹlñın, slime 25.7 (see vapis·qaʹlñin)

was·v

   waʹs·vikın M, to look in 54.7

wañılat

   wañılaʹtikın M (Ch. weñıleʹerkın), to open the mouth 34.7

wañla

   wañlaʹykın M (Ch. wanlaʹrkın), to ask for 74.16

-wyı

   wıʹyıwı (Ch. vıyêʹirgın), breath 33.8

-wi, particle 58.7

withiñ, crack 74.6

wič

   wıʹčwıč, willow-bark

   wıčñaʹlikin M, to fetch willow-bark 72.8

wutin-

   wuʹssın, wuʹtčin (Ch. woʹtqan), this one 22.1

   wutin-nuʹtak (Ch. wuʹtin-nuʹtek), in this country

wutc

   wutčaʹkin (Ch. wutkeʹkin), belonging to this place 49.6

   wuʹtčuk (Ch. wuʹtku), here 49.6

   wŭᵋtču (Ch. wŭᵋtku), then only, now only 35.4

wuʹssıñ (Ch. wuʹrre), on one's back 30.3

wus·q, dark

   wuʹs·quwus, vuʹs·quvus (Ch. wus·quus·), darkness 57.6

   wus·qŭʹmčiku (Ch. wus·qŭʹmčıku), in the dark (see vuʹs·quus)

wus·his·h, clatter

   wus·his·haʹtikın M (Ch. wŭrgırgeʹerkın)ᶜ to clatter 100.6

vųgv, stone

   wuʹgwın, vuʹgvın (Ch. wuʹkwun), stone 25.8

   Gıwıleʹ, Stone-Face 66.1

wulpa, shovel

   wŭlpa (Ch. wıʹlpı), shovel

   wŭʹlpapel, small shovel 14.9

wŭlk

   wŭʹlkuul (Ch. wŭʹlkuul), coal 31.9

wott

   woʹtto, not long ago 68.12

   wottaʹkin, that of not long ago 78.14

woᵋtvan (woᵋt-van), this time 96.8

uya'tik (Ch. e'ettɪk)

    yaqa'n-uya'tikiu, driving-sledges 22.10

uyi

    uyi'ykɪn M, to make fire (cf. Ch. uwi'rkɪn, to cook; uwi'ntɪrkɪn, to feed the fire with more wood)

    ñɪl-oye'ykɪn M, to make a smoky fire 74.3

uyičvat, play

    uyičva'tikɪn M (Ch. uučve'erkɪn), to play 32.7

    uyi'čvina (Ch. uu'čvine), plaything, toy

uiv

    uivu'ui, wooden fence, raised platform

    ui'vɪn (Ch. gui'gun), blockhouse, village of blockhouses (Russian)

    tuive'ñikɪn (t-uive-ñ-ikɪn), to construct a fence, a platform 56.2

ui'ña (Ch. ui'ñä), not 13.9

uwi'k (Ch. uwi'k), body, self 56.10

    uwi'kin, belonging to the body, own 57.2

    čini'nkin uwi'k (Ch. čini'tkin uwi'k), one's own body, one's self

U'weñ P, proper name (female) 92.7

uptɪ

    uptɪ'ykɪn M, to chop off 63.11 (cf. Ch. upti'rkɪn, to cut trees)

umaka

    oma'ka (Ch. omaka), together 23.1

    umaka'tikɪn M (Ch. umeke'erkɪn), to gather together

utt

    u'ttɪut, u'ttuut (Ch. u'ttuut), wood, stick 64.18

u'nmi (Ch. u'nmŭk), quite, very 74.10

u'kkam (Ch. u'kkäm), vessel 17.3

uqugwai

    nuqugwai'qin, unskilful 59.6

uḷwu

    uḷwu'ykɪn A (Ch. ulu'rkɪn), to dig, to bury

    uḷgu'vɪn, uḷhi'wun, cache, underground storeroom 36.3; 80.10

ulqa't, cross-beam

    olqa-tɪle'ykɪn M, to walk along the cross-beam 72.16

o'ya (Ch. o'ra), openly 76.15

oya'mtɪwɪḷaᵋn (Ch. ora'wêḷan), man 42.6

    oya'myan, man (used only in the speech of evil spirits when speaking of human prey) 42.5

oip

    oi'pekɪn (Ch. oi'pŭrkɪn), to prick one's self 24.10

op

    o'pɪtkɪn, o'pɪtčɪn, sharp end, point 72.13

o'pta, also, likewise 21.9; 55.1

o'pta P, it is finished, the end 94.5

otña

    otña'ykɪn, to skip 47.10

oᵘnnen, indeed 59.9

ora'wucak Qar., ora'wač Les., after that, then 96.18

oḷñaq, forked twig, fork

    oḷñaqa'tekɪn, to strangle one's self on a forked twig 35.2

pɪto, pɪttu

    pɪttuña'wikin M, to grow rich 80.7

    nɪpɪto'ñqin, he is rich 22.10

pɪtk

    pɪ'tkikin M, to fall down 84.10

pĭčiq, little bird

    pĭči'q (Ch. pɪčê'qʌlhɪn), little bird (of various species)

    Pĭči'qalaᵋn, Little-Bird-Man 12.1

pɪče' (adv.), for a while 14.11

pɪs·vič

    pɪs·viča'tikɪn M, to shout loudly 39.5

pɪs·q

    pɪs·qi'kɪn M, to hide, to fall down, to lie flat 80.18 (cf. Ch. pɪ'rkɪrkɪn, to fall down from fatigue)

pɪkak

    pɪka'wekɪn, nom. past gapkau'ḷen M, A, to be unable 17.4; 77.11

pɪlvɪnt
pɪlvɪ′ntɪ (Ch. pɪlvɪ′ntɪ), iron, metal 21.8
pa
pa′ykin M (Ch. pa′rkɪn), to dry
patta^ɛl, dried meat 70.21
payɪtt
payɪ′ttɪt, berries of *Rubus Arcticus* 41.6 (cf. Ch. rɪ′ttɪt, berries of *Rubus chamomærus*)
payitto′ykin, to eat berries of *Rubus Arcticus* 41.9
payoč
pai′oč (Ch. pa′rol), extra
pai′oč i′taḷa^ɛn (Ch. pa′rol va′lɪn), being extra, exceeding
paio′čɪpɪt, surplus, remainder 28.7
paivak
pai′vaku ḷɪnɪ′ykɪn A (Ch. pai′vake lɪñɪ′r-kɪn), to feel aversion, to feel envy
Nɪpaiva′thɪtñɪn K, Nipaivatɪ′čñɪn P, Envious-One (mythical being) 33.5; 92.4
Nɪpaiva′tɪnak, subjective form, the suffix of absolute form being dropped 32.9
paivaka′tekɪn M, to feel lonely 74.24 (cf. Ch. paivaqa′arkɪn), to feel aversion, envy)
pani′ta (*adv.*), of future time 78.17
pa′nin K, pe′nin P (Ch. pe′nin), former 15.5; 52.6; 92.7
pani′tčin, pani′tkin, former 86.4
pa′nqa, cap
panqai′pekɪn M, to put on the cap 76.22 (cf. Ch. panqai′pɪrkɪn, to get married by the Russian priest [because the wedded pair have to put on a gilded crown])
pa′quḷ (Ch. pequl), woman's knife 78.23
pa^ɛ
pa^ɛ′ykɪn M, to be thirsty 16.10
paña
paña′tikɪn M(Ch. peñe′erkɪn), to get tired
tapaña′ñikɪn A, to make tired, to be heavy 51.8

paña′wgiykɪn M (Ch. pañêwñɪto′rkɪn), to get the fatigue out, to take rest 53.1
paḷavg
paḷavgun K, paḷa′wkun P, flat stones by the hearth
(Ch. pala′kwun, stones used for surrounding the dead body exposed in the open)
paḷausqa′wikin K, P (M), to roast on flat stone 92.5
paḷto (from Russian пальто), jacket of broadcloth 44.3
paḷqat
paḷqa′tikin M (Ch. pelqäe′rkɪn), to grow old 76.12
pa′La, perhaps 60.5
piwya K, piwte Qar., pivive Les.
piwya′ykɪn K (M), piwte′tɪtkɪn Qar., pivive′tkɪn Les., to spurt with, to squirt 95.3; 96.18; 97.5
pi′pip, comb 78.9
pipi′tcuykɪn M, to comb one's hair 86.16
pipik
pipi′kɪḷñɪn (Ch. pipɛ′kiɪhɪn), mouse 23.3
pinku
pinku′ykɪn M (Ch. piñku′rkɪn), to jump 84.8
piḷh, throat
pi′ḷhɪn (Ch. pi′lhɪn), throat
pi′čhɪpič (Ch. pi′čhɪpič), food, hunger
pi′ḷhikɪn M, to starve 68.14
peye
-peye′ykɪn M (Ch. -pêra′rkɪn), to appear, to show 82.20
peik
peikɪ′ykɪn M, to feel smothered 38.5
pewɪwa
pewɪwa′tekɪn M, to throw into, to splash into 41.6
peny
pe′nyekɪn K (A), penčɪ′ykɪn P (Ch. pê′nrɪrkɪn), to attack 92.11

peḷa

  peḷa′ykın A (Ch. pêla′rkin), to leave 20.9; 34.3

peḷhıno′lñın K, peḷhıno′lñın P (Ch. pêl-hıno′lhın), reindeer-mane 92.11 (see piḷh)

puᶢ

  pu′pgan (Ch. pŭ′g̣pŭg̣), a float, a blubber bag, 58.6

  pupga′tekın M (Ch. pua′arkın), to boil, to bubble 66.13

  yıpga′wekin A (causative), to cause to come up 43.4

poxḷa P, poᵠḷa K

  poxḷa′tkın P, poᵠḷa′ykın K (Ch. pı′r-qırkın), to have diarrhœa 92.23

poḷa′tka (from Russian палатка), tent 19.7

pčep, pḷep

  pče′pekın M, to fit in 34.8

  pḷepa′tekın A, to apply 34.9

pl

  nᴇpplu′qin, it is small 15.2

pḷıtču

  pḷı′tkuykın P, pḷıtču′ykın K (Ch. pḷı′-tkurkın M), to finish, to complete, 50.1; 92.5

pḷak

  pḷa′kıḷñın (Ch. pla′kılhın), boot 13.5

  pḷai′tekın M (Ch. pḷa′gtırkın), to put on boots

  pčaitıva′ykın M (Ch. pčegtuwa′rkın), to take off boots

  pča′gg̣ıtñın, boot-string 59.3

pḷep. See pčep

vıyı

  vı′yıvıy, willow 73.23

vı′yañ, wı′yen (Ch. vi′ᴇn·), notwith-standing 42.8

vıyiw

  vıyi′wikın M (Ch. viri′urkın), to let loose

  yıvıyi′wikın A, to get loose 59.3

vı′thıy, vı′thıñ (Ch. wu′tir), interval, intermediate, middle

  vıthı′ykin (Ch. wuti′rkin), intermediate, middle 50.2

vınyat, help

  vınya′tikın (Ch. vınře′erkın), to help 44.5

-va. See -tva

vay. See vag

vai′am (Ch. ve′em), river 17.1

vaičit

  vaiči′tikın M, to go on foot 12.3

vaiñe

  vaiñe′ykın (Ch. vaiñe′rkın M), to be put out, to be extinguished 57.6

vapis·qa

  vapis·qa′lñın, slime 26.4 (see wapis·-qa′lñın)

vamya

  vamya′ykın M, to get with child 74.9

va′sqiñ, another 47.3

vačap

  vača′pgıčñın, scar 86.1

va′čañ K, P, frequently 92.12

vačin·ñı

  nıvači′n·ñıqin, untidy 59.3

van (particle), there

  ña′no-van, those there 55.8

vant

  vantı′ykın, it dawns

  vantıge′ñın, dawn 18.1

vann

  va′nnilñın (Ch. va′nnuwan), tooth

  vannıñta′tekın M, to lose a tooth 32.8

van·ñı. See yıvan·ñı

vanñat

  vanñatekın M, to peel the skin off one's self (see yıvan·ñı, -nvan·ñı)

vakıth

  va′kıthın, magpie 45.4

  Vakıthı′mtıla⁶n, Magpie-Man 72.9

vaqat, stride

  va′qatekin M (Ch. veᵠäe′rkın), to stride over 47.11

vaqyɪy

va′kyɪy, va′qyɪy, stride

vaqyɪ′yikɪn M, to stride 53.2

vag, vay

va′gɪlñɪn (Ch. va′gɪlhɪn), nail, hoof 84.15

vai′n·aku, big nail 84.15

va′gitčɪn (Ch. ve′gitkɪn), nail-point 57.1

vagitču′ykɪn (Ch. vegitku′rkɪn), to scratch, to rip open with nails 84.17

vaᵉ′ai, vaᵉi. See viᵉ′yai

vaᵉ′ak (= vaᵉ′iuk) 64.9

vaᵉ′yuk, afterwards 13.5

vaxgɪl

vaxgɪle′kɪn A, to have something on in a bandoliere 78.8

valɪ

valɪ′val, seal-oil 80.10

vala (Ch. va′lɛ), knife 46.8

valaikɪla

valaikɪla′ykɪn A (Ch. velerkɪle′rkɪn), to pursue 45.5

valel

vale′le, anus 82.8

valelñaw

valelña′wekin A, to please 48.5

valom

valo′mekɪn M, A (Ch. valo′mɪpkɪn), to hear, to know, to be aware of 39.7

valv

va′lla, va′lvuval, also ve′lla (Ch. ve′ʟɪ), Raven

Valvɪ′mtɪlaᵉn, Raven-Man 12.1

Va′čvɪ-ña′wgut (Ch. Ve′lou-ñaw), Raven-Woman 48.3

vyɪl

vi′yɪlviyɪl, vɪ′yɪlvɪyɪl (Ch. vi′ilviil), shadow, image 32.3

tawyi′lñikɪn M, to make shadow, to throw shadow 48.3

vi′tvit, ringed seal 17.13 ; 24 4

vitkit

vitki′tɪkin, to annoy

vetke′gɪčñɪn, annoyance 20.9

vinv

vi′na (Ch. vi′nɪ), track 68.9

vin·v

vi′n·va (Ch. vi′n·vä), secretly 12.5 ; 41.5

viᵉya, viᵉ

viᵉ′yaykɪn, viᵉ′ykɪn (Ch. viᵉ′rkin), to die 16.9

veᵉyage′ñɪn (Ch. vê′ɪrgɪn), death 18.1 ; 20.9 ; 47.2

viᵉ′yai, vaᵉ′ai, vaᵉi

viᵉ′yai, vaᵉ′ai, vaᵉi′lɪñɪn (Ch. vaᵉ′glɪñɪn), grass, also Grass-Woman (proper name) 53.9

vilɪᵉ′yñ (Ch. vɪ′lɪᵉ), mucus, saliva 88.8

vi′lka (from Russian вилка), fork 19.7

vetat

veta′tekɪn M, to bustle, to busy one's self 78.25

veth

veth- (Ch. vêth-), straight

nive′thaqen (Ch. nuwê′täqên), it is straight

ve′tha-qonom (ve′tha qon-ɪm), just now 56.10

vetho

vetho′ykɪn M, to go through 86.3

vel

ve′livel (Ch. vê′luwêl), thimble 59.5

vel-ɪp-yɪ′lhɪlñɪn (Ch. vêl-êp-rɪlhɪ′lɪñɪn), forefinger (literally, thimble-putting-on finger)

velo

ve′loqal (velo-qal), corner of a bag, of a shed, etc. 74.22 (qal, -side ; the first stem is unknown)

vŭyal (-wyal)

vŭyalya′ykɪn (Ch. vɪyala′arkɪn M) snowstorm begins 13.1

vus P, got K (Ch. ñot) (demonstrative particle), here ! 92.2

vus·q

vu′s·quus. See wu′s·quwus 57.6

vŭgv, stone

voḷq

voḷqɪ'gɪčñɪn, voḷqɪge'ñɪn, evening, darkness, sunset 82.2

vot (Ch. vai), demonstrative particle ᴇnña⁶'n-vot, and there 70.17

v̆-to. See -yɪto

mɪyɪmk

mɪyɪ'mkɪn, shred, tassel 30.9

mɪ'mɪḷ, mɪ'mɪč; stem mḷ (Ch. mŭ'mɪl), louse 55.1

mīḷu'ykɪn M, to look for lice 59.4

mɪmteḷ

mɪmteḷhɪya'tekɪn M, to be resplendent with light 44.3

mɪtqa

mī'tqamit (Ch. mi'tqämit), blubber 70.17

mɪ'čñoḷ, edible seaweed 64.23

mɪng

mɪngɪ'ḷñɪn (Ch. mɪngɪ'ḷɪnɪn), hand 57.3

mɪgɪmg

mɪgɪ'mgɪn, talk (cf. Ch. mŭ'ŭmgɪn, chattering; gibbering of supernatural spirits, mostly of ventriloquistic character)

mɪgɪmga'tikɪn A, to talk to 66.2 (cf. also yɪmgumg)

mīḷa, mḷa

mīḷa'wekɪn M, to dance the ritual dance 37.2 (cf. Ch. mla'arkɪn, to be nimble)

mai, amei' (Ch. mei), O friend! Halloo, friend! 18.4; 63.6

mai

mai'mai (Ch. ma'gnɪ), load left in the open

mai'ekɪn M (Ch. mai'ɪrkɪn), to leave in the open

mai'ken, belonging to the load left in the open 59.7

maiñ

maiñ- (Ch. meiñ-), big

nɪma'yɪñqin (Ch. nɪmei'ɪñqin), it is big 15.4

mama

ma'ma (probably from Russian мама), mamma 26.6; 64.17 (the proper term with endearing sense is a'mma, mamma; cf. Ch. a'mmᴇ, nurse, woman's breast)

ma'mi, elevated storehouse 36.5

mata

mata'ykɪn A (Ch. mata'rkɪn), to take for a wife 16.4

mata'ḷa⁶n (Ch. mata'lɪn), father-in-law 54.9

ma'či, is it not 49.7

ma'ččɪ, and now 19.6

mana

ma'na (Ch. ma'na), asunder

am-ma'na, to different directions 25.2

maniy

mani'y- (Ch. me'nig), cloth, calico

mani'y-i'čan, shirt 44.4; 70.21

ma'nnu K, me'nnu P (Ch. me'ñkɪ), where 92.2

mak

ma'ka (Ch. ma'kɪ), diaper

ma'kil, diaper-string 23.5

makḷa

makḷa'ḷa⁶n (Ch. magḷa'lɪn), traveller (from afar)

maqmi

ma'qim (Ch. mäqɪm), arrow 33.1

mañin- (Ch. me'ñin-), which, what (used only in compounds) 34.2, 5

mañɪ'n·ac, to what degree 66.1

mañe'nko, whence 33.7

male'ta, quietly, noiselessly 54.7

maḷ

nɪma'ḷqin (Ch. nɪme'lqin), good

maḷa'tikɪn (Ch. mele'erkɪn), it grows better (the weather) 13.1

maḷɪtva'tikɪn M, to make the weather better 13.2

maḷ-ña'wɪsqat K, mel-ñe'wɪs·qat P (Ch. mel-ñe'us·qat), a good girl 92.6

maḷ *adv.* (Ch. mel). it seems probable

 maḷ-ki't (Ch. met-ki'it), all right; with great difficulty; hardly 15.6; 74.6

 maḷ-kı'čıḷ, maḷ-kı'tıḷ, all right 66.3

mimḷ, imḷ

 mi'mıḷ (Ch. mi'mıl), water 48.3

 gi'mḷılin (Ch. i'mlıLın), having water

 aqa'-mi'mıḷ (Ch. äᵍq-i'mıl, äqä-mi'mıl), brandy (literally, bad water)

Miti

 Miti' (Ch. Miti'), the name of Big-Raven's wife 12.4

mitiw

 miti'w, to-morrow 21.8; 78.24

mink, miñq

 mi'nki, mi'ñqi (Ch. mi'ñkı), where

 meñqanqa'če, from what side 16.1

 me'ñqañ, why! 16.8

 minka'kin (Ch. miñke'kin), belonging to what country 66.11

 minka'kıḷaᵍn (Ch. miñke'kılın), belonging to what country (person), belonging to any country, belonging to anywhere 40.7

mikina (irreg.)

 ma'ki (Ch. me'ñin), who 12.8; 17.6

 mi'kinak, by whom 12.7

 mi'kın (Ch. mi'kin), whose

 mi'kna (abbreviated from mi'kina) 70.19

mi'qun K, mu'qun P (*adv.*), namely, that is to say, why! 15.2

mi'ñiñ, mi'giñ, storehouse gable 47.11

milya'q, shell 23.8

milh

 mi'ḷhın, fire (cf. Ch. mi'lhımil, fire-drill)

 miḷheᵍ'ey (Ch. mi'lhır), firelock

 meḷha'tekın M (Ch. milhe'erkın), to get fire

 me'ḷhı-ta'n·ñıtan (Ch. mêlhı-ta'n·nıtan), Russian (literally, fire-tools ta'n·ñıtan)[1]

 miḷh-, Russian 17.3

meye

 meye'mey (Ch. mé'rêmêr), tear

 meyeyitva'ykın M (Ch. mêrê'tvŭrkın), to brush away tears 36.10

mesqav Pal., vegetable food 90.21

me'če, whether 32.6

me'nnu. See ma'nnu

muu, mgu

 muu-, mgu- (Ch. muu), belonging to a caravan of pack-sledges 21.2

 mgu'ta tıḷa'ykın M (Ch. muu-tıle'rkın), to move on with pack-sledges

 mgo'-qoy (Ch. mo'o-qoi), pack-reindeer

 mgo-yäᵍ't (Ch. mo'o-rêt), pack-sledge road

 muu-yiḷ (Ch. mu'u-ril), line of pack-sledges 78.5

much

 mu'yi *dual* (Ch. mu'ri *pl.*), we

 močhına'n (Ch. morgına'n), subject

 mučhin (Ch. mu'rgin), our 22.8

muqa

 mu'qamuq, rain

 muqaiu'ykın M, the rain comes 16.5

 muqa'tıykın M, it rains

mu'qun. See mi'qun

muL

 mu'Lımuḷ (Ch. mu'Lımul), blood

 muLıta'wikın K, muLıte'wıtkın P (A), to force blood (into the face) 92.13

mgu. See muu

mḷa. See mi'ḷa

tınaḷat

 tınaḷaᵍ'tekın A, to carry out something 41.8

tınmat

 tınma'tikın M, to tell lies 62.3 (cf. Ch. temyu'ñırkın, to tell lies)

tıñp

 tı'ñpekın A (Ch. tı'npŭrkın), to stab, to peck 47.11

---

[1] Compare Bogoras, The Chukchee (Publications of the Jesup North Pacific Expedition, Vol. VII, p. 18).

tıʟ

tı'ʟıtıʟ (Ch. tı'ttıl), door 100.6

tıla (*initial*), -la (*medial*)

tıla'ykın M, nom. past gala'len, to come (cf. Ch. tıle'rkın M, to move on)

tıʟ- (*initial*), -ʟi (*medial*)

tıli'ykın M, nom. past ga'ʟilin, to follow (the river, the road) 44.1

ta

ta'ykın A, to flood something, to cover something with water 62.8

tayiñtinuñ

tayıñtinu'ñikın A, to deceive 55.8

tayyañ, tayañ

tayya'ñikın M (Ch. tegge'ñirkın), to want, to desire 33.9

tayyeñ

tayye'ñekın M (Ch. teggi'ñirkın), to cough 84.20

tayiliñ

tayili'ñikın (Ch. teili'ñirkın), to grope in the dark

qai-ta'yičina, qai-ča'yičiña, groping slowly 16.10

taitıñıčat

taitıñıča'tikın K (M), taitıñisa'tıtkın P, to boast 101.4, 27

taik

tai'kikın A (Ch. tei'kırkın) to make, to create 13.5

taiñat

tai'ñat (Ch. tei'ñet), food, dried fish (chiefly dog-salmon) 74.11

tawañ

tawa'ñekın M, A (Ch. ta'rkın), to move, to move on 19.9; 53.1

tawal

ta'wal, dried salmon

tawalñıla

tawalñıla'ykın M, to look back 51.8

tawitkıñı'ykın M (probably ta-witkı-ñi-ykın, but the stem witkı remained unknown), to make havoc, to harm, to spoil 34.1

tawatwat

tawtawa'tekın M, to squeal (cf. Ch. tawtawa'arkin, to bark) 23.5

tami'nñı

nıtami'nñaqin (Ch. nıtemi'n·ñäqin), he is skilful, he is a handicraftsman 24.10

taminña'tekın M (Ch. teminñe'erkın), to work skilfully

tamkal

ta'mkal, drying-pole, a set of drying-poles 70.11

tata

ta'ta (Ch. a'tê), daddy 74.12

tata'thilan, step-father

tatol

ta'tol Pal., yayol K (Ch. yai'čol), fox 90.15

tatka

ta'tkan, tatka'gıtñın, root, also Root-Man 54.6 (cf. Ch. tatqa'lhın, point of divergence of root and trunk of tree)

tānaw

tā'naẇ Pal., ya'naw K (Ch. rā'naw), directly, straight on 90.18

tanti

tantı'ykın A (Ch. tentı'rkın), to trample (see čančı's·quykın), to step over)

ta-n-tenmı'ñekın A (Ch. ta-n-tenmı'ñır-kın), to measure, to try on 34.6

takyı

takyı'ykın A (Ch. te'grırkın), to throw at 41.3

takyat

takya'tikın M (Ch. tegre'erkın), to get down, to descend

takno'ñekın, to arrange the birth feast 63.11 (probably ta-kno-ñ-ekın, but the stem *kno* remains unknown)

taqiñ

ta'qiñ-, genuine 23.6

taᵉy

taᵉy (Ch. ter), how much

tayᵋ-a'mu, how much I do not know (= several) 86.3

taᵋḷ

   taᵋḷı'ykın M (Ch. teᵋlırkın), to be unwell; to be suffering 34.10; 84.2

tañ

   tañ- (Ch. teñ-), good 20.7

   nıta'nqin (Ch. nıte'nqin), he is good

   tañıča'tiykın M (Ch. teñıče'erkın), to feel good

   tann·asqa'ñikın A (tañ-yas·qa'ñikın) (Ch. tendilqä'ñırkın), to put to sleep (well) 68.6

tañataw

   ta'ñataw, clothing

   tañata'wikın M, to dress one's self 79.9

taḷa

   taḷa'ykin A (Ch. talä'rkın), to strike, to pound 15.7; 96.3

   taḷai'vekın A (Ch. talaï'wurkın), to strike 53.4

   taḷa'wgun, (iron) hammer 15.7

   Ch. tala'wkun, stone for flattening iron needles with

taḷqiw

   taḷqi'wikın M, nom. past gata'ḷqiwlin, gaḷqiwlin, 57.11 (Ch. res·qi'urkın), to enter 54.10

-taḷı. See -tlı

tiyk

   ti'ykitiy (Ch. ti'rkıtin), Sun 16.6

   tiyk-a'yım (Ch. tirk-e'rım), emperor (literally, sun chief)

ti'ta

   ti'ta, ti'tak (Ch. ti'te), when 48.9; 68.13

   ti'tequn P, ti'taqun K, some time afterwards 92.8

   tito-o'n, after a long time 57.5 (cf. Ch. kıtu'r-go'on, quite a long time ago)

titi

   titi'ña (Ch. titi'ñı), needle

   titi'čaᵋn, ruff (fish) 70.11

titkat

   titka'tikın, titka'ykın A (Ch. titqäe'rkın), to swallow 84.1

tinu

   ti'nuun Qar., rear storeroom 96.23 (see yınu'yı)

tig

   tege'lñın (Ch. tê'gılhın), snowshoe

   ti'git *dual* (Ch. ti'it *pl.*)

   tigi'lñın, snowshoe-string 47.6

   tigilñu'ykın M, to eat snowshoe-strings 47.4

tiḷaiv, -ḷḷaiv

   tiḷai'vikın M (Ch. lei'vŭrkın), to walk around, to travel 21.8

teuḷa

   teuḷa'ykın A (Ch. têwla'rkın), to shake one's coat, to shake off the snow 64.16

tenm

   tenma'wekın A (Ch. tênma'urkın), to prepare 18.3

   ten me'kın A, to take measure

   tenme'čñın (Ch. te'nmıčın), measure

tenmav

   tenma'vıtkın Pal. (A), to finish (cf. Ch. tênma'urkın M, to make ready, to prepare)

   tenma'vıḷaᵋn Pal., finished, the end 90.23

tuy

   tuy- (Ch. tur-), new

   nıtui'qin (Ch. nıtu'rkin), it is new 64.13

tumk

   tu'mgın (Ch. tu'mgın), foreigner, stranger

   tu'mkiñ, tomkai'tı (Ch. tomŭka'gtı), a fabulous tribe 20.9

   tu'mgin (Ch. tumgin, tumgın), stranger's 46.1

tumg

   tu'mgıtum (Ch. tu'mgıtum), friend, mate

   tumgıne'nin (Ch. tumgi'in), belonging to a friend

tučh

tu'yi (Ch. tu'ri), you

tochɪnan (Ch. tərgɪna'n), you (subject)

tu'čhin (Ch. tu'rgin), your

točhɪn-yaq (Ch. tərgɪn-řaq), your turn 80.14

tuḷat

tuḷa'tikɪn M (Ch. tule'erkɪn), to steal

nɪtu'ḷaqin (Ch. nɪtu'läqin), he is prone to stealing 39.1

tọmñ

tomñe'kɪn M, to stop up the smoke-hole 74.4

tomñalqi'wekɪn M, increase of action 57.7

tomñe'nañ, stopper for the roof-hole 37.9

toq, oh 16.5; 21.9

toreḷka

tore'ḷka (from Russian тарелка), plate 19.7

-tvạ (*medial*), -vạ (*initial*)

va'-ykɪn (Ch. va'rkɪn), to be (auxiliary) 12.6, 7

vage'ñɪn, the being, the living (the process of)

vagɪ'tñin, Being, God (cf. Ch. va'ɪrgɪn, god, life, being)

-tvagạḷ

vagạ'ḷekɪn M, to sit 15.11

tvit

tvi'tekɪn M (Ch. vetča'rkɪn), to stand 43.5

tvet

tve'tekɪn A, to stretch 38.8

ṭm (*initial*), nm (*medial*)

tɪme'kɪn A (Ch. tɪmɪ'rkɪn), to kill 12.9

ṭk, ṭč

tɪke'ykɪn M, nom. past ga'tčeḷen (Ch. tɪkê'rkɪn), it smells of

aᵍlatčê'ykɪn (Ch. aᵍlatkê'rkɪn), it smells of excrement 16.1

tkiw, tčiw

ki'wikɪn M (Ch. kiurkɪn), to stay for a night 21.7; 54.4

ñee'tčɪñ (ñee-tcɪñ), two nights passed 54.5

(-t)ku

qu'ykɪn, ku'ykɪn K (A), qu'tɪtkin P, qu'rɪrkɪn Qar. (Ch. ku'rkɪn), to spend, to destroy 100.12; 101.18; 102.11

tñi, tni

tñi'ykɪn, tni'kɪn M (Ch. tni'rkɪn), to sew 61.3

tñiv, tñiw

tñi'vɪtkɪn Pal. (A), tñi'wikɪn K (Ch. tñi'urkɪn), to send 90.22

thɪpaw

thɪpa'wikɪn M, to grow excited 46.8

thɪḷ

gɪḷa'tikɪn M (Ch. gɪle'erkɪn), to be warm

nɪthɪ'ḷqin (Ch. nɪti'ḷqin), it is warm

inathɪḷa'wikɪn A (Ch. inethɪḷe'urkɪn), to make warm 29.3

thait

thaita'tkɪn Pal. (M), to jump out 90.14

-tlɪ, -taṛɪ

tḷɪ'tkɪn Pal. (M), nom. past gata'Lɪḷen, to lie down 90.2 (cf. Ch. rɪḷha'lɪrkɪn, nom. past gaLɪga'Lên, to lie down)

-ssạ. See -yya

čɪtča

čɪtča'ḷñɪn, pelvis-joint

čɪtč-aᵍ'ttam, coccyx (literally, pelvis-joint bone) 49.6

čɪčhu

čɪčhu'ykɪn A, to gnaw 34.2

čɪnk

čɪnku'ykɪn M, to cover the side draught-hole

čɪnku'na, (narrow) side draught-hole 74.6

čınkaitat

   čınkaita'tekın M, to rebound, to jump off 77.2

čịk, yịk

   čıkı'tñın, yıke'ñın (Ch. yıkı'rgın), mouth 56.8

čịḷ, yiḷ

   čı'ḷıyıḷ, yi'yiḷ (Ch. yi'liil), tongue 56.4

   čıḷ-ınmiḷu'ykın M, to lick with tongue 56.3

   cɛp-ñıto'ykın, cep-ñıto'ykın, to peep out 53.5 (cf. liḷa'pikın, to look at)

čayı

   čayı'na (Ch. čeru'ne), hook

čaiučh

   čai'učhın (Ch. tei'učhın), small bag 38.4

čaim. See čeim

čawčuwạ

   čawču (Ch. čawču), reindeer-breeder 45.7; 50.1

ča'myeq, indeed 24.2 (see čem-yaq)

čača

   čača'ykın M (Ch. čača'rkın), to taste of 36.3

čačame

   čača'me, old woman 51.1

čanaḷo'ᵍ (instead of čanaḷa^ᵍ'), abbreviation of imčana'mtıḷa^ᵍ

   Čanaḷo'ᵍ-ña'wıs·qat, Ermine-Woman 63.3

čančis·qu'ykın A (Ch. tenti'rkın), to step over, to trample down 45.2; 84.23 (see tanti)

Čan·ai', proper name (female) 88.4

čaḳet

   ča'kıget, ča'ket (Ch. ča'kıgêt), sister 18.10

čañetat. See čeñ'ačet

čim, čima

   čima-ykın M (Ch. čime'erkın), to break, to get broken 14.3

   čema'thıtñın (Ch. čêma'tirgın), cleft 14.10

čıčhi

   či'čhiñ (Ch. či'čhi), armpits 18.9

činit

   čini't (Ch. čini't), one's self

   gŭmna'n čini't (Ch. gŭmnan čini't), myself

   čini'nkin (Ch. čini'tkin), own 54.9

čintaw

   činta'wikin Les. (M), to grow jealous 97.6 (see qanñı'ykın)

čigai

   čegai'ḷıñın (Ch. čêga'glıñın), small pebbles 26.3

   Čegai'-vai'am (Ch. Čigei'-ve'êm), Pebbly River, Milky Way 106.1

čilila

   čilila'tīkın, čilala'tikın M (Ch. pıḷıle'-erkın), it bubbles 17.2

če, eh 47.6

čeim P, čaim K

   čei'mık P, čai'mık K (Ch. či'mčä), near, close by 100.9

čemya'q (čem-yaq), really, indeed 13.7; 56.1

če'meč-e'en, čemeče^ᵍn (Ch. če'met lü'), so it is, so it happens 46.4

čet

   čet K, čet P (Ch. ret), road

čẹčve

   če'čve, openly 22.5 (cf. Ch. če'čver, in waking state [in contrast to dreaming state])

čenpınm

   čenpı'nmın, shoulders 57.3

čẹnt. See yẹnt

čeñ'ačet Pal., čañetat K

   ceñ'ače'tkın Pal. (M), čañeta'tikın K (Ch. čeñıtte'erkın), to get frightened 90.12

čerepro

   čerepro' (from Russian серебро), silver 22.10

čeḷp

   čeḷpe'kın M, to catch fish with a small round net 66.3

č

čuˊtkın P (Λ), yuˊykin K (Ch. ruˊrkın), to eat, to consume 92.24

čŭmkup

čŭˊmkup (Ch. čïˊmquk), some part 96.3

čopṛǫ

čoproˊykin M, to taste well (this word belongs to the supposed language of supernatural spirits) 80.12

čot

čot-taˊgın (Ch. čot-taˊgın), "pillows' border" (i.e., the sill at the entrance of the sleeping-room formed by pillows laid in a row)
Ch. čoˊtčot, pillow
čotčïˊlqan, cross-pole parting one sleeping-place from another (literally, pillows' top) 84.8

čvi

čviˊykın A (Ch. čuwiˊrkın), to cut 47.7
čviˊpıt (Ch. čuwiˊpit), piece, half
-čvinañ. See yıvinañ

čh(ı)

gıˊčhın (Ch. rıˊgrıg), hair
qeˊ-čhılaᵋn (Ch. qêˊ-rgılın), thick-haired
Λˊxgıke, Hairless-One 24.8

čhıčañaw

čıgıčañaˊwekın K Qar., čigičeñeˊwıtkın Les. (M) (Ch. čıkeyeˊurkın), to recover one's senses 42.10; 96.9

sˁalvıy

sˁalvıyeˊykın M (Ch. aᵋlvıroˊrkın), to pass a day 64.9

sˁv

sˁveˊkın A (Ch. ruˊurkın), nom. past gaˊsˁvılen (Ch. gaˊrvılen), to split, to cut into bands 38.7

nıpaivaˊthıtñın. See paivak

nım

nıˊmnım (Ch. nıˊmnım), settlement
nımyıˊssaᵋn (Ch. nıˊmyırın), village 70.9

nıme (adv.), too much 16.1

nıki

nıkiˊta (Ch. nıkiˊtä), in the night-time 16.7

nıˊklı, stone-pine nut 34.2

nıquˊp, joint 42.7

-naṭv. See yaṭv

naḷ

naˊḷıkın M, nom. past ganaˊḷın (Ch. neˊlırkın), it becomes something (auxiliary) 16.2

naḷp

naˊḷpŭtkın Pal. (M), to suck 90.13

naḷh, nelh

naˊḷhın K, neˊlhın P (Ch. neˊlhın), skin (however neˊlhı- K 49.1)

-nyiw (medial), -nnˑiw (medial). See yıyiw (initial)

niyk, nika

niˊyka K, niˊtke P (Ch. niˊrkıñut), some one
nikaˊykın M (Ch. nikeˊrkın), thou doest something (auxiliary) 17.2

neˊmᵋek Paḷ., also 90.20 (cf. Ch. neˊme, again)

nelh. See naḷh

nuwil (initial), ñvil (medial)

nuwiˊḷıkın M (Ch. nuwiˊlırkın), nom. past ganviˊḷın, gaˊñvılin, to stop 16.10

-numkaw. See yumkaw

nuta

nuˊtanut (Ch. nuˊtenut), country, land
nutıḷaˊtikın M, to go into the (open) country 54.1

nǫǫ K, nuu P

noˊonai K, nuiˊunui P, cooked meat 29.3

-np. See yp

-npıykaḷa. See yıpıykaḷa

nv (medial). See yıv (initial)

-nvanˑñı. See yıvanˑñı

-nviy. See yıviy

-nm. See ṭm

ntıwaṭ. See yıtıwaṭ

-ntıgıwat. See yıthewat

nči. See yıči

-nčimaw. See yıčimaw

-nčičat. See yıčičat

-nnu. See yınu

-nqu. See yqu

-nli. See yıli

kıyaw

   kıya'wikın M (Ch. kıye'urkın), to wake up 12.6

kıyulat

   kıyula'tikın M (Ch. kiule'erkın), to be waking, to live 33.2; 39.4

   nılhi-kyu'qin, quite wakeful 39.9

   kıyula'laɛn, living one 78.7

kıpḷ

   kı'puḷ, tobacco-mortar 50.6

(ykıpḷ)

   kı'pḷekın A, nom. past ga'ykıpḷıḷen (Ch. kı'pḷırkın), to strike 62.4; 64.18

kıpḷu, kipḷu

   kıpḷu'ykın A, to strike 43.5

kım

   kım-, hard

   nıkı'ınqin, he is hard 47.4

kımak

   kıma'k (Ch. kıme'k), almost

kıt, -kt̯

   kıt- (Ch. kıt-) adv. too much

   ga-kt-ača'čhaʟen, he laughed quite loudly (cf. Ch. ga-gtı-qamı'tvalên, he ate quite a good deal 19.2; 74.24)

   kıt-aiña'ykın, to cry loudly, to shriek

   kıt-ınve'tikın A, to pull with violence 74.1; 100.12 (see yı'vikın, to push off)

   kı'tta ḷı'gı K, kıtve'-lıga P, every time again 92.11

kitaiña

   kitaiña'ykın M, to scold 17.8

kıtta'ñ-. See kı'tañ

kıtča

   kı'tčan, slime, saliva 84.9

   kı'svač, cross-pole 68.5

-kıč, there

   ya'qu-kıč, what of that! 49.9

Kïlu', proper name (female) 43.8

kıḷ. See kiḷ

kılv

   kıḷvı'ykın A (Ch. kıḷvı'rkın), to notch

   kıḷvı'gıčñın, notch

   kı'ḷvı-yıpa'ña, (large) grooved hammer 43.2

kıḷt

   kıḷtı'ykın M, to tie

   kı'ḷtıñit, tie, band

   kıḷčı'čñın, band

   ḷa'wtı-kı'ḷčıčñın, head-band 17.13

g̊ıḷka

   kıḷka'kıḷ (Ch. kıḷka'kıḷ), shell-fish 70.2

kŭmat

   kŭma'tikın M, to be angry 24.9

kạw

   ka'wakaw, bed

   taka'wñekın M, to prepare the bed 28.3

   kawa'ssočhın, wallet filled with fish-heads 46.2

kawič

   kawiča'tikın M (Ch. keuče'erkın), to be motionless in pleasant sleep, to lie in dolce farniente

   nikawi'čaqin, he is lazy and sleepy 64.24

kama

   kama'ña, kama'ñı (Ch. keme'ñı), dish 64.3

kạmak

   ka'mak (Ch. ka'mak), (supernatural) spirit 36.6

   kama'w-ña'ut, kamak woman 82.7

kạggup

   kaggu'pekın A, to split in two 54.8

kañat

   kaña't-ingi, drag-net (literally, curved net) (cf. Ch. ke'ñi-ku'pren, curved net)

   kaña'tekın (Ch. keñi'rkın), to fish with drag-nets 44.5

karma'n (from Russian карманъ), pocket
78.9

kali

    kali'ykın M, A (Ch. keli'rkın), to carve, to adorn, to write

    kali'kaḷ (Ch. keli'kel), carving, letter, paper

    kali'- (Ch. keli'-), spotted, adorned 20.2

    Ka'li-ña'ut (proper name), Painted-Woman, 32.5

ki'wan, truly 26.9

kipḷu. See kıpḷu

kimi'ta K, kimite P

    kimi'tan K, kimi'ten P, Qar., clothes 100.11; 101.19; 102.11 (cf. Ch. ki'-mitın, load)

    ki'tañ, kıtta'ñ (Ch. kıta'), now, then! 14.7; 33.8

kičič

    ki'čič K, ki'tkis P, ki'tkit Qar., as soon as 72.21; 100.10; 101.18; 102.9

    ki'kit (= ki'kič)

kinčat

    kinča'tıkın Qar. (M) (Ch. kiñe'erkın), to grow jealous 96.19 (see qanñı'ykın)

kiḷ, kıḷ

    ki'ḷkiḷ, kı'ḷkıḷ (Ch. kiḷkiḷ), navel 63.10

    kıḷis·vi'ykın, to cut the navel 63.3

kiḷt

    ki'ḷtikiḷ, bundle 27.8

keykey, key

    ke'ykey (Ch. ke'rker), dress (mostly female) 76.22

-kwa. See gıva

kum'

    ku'm'ukum Pal, coat 90.19

kumñ

    kumña'tikın M, to call out, to shout 39.2

    ku'mñıkum, voice 72.24

kuka

    kuka'ña (Ch. kuke'ñı), kettle

    kuka'-yıčıu (Ch. kuke'-yırın), kettleful 43.1

kuka'kin, belonging to the kettle 78.1

kukai'vikın K (M, A), kukei'vikın Qar., to cook 51.1; 96.21

kokai'-poi'gın (Ch. kɵkai'-poi'gın), tripod for hanging up the kettle (literally, kettle-spear)

kır

    ku'rıtkın Pal., interrogative verb

kulipči

    kulipči'nañ, plug for the vent-hole 38.1

kuḷ

    kuḷa'tikın, kuḷa'ykın M (Ch. kuwḷıtku'r-kın), to roll 42.3

    ko'ḷoñ i'taḷaᵉn (Ch. kowḷo'ku-wa'lın), round

kuḷak

    kuḷa'k (from Russian кулакъ), fist 36.10

kotha

    kothai'pekın M, to spoil, to pilfer

    Kotha'ño, male name used in tales for Fox-Man 46.8

korowa

    koro'wa (from Russian корова) (Ch. koro'walhın), cow 78.7

koḷo

    koḷo'ykın A, to gnaw, to cut by gnawing 58.6

kmiñ

    kmi'ñın (Ch. kmi'ñın), son child 56.8

    kmiña'tikın M (Ch. kmiñe'erkın), to bear, to be delivered of a child 43.8

-kṭ. See kıt

kḷe'wā̱ (from Russian хлѣбъ), bread 16.2

qıyım

    qıyımeᵉen, qı'yım-e'wun, impossible, not true 14.3 (cf. Ch. qarê'mên, it is not the matter; see also qaye'm)

qım

    nıqı'mqin, it is hard 59.7 (see nıkı'mqin)

qısv. See qas·v

qayıču

    qayıču'ykın A, to chop small 53.6 (see qai)

qaya'n (Ch. qa'aran), covered sledge (literally, reindeer-house; see qo'yaña, reindeer) 52.1

qayem (qayo'm exclamatory form)
    qaye'm K, qate'mmɪ Les. (Ch. qarê'm) (particle of negation), I will not 96.14; 97.19

qai
    qai- (Ch. qäi-), small 17.1
    qaiu'iu (Ch. qäiū', qäiu'u), fawn, calf

qai'gut, indeed 84.19

qai'lɪm, all right 66.4

qa'iñu'n Pal. (Ch. qä'iñun), it seems 90.4

qa'wun, although 78.17

qapay
    qa'pay (Ch. qe'per), wolverene 12.8; 58.7

qapte
    qa'pten (Ch. qe'ptin), back 18.8

qamatča
    qamatča'n, Adam's apple, throat 57.4

qatap
    qata'p (Ch. qata'p), winter fish, fish standing in great numbers in deep still places 61.7

qatv
    qa'tvikɪn A (Ch. qe'tvŭrkin), to stab, to pierce 18.10
    nɪqa'tvuqin (Ch. niqe'twuqin), it is strong, successful 88.21

qatmaw
    qatma'wekɪn M, to feel cold 38.1

qačɪn
    qačɪ'n (adv.), and meantime 14.2

qačɪk
    qa'čɪk (adv.), really, indeed 18.7 (cf. Ch. qäči-qun-u'm, as you like it)

qas·v, qɪsv
    qa's'wuqas, qɪ'svoqɪs (Ch. qɪ'rgoqɪr), stone-pine 21.7

qanya
    qa'nyan, palate 19.2

qanga
    qa'ngaqan, fire, flame 30.8
    qanga'tikɪn M, to burn

yikangawekɪn (causative), to make burn (cf. Ch. qenye'urkɪn M, to flame up) 57.4

qanñɪ
    qanñɪykɪn K (M) (Ch. kiñe'erkɪn), to grow jealous 96.1

qaqla
    qaqla'ykɪn, to be choking 74.28

qage', here! 84.22

qalalv
    qala'lvɪn (Ch. qäle'lvɪn), intestines 78.23

qaleip
    qalei'pekɪn M, nom. past gaqalei'pɪlin, to fall in love 44.4

qaltenñ
    qalte'nñɪn, stopper (in the roof or in the wall of the ante-chamber) 14.8

qalñe
    qalñe'-key (Ch. qalhê-qêr), combination-suit (literally, fastened-together dress) 76.5

qalhaia
    qalhaia'ykɪn M, to cry 20.8

-qi, particle 23.7

qit
    qitɪ'ykɪn M (Ch. qi'tɪrkɪn), to freeze 14.2
    qi'tɪ-nuta'lqan (Ch. qi'tɪ-nute'sqän), frozen ground

qe'e (Ch. qeqe'), interjection of wonder (used by women) 82.14

qes·h
    qe's·hɪqes (Ch. qê'rgɪqêr), light
    qes·ha'vekɪn M (Ch. qêrga'arkɪn), it makes light
    nɪqe's·hɪqen, ne's·hɪqen (Ch. nɪqê'räqên), it is bright (see ečh, es·h)

quyqiy
    Quyqɪ'nn·aqu (Ch. Ku'rkɪl, Ku'urkɪl), Big-Raven 12.1, 2.

qut, quli
    qo'lla, qoʟa' (Ch. qol), other, another
    qu'tti dual (Ch. qu'tti pl.), 12.7; 32.8
    plural quttu, qutčan

-qun (Ch. -qun), particle 14.8
   qu'nam (qun-am), even 49.1 (cf. Ch. -qun-ım-ELO'n)
qun·
   qun· (Ch. qun·), one, single one
   qu'n-ač (Ch. qun·a'čä), one time, single time 53.2
quli. See qut
quli
   quli'quḷ (Ch. quliqul), voice, singing 48.7
   quḷila'tikın M (Ch. qulile'erkın), to sing, to make noise, to shout 68.17
qu'lin (Ch. quli'nikek), afterwards 60.2
qulu' Ch. qolo'), something big 29:9
   qulumti'ykın (qulu-imti'ykın) M, to carry something big, striking, (a club), on one's shoulders 57.9; 82.8
qoḷowočŭ'mñın (probably qoḷo-wočŭ'm-ñın), big club 29.7
quḷta
   qoḷta'lñın (Ch. qoḷta'lhın), thong-seal skin, sole leather, sole 50.3
qo' (Ch. qo'), I do not know 49.6
qo'yıñ, to this side 19.2
qoya
   qoya'ña (Ch. qora'ñi), reindeer 22.4
   qo'ya-nma'tekın (Ch. qa'a-nma'arkın), to slaughter reindeer
   qo'ya-ya'mkın (Ch. qa'ra-ra'mkin), Tungus, Lamut tribe (literally, reindeer people)
   qoyaḷa'tekın M, to herd reindeer 74.20
qo'oñ, caw! raven's cry) 48.2
qonp
   qo'npŭ (Ch. qo'npŭ), altogether 13.1; 41.8
   qonpŭña'wekın A (Ch. qonpŭña'urkın), to end, to finish 96.12
qoqḷa
   qoqḷa'tkın Qar. (M), to call, to shout 97.2
qoqḷo
   qoqḷo'ykın A, to pierce
   qoqḷo'wıčñın, hole 15.9

qlik (Ch. qlik), male, man 72.3
qḷa'wuḷ (Ch. qḷa'ul), man 17.4
gıyapča
   gıyapča'ykın M (Ch. wıyopča'rkın), to sing, to whistle 17.1; 72.16
gıyaḷ
   gıya'ḷıkin M (Ch. gre'lırkın), to vomit 43.4
gıyip, -yyip
   gıyi'pikın A, to keep back
   yini'pikın, yiñi'pikın (causative), to make one be kept back 41.9; 60.5
gıynik
   gı'ynik K, gı'rnik Qar. (Ch. gınni'k), game 61.8
GıwıḶe' (proper name), Stone-Face 66.2
gıva, -gva, -kwa
   gıva'ikin K (M), gıva'tkın P (Ch. uwa'r-kın), to catch at 36.6; 100.12; 101.19
gıt, gın, gı
   gı'ssa, gi K, gıtča P (Ch. gıt, gır), thou 18.7; 66.21
   gıni'n (Ch. gıni'n), thy, thine
   gı'niw (Ch. gi'niw), like thee 14.5
gıttat
   gıtta'tikın M (Ch. gıtte'erkın), to feel hungry 35.5; 74.15
gıtča
   gıtca'lñın (Ch. gıtka'lhın), leg 53.3
gı'čhın. See čh(ı)
gıčhoḷ
   gıchoḷ (Ch. gırgo'ḷ), above 20.1; 80.5
gın. See gıt
gınun
   gınu'n, lıñu'n (Ch. gınu'n), half, middle 43.4
   gıno't-aᵉlo' (Ch. am-gıno't-aᵉlo'), midday
   gınu'n-nıki'ta (Ch. gımi'n-nıki'tä), midnight
gıntaw
   gınta'wekın M, to run (cf. Ch. gınte'urkın, to flee) 36.6; 55.2

gɪnk

    gɪ́nku ḷɪñɪ́ykɪn A, gɪnkɪča'tikɪn M, to bid welcome 64.16

gɪḷh

    gɪ́ḷhɪn (Ch. gɪ́lhɪn), skin

    gɪḷhɪtča'n, carcass (literally, skin taken off) 49.10

gŭm

    gŭm, gŭ'mma (Ch. gŭm), I (subjective intransitive) 68.13

    gŭm-na'n (Ch. gumna'n), I (subject transitive) 12.3

    gŭmna'n čini't (Ch. gŭmna'n čini't), myself

    gŭm-ni'n (Ch. gŭmni'n), my, mine

gŭ'mḷañ (Ch. lŭ'mñä), again 15.1

gaimat

    gaima'tekɪn M (Ch. [Anadyr] gaima'tɪr- kɪn), to desire 12.2; 38.4

gaimɪ

    gaimɪyo'oykɪn M, to be joyful 23.2 (cf. Ch. gaimɪča'urkɪn, to become rich)

gamga

    ga'mga- (Ch. ge'mge-), every, each 34.9

    ga'mga-qḷawuḷ (Ch. ga'mga-qḷa'ul), every man

gatha

    ga'ttɛ (Ch. ga'ttɪ), hatchet 56.3

gačñɪn, ña'čñɪn

    ga'čñɪn, ña'čñɪn (Ch. ña'rgin), outside 33.2

    ña'čñɪnen (Ch. ña'rgɪnên), world

ga'nka, there 40.10 (cf. Ch. gā'nqan, there, quite, afar)

    ganka'kɪḷaᵍn, a man belonging there 40.8

gaḷa

    gaḷa'ykɪn M (Ch. gala'rkɪn), to pass by 66.12; 84.18

gaḷñɪḷ

    ga'ḷñɪḷ (Ch. ña'lhɪl), in both directions, in all directions 23.1

gi. See gɪt

gita

    gita'ykɪn A (Ch. gite'rkɪn), to see 44.10

gep

    ge'pekɪn M, to go upstream 61.7

gek (Ch. gɪk, gɪč), oh! 33.3

got! off! 48.9 (see vus)

-gva. See gɪva

ñɪyo'x, three

ñɪyo-s'ho'yu (absolute pl.) (Ch. ñɪro'rgarɪ [absolute]), they three

ñɪpa

    ñɪpa'ykɪn M (Ch. ñɪpe'rkɪn), to land

    kukañpa'ykɪn (kuka-ñpaykɪn) M, to take the meat out of the kettle 51.3 (cf. Ch. ere'mperkɪn [ere-mperkɪn; e'ret cooked meat])

ñɪvo, -ñvo

    ñɪvo'ykɪn M (Ch. no'orkɪn), to begin 33.7

ñɪt

    -ñɪti'ykɪn M (Ch. -ñɪttɪ'rkɪn), to get by hunting

    ɪḷva'-ñɪtɪ'ykɪn, to hunt wild reindeer

    qata'p-ñɪtɪ'ykɪn, to catch winter fish 61.7; 70.10

ñɪta

    ñɪta'ykɪn M (Ch. ñɪta'rkɪn), to go and fetch something

    notantay·kɪn M (Ch. notanta'rkɪn), to go· and fetch something from the open country, such as berries, roots, and such like 86.8

    yaxñɪta'ykɪn M (Ch. raᵍñɪta'rkɪn), for what do you come

ñɪtat

    ñɪta'tikɪn M (Ch. ñɪte'erkɪn), to break off, to detach

    imtiliñta'tikɪn M, the strap breaks off, the strap is snapped (in two) 66.8

ñɪto

    ñɪto'-ykɪn M (Ch. ñɪto'rkɪn), to go out 12.5

ñıtoｌñ

ñıto'ｌñın (Ch. gıto'lhın), flank, side of meat 66.9, 16

ñınvo'q, a number of 13.5

ñay

ña'yañ, second time 64.5

ña'yey, two 74.11

ña'yañ, again, the second time 64.5, 17

ñeyas·hei'tı K (allative), nečıshei'tı (allative) P, ñiterge'ta (subjective) Qar. (Ch. ñırɛrge'rı [absolute]), they two 101.1, 25; 102.16

ña'yen, ña'nyen, that one

ñai

ñai'ɴai (Ch. ñe'gnı), mountain 42.2

ñaw

-ñaw- (Ch. -ñew-), woman, female (only in composition)

ı'npı-ñaw (Ch. ı'npı-ñew), old woman

tu'la-ñaw (Ch. tu'lı-new), female thief

ñaw-a'kak (Ch. ñe'ekik), daughter (literally, female son) 12.3

ñaw-aᵍttaᵍn (Ch. ñeuᵍttın), she-dog

ña'wan (Ch. ñe'wän), wife

ña'w-ı-tqat (Ch. ñe'us·qät), woman 21.4

ñaw-ı-nyu'ykın (Ch. ñeund·u'rkın), to woo, to ask for a wife (literally, thou herdest [the reindeer-herd] for a wife) 12.1

ya-ñawt-ı-ña't-i-kın (Ch. rañawtıña'ar-kıɴ), thou makest him to have the wife 13.3

ñaw-yiｌa'ｌñı-to'mgın (Ch. ñawgê'lhı-tө'mgın), female cousin 82.16

ña'čñın. See gạčñın

ñan

ña'nako (Ch. ñe'n·ku), there 70.8

ña'nakañqo, from there 42.3

ñe'nako, there 19.10; 74.20 (see ña'nako)

ña'nyen, that one 13.3; ñanyat, ña'n-yaqıt (dual), ñanyau, ña'nyeu (pl.) 74.9, 10

ñanka'ken (Ch. ɛn·ke'kin), that belonging here 70.22

ñaｌqıw

ñalqı'wekın M (Ch. ñelqi'urkın), to sit down upon a sledge (mostly astride) 52.1

ñiyaq

ñi'yaq (Ch. ñi'räq), two

ñiye'ča (Ch. ñirä'čä), two times, twice

ñiyeqı'wikın M (Ch. ñireqäurkın), numeral verb

ñi'yuq, the deuce! (combined with verbs) 55.8

ñinvit

ñi'nvit, ñenve'thıčñın, evil spirit 38.3

ñilñ

ñi'ｌñın (Ch. ñi'lhın), thong 38.6; 40.5

ñe'keｌ, ñeykıｌ

ñekeｌa'tekın, ñeykıｌa'tekın M (Ch. ñır-kıｌa'arkın), to feel shame, to feel fright 46.6; 82.6

ñeｌv

ñe'ｌa (Ch. ñe'lvŭl), herd 21.8

ñunin-

ñu'nin- (Ch. ñu'nqin), that one (apart from the speaker) 34.7

ño

ñova'ykın M (Ch. ño'rkın), to lack something, to be suffering 33.7

ñoiñ

ñoiñın P, K (Ch. ñoi'ñin), pelvis, buttocks, tail 92.17

ñvil. See nuwil

-ñvọ. See ñivọ

ñḷ

ñi'ｌñıｌ (Ch. ñı'lhıｌ), smoke

ga'nｌıｌen (Ch. ga'nlılên), smoky

ñıｌa'tekın (Ch. ñıla'arkın), to be smoky, to feel smoky 38.1

ñıｌoye'ykın (ñıｌ-oye'ykın) M, to make a smouldering fire with plenty of smoke 74.3

nıｌñıｌqa'wikın M (Ch. ñılhıla'arkın), to be full of smoke 74.4

li

li'li (Ch. li'glig), egg 74.10

lili

lele'lñin (Ch. lele'lhin), mitten 22.2

lila

lela'lñin (Ch. lêla'lhin), lila't (*dual*) (Ch. lile't *pl.*), eye

gaḷa'lin, with eyes 24.2

lela'shin (Ch. lêla'rgin), eyelash 32.10

lela'pekin M (Ch. lile'purkin), to look upon 13.8

yičiča'tikin A (Ch. ričiče'erkin), to inspect 33.10

luta

luta'ykin M, to pass water 66.6

lipyui

lipyui', hood 70.5

limñena

limñena'ykin A (Ch. lŭmñena'rkin), to follow 17.6

ligı'mmen Les. (Ch. lŭ'mñä), again 97.12 (cf. gŭmḷañ)

lı'gıqar, still the less 49.1

lı'gan (Ch. li'ɛn), even as, as soon as 44.3

liñat

lıña'thısñın P, lıña'thıtñın K, parting of the hair

taḷñathisñı'ñekin M, to arrange the parting of the hair 92.19

-ḷa. See tıḷa

lawt

ḷa'ut (Ch. le'ut), head 17.13

ḷawti-kı'lčıčñın, head-band 17.13

ḷawti'ḷñın (Ch. leuti'lhın), halter 72.1

ḷawtıme'ykin M, to shake one's head 25.6

ḷawtıntı'ykin K (M), lewtıntıtkin P, to wring the neck 46.8, 26

ḷaqḷañ

ḷa'qḷañ (Ch. leᵋle, läᵋleñ), winter

ḷaqḷañyo'ykın M (Ch. läᵋlenru'rkın), winter is coming 72.5

ḷäᵋ. See ḷōᵋ

ḷaᵋo. See ḷōᵋ

ḷaxt

ḷa'xtekın M, nom. past gaḷḷa'xtılin, to come back 88.11

ḷaḷu

ḷaḷoḷñın (Ch. laḷo'lhın), whiskers, mustache 24.2

ḷōᵋ, ḷäᵋ

ḷōᵋ'ykın A (Ch. luᵋ'rkın), nom. past gaḷäᵋ'wlin, gača ᵋ'awlin to find, to see 51.9

ḷōᵋ'ḷqaḷ (Ch. luᵋ'lqäl), face 53.5

ḷōᵋ, ḷaᵋo

ḷōᵋ'ḷon, ḷōᵋoḷon (Ch. lolo'lhın), (woman's) breast

ḷōᵋ'o-ḷpine't, women's hearts fastened together 68.16

ḷo'wekin M (Ch. lo'urkın), to suck

ḷo'ḷo (Ch. lo'lo), penis 82.6

-ḷpinit, -ḷpınit

pıni'tikın, pini'tikın M (Ch. pini'irkın), to tie (boot-strings)

aḷpini'tča (Ch. elpini'tkä), not tied up (when speaking of boot-strings or any other lacings of such kind) 60.1

-ḷpirt

pirte'tkın Pal. (A), to wring out 90.19

ḷv̥

lı'vitkın P, lve'kın K (A), nom. past ga'ḷviḷen P, K, to vanquish, to be superior to 92.20

ḷqain

qaina'wikın A (Ch. qäine'urkın), to shoot at 33.1

(ḷ)qat (the whole stem is weak, but *a* is short and neutral)

qati'kın M (Ch. qäti'rkın), to go away 13.5

Ch. qati'rkın, thou goest away, thou departest 13.5

ḷñ

lıñı'ykın A (Ch. lı'ñirkın), nom. past ga'ḷñilin (Ch. ge'lhilin), to do some action (auxiliary)

a'nku lıñı'ykın A, to refuse 64.16

ḷñı = lı'gı (see ḷh) 88.21

ḷh

ḷı′gı- (Ch. li′i-), known (used only in compounds)

ḷıgı yıtčı′ykın A (Ch. li′i lı′ñırkın), to have in mind 36.7

ḷhi

ḷhi- (Ch. lii-, lhi-), genuine, numerous, strong, quite

nı-ḷhi-nımai′ɛnqin (Ch. nı-lhi-nımei′ın-qin), a quite big one

ne-ḷhe-pıto′nqen, he is quite rich 22.10

-ḷḷaiv. See tīḷaiv

-ḷḷaxtat. See yıḷaxtat

-ɪ̣.i. See tıli′ykın

rıyat

rıya′-vıḷ Pal., return payment 90.22

rıya′tıtkın Pal. (M), to thank 90.21

rı̣kr

rı′kriñ Pal., yıke′ñın K (Ch. yıkı′rgın), mouth 90.12

riri

riri′ñe Pal., white whale 90.6 (see yiyi′ña)

Suffixes.

-ı, intransitive subject; 2d and 3d per. sing. past; 2d per. sing. exhortative 20.4, 6. See -i

-ı ([ı]g̑), locative of nouns and verbal stems 74.10. See (ı)k

-ıy- (Ch. -ırg-), they (3d per. pl.); the family of, the house of 19.9; 38.9

-(ı)mtı-, a personified animal or inanimate object 44.6; 46.7

Vaḷvı′mtıḷaɛn, Raven-Man 12.1

-(ı)t, -ti (Ch. -[ı]t, -ti, pl.), dual absolute form 17.1; 80.10

-(ı)n, -(ɛ)n, -(a)n (Ch. -[ı]n, -[ɛ], -[ä]n), absolute form 15.4; 39.1; 48.8

-(ı)n, personal noun

-(ı)na(ñ) (Ch. -[ı](na), allative of personal nouns in -(ı)n

-(ı)nak (Ch. [ı]na), subjective and possessive form of personal nouns in -(ı)n 12.7; 15.11; 16.4

-(ı)na-k (Ch. -inä), subjective; possessive of personal nouns in -(ı)n 24.2, 10; 25.2

-(ı)nu, plural absolute form of personal nouns in -(ı)n 33.3; 43.7. See -(ı)n

-ın-u, -in-u, plural of proper names 24.7; 45.1

-(ı)nti (Ch. -[ı]nti pl.), dual absolute form of personal nouns in -(ı)n 12.1; 19.5

-(ı)k, -kı (Ch. -[ı]k, -kı, -qı), locative and possessive 18.9; 19.4, 9; 21.7; 25.2; 32.1, 2; 38.4; 80.10, 13

-(ı)k, -ka (Ch. -[ı]k), supine (locative form of the verbal stem) 17.1, 2; 74.8

-(ı)k (Ch. -gäk), intransitive subject; 1st per. sing. past; exhortative, conjunctive 18.6

-iñ, indefinite form of the adjective (in Ch. only in composition: ta′ñum-va′lın, Kor. te′ñıñ-va-lın, the better one) 82.4

-a. See ga—a

-a, -ta (Ch. -e, -ä, -tä), instrumental 12.5; 18.10; 20.7; 39.7; 41.3

-a, -ta (Ch. -ä, -tä), modal (instrumental of verb stem) 21.3; nominalizing indefinite form (used chiefly as imperative) 32.1

-aw (Ch. -eu). See y(ı)-

-au, plural absolute 12.7; 28.5. See u

-au K, -eu P, intransitive 3d per. pl. nominalizing form, also plural adjectival 30.1; 44.2; 94.1

-ač, adverb of time, place, manner 18.10; 27.4, 5; 70.4, 14

-an (Ch. -än) 36.8. See -gan (Ch. -gän)

-(a)n. See -(ı)n

-(a)k (Ch. -[ɪ]k), supine (possessive of verbal stem) 58.1

-yɪ'čɪn (Ch. yɪ'rɪn), full, contents of 43.1

-yu- (Ch. -ru-), increased action; also seasons, parts of time 13.1; 72.5

-yon, destined for (future passive participle). (Cf. Ch. -yo, general passive participle)

-yk-, (-ik-) (Ch. -rk-), present, all persons 12.1, 2, 6, 8

-yk-i. See -i

-yk-e. See -e

-yñ- (Ch. -yñ-), augmentative 72.12. (*Rare*)

-ɪ́ (Ch. -ɪ́), exclamatory form of noun 28.9; 88.1

-ɪ́ (shortened i), transitive object, 1st per. sing., various tenses 84.14; 88.20

-ɪ́ (shortened -i and -e), intransitive subject, 3d per. dual pl., various tenses 22.8; 100.6, 12

-ɪvɪ- (Ch. -ivɪ-, -ɪwu-), increase of action 44.7

-ɪ́tɪ, -etɪ (Ch. gtɪ, -êtɪ, -wtɪ), allative 20.1; 35.6; 36.3; 43.3

-i, intransitive subject, 3d per. dual (present -yk-i, past -(g)i, future -ñ-i) 57.9; 82.17; 100.2

-i, intransitive subject; 2d and 3d per. sing. past; 2d per. sing. exhortative 18.5; 26.2; 35.1: also transitive object 1st per. sing., various tenses 25.1. See -gi

-in (Ch. -in), adjectival, material, and possessive 24.10; 25.3; 46.2; 53.3; 64.2; 78.1

-in- (Ch. -in-), demonstrative and interrogative pronouns, compound form 34.5, 7

-in (-ɪn), *dual* -inat (-ɪnat), *pl.* -inau (-ɪnau) (Ch. -in, *pl.* -inet), transitive object, 3d per. (with the subject 3d per. sing.), present, past, exhortative, future, conjunctive 18.8; 19.2; 46.4; 94.2

-inañ (Ch. -ineñ), instrument, means of 37.9; 38.1: verbal noun, abstract action 30.7

-in-u, *n.* See -in-u

-ik- (-yk-) (Ch. -rk-), present all persons (sing. dual) 57.9

-i—gi (Ch. -i—gɪt), 2d per. sing. nominalizing form of verb, and conjugated form of noun 60.2; 82.8

-i-gŭm (Ch. -i-um), 1st per. sing. nominalizing form of verb, and conjugated form of noun 17.7; 30.1; 47.5; 60.5

-(ᴇ)n. See -(ɪ)n

-e, intransitive, 3d per. pl. (*present* -ḷa—yk-e, *past* -ḷa—(g)e, *future* -ḷa—ñ-e) 12.6; 80.11; 82.1

-e'pu (Ch. -ɪ́pu, -epŭ, -gŭpŭ), ablative, only in Kor. II

-wi. See -wgi

-wgi, vvi, Wi, plural after final vowel 22.4; 25.4; 42.7; 50.7; 66.18

-u, plural absolute form after final consonants 28.5; 44.2, 3

-u (Ch. -u), designed for (post-position, both verbal and nominal) 15.10; 20.2; 38.1; 101.6

-u- (Ch. -u-), to eat something 30.2; 46.10

-pil K, P, -pi Pal. (Ch. -pil), diminutive 23.7, 8; 78.7

   piliñ, pila'qu, diminutive, mostly of endearing sense 17.2; 22.7; 74.8

-vvi, *n.* See -wgi

-mɪk (Ch. -mɪk), 1st per. dual pl.; intransitive subject; past exhortative; future conjunctive; transitive object; all tenses 26.7; 29.9; 64.16

-ma K, P. See a'wun—ma, ga—ma

-mu'yi *dual*, -mu'yu *pl.* (Ch. -mu'ri *pl.*), verbal suffix; 2d per. dual and plural; intransitive subject, nominalizing past and present; transitive object, nominalizing past and present 29.6

-t Les. (abbreviation of -ta), instrumental 97.5
-tık (Ch. -tık), 2d per. dual and plural; intransitive subject, transitive object 13.2; 27.1
-ta. See ga——a
-ta, -a (Ch. -tä, -e, -ä), instrumental 12.5; 18.10; 20.7; 39.7; 41.3
-ta, -a (Ch. -tä, -ä). See -a, -ta
-ti. See -(ı)t
-tuḷ (Ch. -tul), piece of, part of 92.11
-tvat- (Ch. -tvet-), causative of "to acquire some quality" 13.2
-tvi- (Ch. -tvi-), to acquire some quality 13.2
-tč(ın) (Ch. -tk[ın]), point of (absolute form) 57.1
-tčın, numeral iterative 54.5. See -če
-tča (Ch. -tkı), transitive subject; 2d per. dual and plural of various tenses 23.4, 7, 8
-tča (in negative stems ending in *t* with the suffix -ka; change -*tka* to *tča*) 13.1
-tču K, -tku- P, Les. (Ch. -tku-), increased action, long duration 13.6; 96.1; 97.18; 101.11
-tčutču. See čuču
-tk- P, Pal., present, all persons 90.15; 92.19. See -yk-
-tku- P, Les. See -tču K

-s P, intransitive subject, 3d per. dual and plural 101.18. See -ı̆ *v.*
-ssaᵋn, passive participle 96.6. See -ḷaᵋn

-sꞏh- (Ch. -rg-), 3d per. (personal pronoun) sing. and pl.; possessive form of personal nouns 28.7

-sꞏqiw- (Ch. -sꞏqiu-), unity of action 64.25. See -ḷqiw-

-č, -ča, K. See -če P
-čıku (Ch. -čıku), within (post-position) 16.10
-čıkoı̆tıñ (Ch. -čiko'w̩tı), into 15.2
-čaᵋn (Ch. čeᵋn, -čın), adjectival, mostly comparative 30.7
-čaᵋn, verbal noun 76.2, 19
-če P; -ča, -č, K (Ch. -če), numeral iterative, adverbial iterative 53.2; 92.19
-ču-, 27.7. See -tču-
-čuču, tčutču, great increase of action 59.7
-čh-, 28.7. See -sꞏh-
-čñ(ın) (Ch. -čh[ın]), emphatic form or definite form 15.8; 17.2

-n (abbreviation of -gan), *dual* -nat, *pl.* -nau (Ch. -n [abbreviation of -gın]), transitive object, 3d per. past exhortative, conjunctive 18.2
-n(ı)- P. See y(ı)-
-n(ı)-. See y(ı)-
-nau. See -n
-nat. See -n
-nan (Ch. -nan), personal pronoun, subjective 17.5
-nu (Ch. -nu), designed for (after final vowel), 86.9, 11
-nv- (Ch. -nv-), verbal noun, abstract action 31.3
-nki. See -ñki
-nko. See -ñqo

-nꞏaqu (Ch. -yñ), augmentative 12.2

-k, locative, subjective
-k (Ch. -k), intransitive subject, 1st per. sing., past exhortative, conjunctive 16.8
-kı. See -(ı)k

-kɪñ, allative form of personal nouns and pronouns 29.2; 74.22

-kɪ̆-laᵋn, -kɪ̆-lin. See a—kᴇ̆-lin

-kᴇ̆-lin, -kɪ̆-lin, -kɪ̆-laᵋn. See a—kᴇ̆-lin

-ka (Ch. -kä). See a-ka (Ch. e-kä)

-ka (Ch. -kɪ), supine 40.2. See (-ɪ)k

-ki. See a-ki

-kin (Ch. -kin), pertaining to (adjectival) 60.4; 66.11; 70.22; 76.17

-qače. See -qaḷ

-qaḷ, -qače (Ch. -qaḷ, -qač̆, -qa'ča), by the side of, close to

    meñqañqa'če, from what side, wherefore 16.1

    ñanɪkañqaḷai'tɪñ, to his side 100.8

-qin. See nɪ—qin

-qinau. See nɪ—qin

-qinat. See nɪ—qin

-qu, nominalizing present, all persons 18.10

-g, locative, subjective 19.3. See -k

-gɪtñ(ɪn). See -geñ(ɪn)

-gɪčñ(ɪn). See geñ(ɪn)

-gɪn, dual -gɪnat, pl. -gɪ'nau (Ch. -gɪn, pl. -gɪnet), transitive object, 3d per. all numbers, with the subject 1st and 2d per. past exhortative 74.1

-gan (Ch. -gän), transitive object, 3d per. sing. past exhortative, conjunctive 20.7

-gi (Ch. -gi), intransitive subject, 2d and 3d per. sing.; transitive object, 1st per. sing.; various tenses 22.1; 27.3; 47.9; 84.25; 90.21

-gi (Ch. -gi, -gɪt), intransitive subject, transitive object, 2d per. sing., various tenses 16.7; 21.4; 84.24, 27

-(g)i. See -i

-gi. See -i—gi

-gis P, intransitive subject, transitive object, 2d per. sing., various tenses 101.12. See -gi

-gɪ'niw (Ch. -gɪ'niw), a group of, a number of 70.10

-gɪnkɪ, -gɪ'ñki, to the foot of 21.7 (cf. uttɪ'gi[ñ], the foot of a tree)

-gɪ'nka, under 13.6 (cf. Ch. -gi[ñ], the base or foot of something)

-gɪ'nko, -gɪ'ñko, from the bottom of 53.3 (cf. ɵttɪgê'ñgŭpŭ, from the foot of the tree)

-(g)e. See -e

-geñ(ɪn),-gɪtñ(ɪn), -gɪčñ(ɪn) (Ch. -gɪrg[ɪn]), verbal noun, abstract 18.1; 20.9; 47.2

    viᵋyage'ñɪn (Ch. vê'ɪrgɪn), death

-geñe'ti, to the bottom of 40.9; 41.5

-gum. See -i-gŭm

-ñ. See t(a)—ñ

-ñ-. See ya—ñ-, ya—ñ-

-ñɪ. See -ña

-ñɪvo-. See -ñvo-

-ñɪn, dual -ñɪnat, pl. -ñɪnau (Ch. -ñɪn, pl. -ñɪnet), transitive object, 3d per. future 27.1; 39.10

-ñɪnau, pl. of -ñɪn, q. v.

-ñɪnat, dual of -ñɪn, q. v.

-ña, -ñɪ (Ch. -ñɪ), absolute form 22.4; 28.6; 43.2; 64.3

-ñat (Ch. -ñet). See y(ɪ)-

-ñ-i. See -i

-ñit (Ch. -ñit), duration, space of time, season 31.10

    aḷañit (Ch. ele'ñit), summer season

-ñ-e. See -e

-ñvo-, -ñɪvo- (Ch. -ñño-), inchoative (cf. ñɪvo'ykɪn, to begin) 38.1; 39.3

-ñki, -nki, adverbial demonstrative and interrogative 25.6; 26.3

-ñqo, -nko, ablative (cf. Ch. -nqo, only in adverbs) 33.4, 7; 53.3

-lɪ Qar. See -ḷa-, -lin, -linau, Kamen. 96.16, 18, 20

-lɪn (Ch. -lin), adjectival (only in compounds) 82.13

-ḷa- plural of verb, all tenses and persons 12.6; 16.9; 22.5; 23.4

-ḷa—yk-e. See -e

-ḷa—(g)e. See -e

-ḷa—ñ-e. See -e

-ḷat- (Ch. -let-), increased action, long duration, frequentative of action 18.1; 53.1

-ḷaᵋn (Ch. -lɪn, -leᵋn), adjectival 44.3, 4, 10; 45.3; present participle 52.5; 57.9; used for, destined for 50.1

-lin. See ga—lin

-linau. See ga—lin

-linat. See ga—lin

-lk- Qar., present, all persons 95.16. See -yk-

-ḷkɪḷɪ, 3d per. plural, present and past (nominalizing) 96.16, 18

-ḷkaḷ P. See ḷqaḷ K

-ḷqɪ Pal., nominalizing past 90.1, 10, 11

-ḷq(an) (Ch. lq[än]), place abundant with mimḷɪ'ḷqan (Ch. mimlɪ'ḷqän), place abundant with water, swampy ground

-ḷq(an) (Ch. -s·q[än]), top of ña'nkalqan, the top of the 78.15

-ḷqal K, ḷkaḷ P (Ch. -lqäl), designed for ḷoᵋ'ḷqaḷ (Ch. luᵋ'lqäl), face (designed for being seen) 53.5; 96.19

-ḷqiw- 57.7. See -s·qiw-

Prefixes.

ɪna'n-, superlative

a'wun—ma K, e'wun—ma P, comitative 100.14. See ga—ma

a—ka (Ch. e—kä), negative, verbal and nominal 13.1; 51.7; 80.12

a—ki (Ch. e—ki), negative (used as a noun) 24.8

a—kĕ-lin, a—kĭ-lin, a—kĭ-ḷaᵋn, negative, verbal and nominal 70.24; 74.26; 76.21

aᵋn- (Ch. äᵋn-), transitive subject, 3d per. dual pl. exhortative 38.4

y(ɪ)- P (Ch. r[ɪ]—) (both *medial*), transitive 15.7; 18.2, 8; 36.5: causative 13.3; 70.23; 72.1, 10. n(ɪ)— (*initial*)

y(ɪ) —aw (Ch. r[ɪ] —eu) (both *medial*), causative 13.3; 70.23; 72.1, 10. n(ɪ)— (*initial*)

y(ɪ) —ñat (Ch. r[ɪ] —ñet) (both *medial*), causative 13.3; 70.23; 72.1, 10. n(ɪ)— (*initial*)

ya- See sa-

ya—ñ- (Ch. re—ñ-), future 12.3; 13.3; 30.2, 5; 33.1; 38.5; 60.5

ya—ñ- (Ch. re—ñ-), optative 44.8; 64.15

ina- (Ch. ine-), pronominal, transitive (thou, he, you — me) 33.1; 41.5; 88.9: transforms the transitive into intransitive 49.4

m(ɪ)- (Ch. m[ɪ]-), 1st per. sing. exhortative 13.5; 29.7; 56.1

mɪt- (Ch. mɪt-), 1st per. dual pl., present, past 16.9; 21.4

mɪssa- (Ch. mɪrre-), cf. mɪn-sa (Ch. mɪn-re) 16.9; 40.8 (sa = ya, prefix of future)

mɪn- (Ch. mɪn-), 1st per. dual pl. exhortative future 22.5; 33.6

t- (Ch. t-), 1st per. sing. 12.3; 16.2

t(a)—ñ (Ch. t[e]—ñ), to make, to create, to construct (ta probably abbreviated from taik TO MAKE)

gatui'veñlinau (ga-t-ɪɪve-linau), they constructed a raised platform 13.4; 50.6; 55.4

sa- (= ya-), prefix of future 16.9; 40.8

nɪ—qin, *dual* nɪ—qinat, *pl.* nɪ—qinau (Ch. nɪ—qin, *pl.* nɪ—qinet), adjectival quality 64.24; 88.3; 90.7: verbal, 3d per. subject, nominalizing present 25.5; 66.3; 74.12

ni—qinau, *pl.* of ni—qin, *q. v.*

ni—qinat, *dual* of ni—qin, *q. v.*

na- (Ch. ne-), transitive subject, 3d per. pl., present, past, future 22.7; 40.3, 5; 64.17; 78.17

nina- (Ch. nine-), nominalizing present, transitive subject 46.10; 60.6, 8, 9

qa-, q(i)- (Ch. qä-, q-), exhortative, 2d per., all numbers 13.2; 21.10

ga—a, ga—ta P (Ch. ge—ä, ge—tä), comitative 37.3, 7: nominalizing past,

indefinite form (used chiefly as imperative) 30.3; 31.8; 35.6

ga—ma (Ch. ga—ma), comitative 100.13

ga—lin (Ch. ge—lin), possession 24.2, 3; 50.2

ga—lin, *dual* ga—linat, *pl.* ga—linau (Ch. ge—linet), nominalizing past, 3d per.; intransitive subject; transitive object; adjectival absolute form 13.2; 14.3; 15.1

ga—linau, *pl.* of ga—lin, *q. v.*

ga—linat, *dual* of ga—lin, *q. v.*

English–Koryak Stems.

above, gɪčho'l

actual, real, ipa

actually, yep

Adam's apple, qamatča

adorn, to, kali

afraid, to be, aqa

afraid, to feel (before some supernatural being), yɪmgumg

after that, ora'wucak

afterwards, yawal, va⁵'yuk, quli (?), (some time) ti'ta

again, i'nnɪk, gŭ'mḷañ, ñay, ḷɪgɪ'mmen

ah, ann

all, am, ɪm̥

all right, a'nau, awwa', atau'-qun, maḷ, qai'ḷɪn

almost, kĭmak

alms, aiv

also, a'kyeḷ, op, ne'm⁵ek

although, qa'wun

altogether, qonp

and so, a'naqun

angry, anñen, kŭmat

annoy, to, vitkit

another, a'ḷva, va'sqiñ, qut

antler, yɪnn

anus, vaḷeḷ

appear, to, iwini, inini, peye

apply, to, pčep

armpits, čiči

arrow, maqmi

as long as, aia'ñač

as soon as, kičič, ḷɪ'gan

ask for, to, wañḷa

asunder, yanya, mana

at least, ayi'kvan

attack, to, peny

aversion, to feel, paivak

aware of, to be, vaḷom

awful, awfully, añaika

awkward, awkwardly, aḷait

axe, a⁵al

bachelor, yanya

back, qapte

back, on one's, wu'ssiñ

backbone of fish, a⁵m

bad, aqa

bag, agɪm, (small) čaiučh

bald-headed, im

band, kɪḷt

bandolier, vaxgɪḷ

bar, to, yɪp

be, to, it, (auxiliary) -tva

become, to, naḷ

bed, kaw

begin, to, ñɪvo

behind, yawal

being, -tva

berries of *Rubus Arcticus*, payɪtt; of *Rubus chamæmosus*, yɪttɪt (see *cloud-berry*)

better, maḷ

between themselves, es·he'lvɪñ (see Es·h = ačh, they)

big, maiñ, qulu'

Big-Raven, quyqiy

bird, little, pĭčiq

birth, to give, kmɪñ (see *bring forth*)

birth-feast, to arrange, takno'ñekɪn

bite, to, -ygu

blame, to, ayɪw

blockhouse, uiv

blood, muʟ

blubber, mɪtqa

blubber bag, float, puɢ

boast, to, taitɪñɪčat

body, uwi'k

boil, to, puɢ

boiled water, apa

bone, atta^ᵉm

boot, atv, pḷak

boot-string, pḷak

boots, to put on or take off, pḷak

brandy, mimḷ

bread, kḷe'wā̱ (from Russian)

break, to, čim

break off, to, ñɪtat

break open, to, yɪčimaw

breast, woman's, ḷō^ᵉ

breath, -wyɪ

bring, to, yat

bring forth children, to, -yɪto (see *birth, to give*)

bring in, to, yatv

bright, ečh, qes·h

broth, apa, ipa

brother, yɪčamyi

bubble, čilila

bubble, to, puɢ

bumblebee, yuqy

bundle, kiḷt

burn, to, qanɢa

bury, to, uḷwu

bustle, to, veṭat

busy one's self, to, veṭat

but, a'wun, yaq

buttocks, ñoiñ

cache, uḷwu

calf, qai

calico, maniy

call, to, aiñaw, qoqḷa

call out, to, kumñ

cap, pa'nqa

carcass, gɪḷh

care, do not, am

caribou, eḷv

carry, to, imti

carry away, to, yɪḷaxtat

carry out, to, tɪnaḷat

carrying-strap, imti

carve, to, kali

catch at something, to, aḷhaḷ, gɪva

catch fish with small round net, to, čeḷp

catch winter fish, to, ñɪt

cave, agiñ

caw! (raven's cry), qo'oñ

cease, to, ankaw

chamber-vessel, ača

charm, small wooden, ikḷañ

cheek, cheek-bone, aḷp

cheer up, to, anya

chew, to, yaḷu

choking, to be, qaqḷa

chop fine, to, qayɪču

chop off, to, uptɪ

clatter, wus·his·h

cleft, čim

cliff, enm

close by, čeim

close to (*adv.*), eñyei'ña

cloth, maniy

clothes, kimi'ta

clothing, tañataw

cloud-berry (*Rubus chamæmosus*), yɪttɪɪ

club, big, qulu

coal, wŭlk

coast, down the, atta⁶yoḷ

coat, kum'

coccyx, čɪtča

cold, to be, iskuḷa'tikɪn

cold, to feel, qatmaw

collar-string, (l)inn (under inn)

comb, pi'pip

combination-suit, qaḷñe

come, to, tɪḷa

come back, to, ḷaxt

come home, to, ya

come out, to, iwini

common sense, anñen

compassion, yai'vač

consent, I, i'nmi-qu'nŭm

consume, to, yu (nu)

contemporary, yɪshɪ

contents, yɪss

cook, apa, kuka

cormorant, ivvalu

corner (of a bag, of a shed), veḷo

cough, to, tayyeñ

count, to, yɪḷh

country, nuta

cousin, yeḷh

cousin, female, ñaw

cover all around, to, aimak

coverlet, iniyi

cow, korọwa (from Russian)

crack, withiñ

create, to, taik

cross-beam, uḷqa't

cross-pole, kɪ'svač, (between sleeping-
places) čot

crucifix worn on neck, -(l)i⁶nn (under
i⁶nn)

cry, to, qaḷhaia

cud, yaḷu

cut, to, čvi

cut into bands, to, ̣s̨'v

cut navel, to, kiḷ

daddy, tata

dance the ritual dance, to, miḷa

dark, wus·q

darkness, wus·q, vuḷq

daughter, ñaw

dawn, to, ečh

dawn, ečh, vant

daylight, a⁶ḷo

death, vi⁶ya

deceive, to, tayiñtinuñ

define, to, yɪyiw

deny, to, ankaw

descend, to, takyat

desire, to, tayyañ, gaimat

destroy, to, (-t)ku

detach, to, akmitkat, ñɪtat

deuce, the, ñi'yuk

diaper, mak

diaper-string, mak

diarrhoea, to have, poxḷa

die, to, vi⁶ya

difficulty, with great, maḷ

dig, to, uḷwu

directions, in both or all, gaḷñɪḷ

directions, to different, mana

directly, straight on, tặnaw

dirty, to grow, to soil itself, aqačñ

dish, kama

distance, far off, ɛg

divination, divining-stone, an·a

do something, to, yɪt, (auxiliary) ḷñ

dog, a⁶tt

dog, female, ñaw

dog-shed, a⁶tta'yan

door, tiḷ

down river, atta⁶yoḷ

drag-net, kañat

draught-hole, to cover side, čɪnk

dress, iss

dress (mostly female), keykẹy

dress one's self, to, tañataw

dried meat, pa

drink, to, iwgiči

drive in, to, yp

driving, yaqañ
drum, ya'yay
drum, to beat the, iḷutču
dry, to, pa
drying-pole, tamkaḷ

each, gamga
early, i'naᵋ
eat, to, awyi, yu(nu), ču
eat cooked fish, to, aᵋs
egg, li
eh, če
elated, to feel, añınmıḷat
emperor, tiyk
end, a'ččıč, op, tenmav
end, to, qonp
enough, in·ač
enter, to (mostly the sleeping-house), yaḷq
enter, to, taḷqiw
Envious-One, paivak
envy, to feel, paivak
envy, to, akin
ermine, ımča
even, -qun
even as, ḷı'gan
evening, vuḷq
every, every man, gamga
every time, all the time, am
every time again, kıt
everywhere, e'wḷañ
evil spirit, ñinvit
excited, to grow, thıpaw
exclusive, am
excrement, excrement-net, aᵋḷ
extinguished, to be, vaiñe
extra, payǫč
eye, eyelash, liḷa

face, ḷoᵋ
fall down, to, ayat, iññat, pıtk, pıs·q
family, yıss
far, yawa, eg
fastened, to be, ap

fat, ač, ača
father, eꜱ, appa
father-in-law, mata
fawn, qai
feed, to, awyi
feed the fire (with sacrifice), to, inaḷvat
female, ñaw
fence, wooden, uiv
fetch, to, yat, -(y)ęt (under ęt)
fetch, to go and, ñıta
fetch water, to, aim
fill, to, yıss
find, to, ḷōᵋ
finger, yıḷh
finish, to, pḷıtču, tenmav, qonp
finished, it is, op
fire, miḷh, qanga
fire, to make, uyi
firelock, miḷh
first, at, yanot
fish, ᴇnn
fish, cooked, aᵋs
fish, dried (chiefly dog-salmon), taiñat
fish, winter, qatap
fish, winter, to catch, ñıt
fish with drag-nets, to, kañat
fish-tail, ạwulpel
fist, kuḷak
fit, to, yıpạt
fit in, to, pčęp
flame, qanga
flank, side of meat, ñıtoḷñ
flipper, aᵋpa
float, pug
flood, to; to cover something with water, ta
fly, to, yiña
fly-eggs, aikıp
follow (the river, the road), to, (-ḷi)
follow, to, ḷımñana, yạwal
follow (some road) in full length, to, -yya
food, taiñat, piḷh
foot, to go on, vaičit
force one's self on, to, ęwgupat

fore, front, yanot
forefinger, vel
foreigner, tumk
foreleg, yanot
forget, to, yɪthewat
fork, vi'lka (from Russian)
fork, forked twig, olñaq
former, pa'nin
fox, yayol, tatol
Fox-Man (used in tales), kotha
freeze, to, annɪn, qit
frequently, va'čañ
friend, tumg
fright, to feel, ñe'kel
frightened, to become, čeñ'ačet
fringe, fringed, aᵋtt
from this time on, am, a'mlɪñ-van
front side, to the, yaina
Frost-Man, annɪm
frozen ground, qit
future time, of, pani'ta

game, gɪynik
gather together, to, umaka
genuine, taqiñ, lhi
get, to, -(y)et (under et).
get by hunting, to, ñɪt
get out, to, -yɪto
girl, O! O woman! ɪlla'
give, to, yɪl
glove, yɪlh
glue, ɪñ
gnash (one's teeth), to, yɪpɪtčav
gnaw, to, čɪčhu, kolo
go and fetch, to, ñɪta
go away, to, (l)qat
go out, to, ñɪto
go out of house, to, ya-nto'-ykɪn
go through, to, vetho
God, añañ, -tva
good, tañ, mal
grandfather, appa
grandmother, an'a
grass, viᵋyai

grooved (hammer), kɪlv
grope in the dark, to, tayiliñ
guest, to come as, yamkɪči
gull, yaqyaq
gums, yɪnnɪm

habitation, summer, ala
hair, čh(ɪ)
hairless, im
Hairless-One, çh(ɪ)
half, čvi, gɪnun
halloo! añe', wayo'
halloo, friend! mai, amei'
halter, lawt
hammer, iron, tala
hammer (chiefly of stone), yɪpañ
hammer, grooved, kɪlv
hand, mɪng
handle, yekui
hang upon, to, yopat
happens, so it, če'meč-e'en
hard, kɪm, qɪm
hardly, mal
harm, to, tawitkɪñi'ykɪn
hastily, avi'ut
hatchet, gatha
hate, to, aqann·
haul, to, aᵋya, yɪña
havoc, to make, tawitkɪñi'ykɪn
he, his, that one, ɛn
head, lawt
head-band, kɪlt, lawt
hear, to, yɪt, valom
hearth-stones, palavg
hearts, women's, fastened together, lōᵋ
heaven, iyaᵋ
heavy, paña
heedless, headlong, as·ka'čɪkɪlin
help, vɪnyat
herd, ñelv
herd reindeer, to, qoya
here, wutc
here! vus, qage'
hide, to, yɪyɪlpat, pɪs·q

hit, to, iy
hold, to, yınn·, enaaye
hole, qoqlo
hood, lıpyui
hoof, atvai, vag
hook, čayı
house, ya (in composition)
houseful, yıss
house-top, ya
how is he? ame'yaq = a'me-yaq
how much, ta⁰y
hunger, pilh
hungry, to feel, gıttat
hunt wild reindeer, to, ñıt

I, my, mine, myself, gŭm
I do not know, am
ice on frozen sea, upright blocks of, ayiyai
ice-hole, aim
image, vyıl
immediately, just then, a'wwi
impossible, qıyım
in a good manner. See *well*
in the same place, ᴇnnan
increase of action, yat
indeed, really, ipa, i'nmi-qu'nŭm, e⁰'en,
    o⁰'nnen, ča'myeq, čemya'q, qai'gut,
    qačık
inspect, to, yıčičat, lila
intermediate, vıthıy
interval, vıthıy
intestines, qalalv
iron, pılvınt
is it not, ma'či

jacket of broadcloth, palto
jealous, to grow, čintaw, kinčat, qanñı
joint, nıqu'p
joyful, to be, gaimı
jump, to, pinku
jump off, to, čınkaitat
jump out, to, thait
just now, akila⁰'č

keep, to, yawa
keep back, to, gıyip
kettle, kuka
kick, to, aate
kick with one's feet, to trample half-
    scraped skin, apt
kill, to, ţm
kill wild reindeer, to, clv
knife, vala
knife, woman's, pa'qul
know, to, to understand, yeyol
know, to, valom
know, I do not, qo'
known, lh

lack something, to, ño
Lamut tribe, qoya
land, nuta
land, to, ñıpa
laugh, to, ačačhat
laugh loudly, to, kıt
laughing-stock, atas·h
lazy, kawič
leather, sole, qulta
leave, to, pela
leave (some part), to, yınu
leave in open, to, mai
leg, gıtča
letter, kali
lick with tongue, to, čıl
lie down, to, yıltel, -tlı
lie flat, to, pıs·q
lie on side, to, ayıčña
lie, to tell, tınmat
light, qes·h
light, to be resplendent with, mımtel
light of foot, in
likewise, ᴇ'nkıta, op
live, to, kıyulat
live in joy, to, yınnaw
live together (in one house), to, yaip
living one, kıyulat
living thing, ilu
load left in the open, mai

lonely, to feel, paivak
long, iwḷ
long ago, ai′ñun, ti′ta
look back, to, tạwaḷñiḷa
look for, to, yıči, enayey
look in, to, yıvinañ, was·v
look upon, to, liḷa
loose, to let or get, vıyiw
loud, is·h
louse, mı′mil̨, mḷ
love, to fall in, qaḷeip
love, to make, agınñı

magpie, vakıth
make, to, taik
make soup, to, apạ
male, qlik
mamma, mạmạ (probably from Russian)
man, o′ya, qḷawul̨, qlik
many, i′n·ač
marlin-spike, yıs
mate, tumg
meantime, and, qačın
measure. to, ṭenm
meat, cooked, noo
meat, to take, out of kettle, kukañpa′y-
    kın (see *kettle*)
meet, to, yaina
mere, am
metal, pịḷvịnt
mid-day, gınun
middle, vıthıy, gınun
midnight, gınun
Milky Way, čigai
mind, common sense, ạnñen
mind, do not, am
mind, to have in, ḷh
mitten, lili
monster, monstrous, yẹnt
month, yiḷ
moon, yiḷ
morning dawn, ečh (see *dawn*)
mortar, tobacco, kıpḷ
mother, ıṛ.

mountain, ñai
mouse, pipik
mouth, čık, rịkr
move, to, iḷu
move on, to, yali, tawañ
much, too, kịt, nıme′
mucus (nose), vıḷıᵋ′yñ
mustache, ḷaḷu
myself, činit

nail, vag
nail-point, vag
namely, mi′qun
navel, kiḷ
nay! oh, well! a′ḷımıñ
near, close by, čeim
neck, (l)inn (under inn)
necklace, -(l)iᵋnn (under inn)
needle, titi
nevertheless, at least, ayi′kvan, yaq
new, tuy
news, to bring, ẹshıpạt
night-time, in the, nıki
noise, to make, quli
noiselessly, male′ta
nose, iᵋñ
nostril, e′ñval
not, igu′t, ui′ña
not, I will, qayẹm
not as yet, yep
not long ago, wọtt
notch, to, kıḷv
notwithstanding, vı′yañ
now, ačhi, -yaq
now, and, ma′ččı
now, just, vẹth
now only, wŭᵋ′tču
now, then! ki′tañ
number of, a, ñınvo′q
numerous, i′n·ač, ḷhi

odor, aig
off! got!
oh, toq, gek

oh, there! eᵋn
oh, well! eᵋn
old, ınp
old, to grow, paḷqat
old woman, ñaw
one, ᴇnnan
one, single one, qun·
one to each (of the two), am
one's self, uwi'k
one time, e'enač, qun·
one — another, ya — ya
only, am, yep
open mouth, to, wañıḷat
openly, o'ya, čečve
other, qut
outside, gačñın
own, uwi'k, činit

pack-reindeer, muu
pack-sledge, muu
Painted-Woman, kali
palate, qanya
paper, kali
part, some, čŭmkup
parting of hair, ḷıñat
pass a day, to, s·aḷvıy (see *spend*)
pass the night, to, tkiw
pass by, to, gaḷa
pass over (sea, river, cliff, etc.), to, iᵋy
pebbles, small, čigai
Pebbly River, čigai
peck, to, iᵋñ, ṭıñp
peep out, to, cᴇp-ñıto'ykın
pelvis, ñoiñ
pelvis-joint, čıtča
penis, ača, ḷo'ḷo
people, yamk
perhaps, pa'ʟa
piece, čvi
pierce (by pecking), to, yıvıy
pierce, to, qatv, qoqḷo
pilfer, to, koṭha
pillow, čoṭ
plate, toṛeḷka (from Russian)

platform, raised, uiv
play, to; plaything, uyičvat
please somebody, to, vaḷeḷñaw
pocket, karmaʼn (from Russian)
point, iᵋñ, op
pointed, isv
Polygonum viviparum, root of, a'wyek
porch, ya
pound, to, taḷa
praise, to, to cheer up, anya
pregnant, to become, vamya
prepare, to, ṭenm
presence, in the, yaina
present, at, yıshı
pretend, to, ewgupat
prick one's self, to, oip
pricked, to be, isv
probable, it seems, maḷ
provisions, travelling, inu
pudding, yiḷk
pull with violence, to, kıt
punish, to, yıgıḷ
pursue, to, vaḷaikıḷa
push off, to, yıv
put on, to, ·yıp

quick, i'naᵋ
quickly, in haste, avi'ut
quid, yaḷu
quietly, maḷe'ta
quite, very, awnu'p, u'nmi, ḷhi

rain, ɴuqa
raven, vaḷv
Raven. See *Big-Raven.*
real, actual, ipa
really, čemya'q, qačık
rear, in the, yawaḷ
rebound, to, čınkaitat
recent, ass
recover senses, to, čhıčañaw
refuse, to, ankaw, ḷñ
reindeer, qoya
reindeer, pack, muu

reindeer, wild, eḷv

reindeer-breeder, čawčuwa

reindeer-mane, peḷhɪno'ḷñɪn

remainder, payoč

rest, to, paña

return payment, rɪyat

revive, to, ayu

rich, to grow, pɪto

rip open, to, yɪčimaw

rise, to make, puᵤ

river, vai'am

road, čet

roast, inay

roast (on flat stone), to, paḷavᵤ

rob, to, itča

roll, to, kuḷ

root, Root-Man, tatka

round, kuḷ

ruff (fish), titi

run, to, -ykɪḷ, ᵤɪntaw

Russian, miḷh-

said, he, e'wañ

saliva, vɪḷɪᵘ'yñ, kɪtča

salmon, dried, tawaḷ (see also taiñat)

sand-spit, e'rgiñ

say, to, iw

scar, vačap

scold, to, aqɪt-aiña, kitaiña

scrape skins, to, yɪv

scratch with nails, to, vag

sea, aᵤqa

seal, ringed, vi'tvit

seal-oil, vaḷɪ

seamstress, awa-nñi

seashore, ačhɪñ

seaweed, edible, mɪ'čñoḷ

second time, ñay

secretly, vin·v

see, to, ᵤita, ḷōᵍ

seek, to, enayey

seems, it, iw, qa'iñu'n

self, uwi'k

self, one's, činit

send, to, tñiv

separately, yanya

settlement, nɪm

several, taᵘy

sew, to, yagɪt, tñi

sew well, to, awa-nñi

shadow, vyɪḷ

shake (one's coat, snow off), to, tɛuḷa

shake head, to, ḷawt

shaman's assisting spirit, añañ

shaman's stick, iluᵘp

shamanism, to practise, añañ

shame, to feel, ñe'keḷ

sharp, isv

sharp end, op

shell, milya'q

shell-fish, ḳɪḷka

shine full, to, ečh

shirt, maniy

shoot at, to, ḷqain

shoulders, čenpɪnm

shout, to, pɪs·vič, kumñ, qoqḷa, quli

shovel, wulpa

shovel snow, to, aᵘlɪn

show, to, peyɛ

shred, mɪyɪmk

shriek, to, kɪt

silver, čerepro (from Russian)

since (adv.), ass

since, as long as, aia'ñač

sinew thread, to prepare, ɪlñɪtat

sing, to, quli, ᵤɪyapča

single one or time, qɪn

sister, čaket

sit, to, -tvagaḷ

sit down on sledge (mostly astride), to, ñaḷqɪw

skilful, tami'nñɪ

skin, naḷh, ᵤɪḷh

skin, inner, yɪpn

skin, to, yɪvan·ñi

skin, to peel off, vanñat

skip, to, otña

slaughter reindeer, to, qoya

sledge, covered, qaya'n (literally, reindeer-house)
sledge, driving, uya'tik
sledge-load, i'nañ
sleep, sleepy, kawič
sleep, to, yılqat
sleep (well), to put to, tañ
sleeping-room, in the, yaḷq
sleeping-tent, iniyi
slide, to, yali
slime, wapıs·qa, vapis·qa, kıtča
small, pl, qai
smell of, to, ṭk
smoke, ñl
smothered, to feel, peik
snare, enat
snares, to spread, yıtıwat
snore, to, ɛnkaya
snow, ä⁸ḷ
snow soaked with urine, ača
snowdrift, a⁸lm
snowshoe, snowshoe-string, tig
snowstorm begins, vŭyaḷ
so, a'naqun
soar, to, yiña
soft, yiyk
some one, niyk
something, to do, niyk
son child, kmiñ
soon, i'na⁸
spend (a day), s·aḷvıy; (the night), tkiw
spend, to, to destroy, (-t)ku
spirit (supernatural), kamak
spit out bones, to, atta⁸m
splash into, to, pewıwa
split, to, ş·v
split in two, to, kaggup
split lengthwise, to, -yya
spoil, to, tawitkıñı'ykın, kotha
spotted, kaḷi
squeal, to, tawtawat
squirt, to, piwya; (upon something),
  epetčayta
stab, to, tıñp, qatv

stand, to, tvit
starve, to, piḷh
state, to, yıyiw
steal, to, tuḷat
step over, to, čančis·qu'ykın
step-father, tata
stick, utt
stick, to, akmitkat
still, yaq, yep
still the less, lı'gıqar
stingy, aḷña
stir, to, iḷu
stone, vʋgv
Stone-Face, vʋgv, Gıwıɭe'
stone-pine, qas·v
stone-pine nut, nı'kḷı
stones, flat, paḷavg
stop, to, nuwil
stop up, to, yıp; (smoke-hole) tomñ
stopper for roof-hole, tomñ; (in roof or
  wall) qaḷtenŭ
store, to, yumkaw
storehouse, aia; (elevated) ma'mi
storehouse gable, mi'ñiñ
storeroom, rear, tinu; (within the outer
  tent, rear) yınu; (underground) uḷwu
stow, to, yumkaw
straight, veth
straight on, tän̥aw
stranger, tumk
strangle, to, yıpıykaḷa; (one's self on a
  forked twig) oḷñaq
strap for carrying, imti
stretch, to, tvet
stride, vaqyıy
stride over, vaqat
strike, to, taḷa, (y)kıpḷ; (A) kıpḷu
strong, qatv, ḷhi
successful, qatv
such a one, iñi'nñin
suck, to, naḷp, lō̥⁸
suffering, ta⁸ḷ, ño
summer, aḷa
sun, tiyk

sunset, vuḷq
superior to, to be, ḷy̆
supernatural spirit, kamak
surplus, payŏč
swallow, to, titkat

tail, ñoiñ
take, to, akmit
take away (by force), to, itča
take (it) on back, to, imti
talk, mɪgɪmg
tassel, mɪyɪmk
taste of, to, čača
taste of excrement, to, aᵋḷ
taste well, to, čopro
teach one a lesson, to, yɪgiḷ
tear (of eyes), meye
tent, poḷa'tka (from Russian)
tent, outer, ya
thank, to, rɪyat
thanksgiving ceremonial, to arrange,
    inačɪxčat
that one, ᴇnin-, ñayen, ñan; (apart
    from speaker) ñunin-
their, ačh
then, a'ttɪ, inya'wut, ora'wucak
then only, wŭᵋ'tču
there, ᴇ'nkɪ, yeḷh, van, -kɪč, ga'nka, ñan
there, and, vot
therefore, iñi'ññin
they, ačh, ᴇčh, ñay
thief, female, ñaw
thigh, assa
thimble, veḷ
thirsty, to be, paᵋ
this country, in, wutin-
this much, to such degree, ᴇnin
this one, wutin-
this place, belonging to, wutc
this side, to, yeḷh, qo'yɪñ
thong, ñilñ
thong, hairless, i'ḷñin
thong-seal skin, quḷta
thou, thy, thine, thee, gɪt

three, ñɪyo'x
throat, piḷh, qamatča
throw, to, yinḷa
throw at, to, takyɪ
throw into, to, pewɪwa
thrust, to, yp
thud, to, añaika
thus, ᴇñaᵋ'an
tickled, to be, yɪgɪčh
tie, to, kɪḷt; (boot-strings) -ḷpinit; (load
    on sledge) enomat
time, every, all the, am exune'če
time, in that, inya'wut
time, this, e'čhivan, woᵋtvan
tired, to get, paña
tobacco-mortar, kɪpḷ
together. umaka
to-morrow, mitiw
tongue, čiḷ
too much. See *much*
tooth, vann
touch, to, iy
toy, uyičvat
track, vinv
trample, to, tanti
trample down, to, čančis·qu'ykɪn
traps, to set, yɪtɪwat
travel, to, tïḷaiv
traveller (from afar), makḷa
trifle, yaq
tripod, for kettle, kuka
truly, i'nmi-qu'nŭm, ki'wan
truth, in, i'nmi-
try on, to, tanti
Tungus, qoya
turn, to, yɪli, yɪḷt
tusk, yɪnn
twice, °ñiyaq
two, ñay, ñiyaq

unable, to be, pɪkak
underground storeroom, uḷwu
understand, to, yeyoḷ
unreasonably, atau'

Reprint Publishing

For People Who Go For Originals.

This book is a facsimile reprint of the original edition. The term refers to the facsimile with an original in size and design exactly matching simulation as photographic or scanned reproduction.

Facsimile editions offer us the chance to join in the library of historical, cultural and scientific history of mankind, and to rediscover.

The books of the facsimile edition may have marks, notations and other marginalia and pages with errors contained in the original volume. These traces of the past refers to the historical journey that has covered the book.

ISBN 978-3-95940-197-5

Made in Germany

www.reprintpublishing.com